BUSINESS ETHICS

Can business activities and decisions be virtuous?

This is the first business ethics textbook to take a virtue ethics approach. It explains how virtue ethics compares with alternative approaches to business ethics, such as utilitarianism and deontology, and argues that virtue ethics best serves the common good of society.

Looking across the whole spectrum of business—including finance, governance, leadership, marketing, and production—each chapter presents the theory of virtue ethics and supports students' learning with chapter objectives, in-depth interviews with professionals and real-life case studies from a wide range of countries.

Business Ethics: A Virtue Ethics and Common Good Approach is a valuable text for advanced undergraduates and Masters-level students on business ethics courses.

Alejo José G. Sison is Professor (School of Economics and Business, University of Navarra) and former president of the European Business Ethics Network (EBEN) (2009–2012). He is Section Editor at the *Journal of Business Ethics* and editorial board member of *Business Ethics Quarterly*.

Ignacio Ferrero is Professor of Business Ethics (School of Economics and Business, University of Navarra) and Visiting Scholar at Bentley, Harvard and Notre Dame University. He is co-founder of the research group on virtue ethics in business and management.

Gregorio Guitián is Associate Professor of Moral Theology (School of Theology, University of Navarra). He has published several books and articles on Catholic Social Teaching in international journals. His research interest includes Catholic Social Teaching on economic issues. He is Associate Editor of the journal *Scripta Theologica*.

BUSINESS ETHICS

A Virtue Ethics and Common Good Approach

Edited by Alejo José G. Sison,
Ignacio Ferrero and Gregorio Guitián

Routledge
Taylor & Francis Group

LONDON AND NEW YORK

First published 2018
by Routledge
2 Park Square, Milton Park, Abingdon, Oxon OX14 4RN

and by Routledge
711 Third Avenue, New York, NY 10017

Routledge is an imprint of the Taylor & Francis Group, an informa business

British Library Cataloguing in Publication Data
A catalogue record for this book is available from the British Library

Library of Congress Cataloging in Publication Data
A catalog record for this book has been requested

ISBN: 978-1-138-24256-2 (hbk)
ISBN: 978-1-138-24257-9 (pbk)
ISBN: 978-1-315-27785-1 (ebk)

Typeset in Bembo
by codeMantra
Printed and bound by CPI Group (UK) Ltd, Croydon, CR0 4YY

For F.O.B., *Pater et Magister*

CONTENTS

ILLUSTRATIONS

Figures

Table

ABBREVIATIONS

CA	Centesimus Annus
Civ	Caritas in Veritate
CSDC	Compendium of the Social Doctrine of the Church
CST	Catholic Social Teaching
DCE	Deus Caritas Est
EG	Evangelii Gaudium
GeS	Gaudium et Spes
LE	Laborem Exercens
LS	Laudato Si
MeM	Mater et Magistra
NE	Nicomachean Ethics
OA	Octogesima Adveniens
Pltcs	Politics
QA	Quadragesimo Anno
RN	Rerum Novarum
SRS	Sollicitudo Rei Socialis
WF	Wells Fargo

CONTRIBUTORS

Editors

Sison, Alejo José G., Ph.D., is Professor of Business Ethics at the School of Economics and Business of the University of Navarra. He was president of the European Business Ethics Network (EBEN) between 2009 and 2012. He has been Fulbright Senior Research Fellow and Visiting Scholar at Harvard University and has received fellowships from the 21st Century Trust Foundation (London); the Academic Council on the United Nations System (Yale University); the American Society of International Law (Washington, DC); the Salzburg Seminar, Bentley University (Waltham, MA); the Policy and Leadership Studies Department of the National Institute of Education, Nanyang Technological University (Singapore); and the Institute of Education of the University of London. He is editor of the *Journal of Business Ethics* and *Business Ethics Quarterly*. His research deals with the issues at the juncture of ethics with economics and politics, such as the virtues and the common good. His latest books include *Happiness and Virtue Ethics in Business* (Cambridge University Press, 2015), *The Challenges of Capitalism for Virtue Ethics and the Common Good* (Edward Elgar, 2016), co-edited with Kleio Akrivou, and the *Handbook of Virtue Ethics in Business and Management* (Springer, 2016) of which he is editor in chief.

Ferrero, Ignacio is Professor of Business Ethics and the Dean of the School of Economics and Business Administration at the University of Navarra. He has been Visiting Scholar at Bentley University, Harvard University (Real Colegio Complutense) and Notre Dame University (Mendoza College of Business). He has published several books on the History of Economic Thought and articles in such academic journals as *Business Ethics Quarterly, Journal of Business Ethics, Business Ethics: A European Review* and *Business and Society Review*. He is currently working on virtue ethics and the common good in finance. He is co-founder of the research group on virtue ethics in business and management, with a worldwide network of collaborators. He holds a B.S. in Philosophy and in Business Administration and a Ph.D. in Economics (University of Navarra).

Guitián, Gregorio is Associate Professor of Moral Theology at the School of Theology of University of Navarra. He obtained a Degree in Business Administration from Universidad Autónoma de Madrid (Spain) in 1997 and a Ph.D. in Theology from Pontifical University of the Holy Cross (Italy) in 2004. He has published several books and articles in international journals. His research interest includes Catholic Social Teaching on economic issues.

Contributors

Bosch, María José is Director of the Work and Family Research Center and Associate Professor in the Department of Organizational Behavior at ESE Business School in Chile. She holds a Ph.D. and MSc. from IESE, University of Navarra, and a B.S. from Pontificia Universidad Católica de Chile. She has published and researched on leadership and work-family issues. Her areas of interest are work-life balance, women in leadership, leadership competencies, organizational behavior and motivations across different cultures.

Cuervo, Javier Calero is Assistant Professor in Management and Programme Co-ordinator for Global Business Management at the Department of Management and Marketing of the Faculty of Business Administration of the University of Macau. He completed his Ph.D. from the National University of Singapore (NUS). Dr. Cuervo was educated at De La Salle University (Manila), University of Asia and the Pacific (Pasig) and NUS. He is author/co-author of several book chapters and cases. His research interest strides International Business (including Construction Management and Real Estate studies), Entrepreneurship and Management. His articles have appeared in *Construction Management and Economics*, *International Journal of Employment Studies, Engineering, Construction and Architectural Management, Journal of Property Investment & Finance* and *The International Journal of Urban Policy and Planning (Cities)*.

Garcia-Ruiz, Pablo is Associate Professor of Sociology at the School of Social Science, University of Zaragoza (Spain). He obtained his Ph.D. in Philosophy from the University of Navarra in 1992. He served as Research Scholar at the London School of Economics and the University of Macao. His present research interests include consumer ethics and identities.

Hamilton, J. Brooke, III, Ph.D., MBA, Emeritus Professor of Management, B.I. Moody III College of Business, University of Louisiana at Lafayette, USA. He earned his Ph.D. in Philosophy at Emory University in 1972 and his MBA at the University of Louisiana at Lafayette in 1990, where he taught for the next 25 years. His research focuses on synthesizing philosophical traditions with recent findings in neuroscience and psychology on brain processes involved in ethical action, to develop practical ethical standards for business and personal use. Some are found at www.EthicsOps.com.

Hühn, Matthias P., Ph.D., is Professor of Management in the School of Economics and Business at the University of Navarra, Spain. He obtained his Ph.D. in Strategy from the University of St. Gallen in 1996 and is an associate editor at *Business Ethics: A European Review*. His research interest is Management Philosophy and Management Education.

Kim, Richard, Ph.D., is Postdoctoral fellow at Saint Louis University in St. Louis, US. He obtained his Ph.D. in Philosophy from the University of Notre Dame in 2012 and is the author of a number of articles and book chapters. His research interests include ethics, East Asian philosophy and comparative philosophy.

Meyer, Marcel obtained a Ph.D. in Organizational Governance and Culture from the University of Navarra in 2017. Currently, he works as a language and cultural training professional in multinational companies in Spain. His research has been published in journals such as *Business Ethics: A European Review* and the *Journal of Business Ethics*. His main research interests include Leadership, Business Ethics and Organizational Psychology.

Mondejar, Reuben is Professor (for Asian programs) at IESE Business School and formerly Associate Professor of Management, City University of Hong Kong, where he was Director of the Global Business Management Program (MAGBM) from 1995 to 2016. He holds degrees in Economics, Finance, International Studies and Organization Theory. Dr Mondejar was educated at De La Salle University (Manila), Harvard University (US) and IESE-University of Navarra (Spain). He is the author/co-author of eight books, among which are *Business Creativity* (with A. Gogatz), 2005 (Russian ed., 2007) and *Introduction to International Business & Globalization* (with J. Onishi et al.), 2010. His research interests include: Comparative Management through Asian Perspectives, International Business and Globalization, Entrepreneurship and Creativity. His articles have appeared in the popular press as well as in academic journals such as *Journal of Management*, *Journal of Management Studies*, *Management International Review*, *Journal of Entrepreneurship* and *Journal of Business and Economics*, among others.

Ogunyemi, Kemi is Director of the Christopher Kolade Centre for Research in Leadership and Ethics at Lagos Business School, Nigeria. She holds a degree in Law from University of Ibadan, Nigeria; an LLM from University of Strathclyde, UK; and MBA and Ph.D. degrees from Lagos Business School, Pan-Atlantic

University, Nigeria. She is the Academic Director of the School's Senior Management Programme at Lagos Business School. She has authored over thirty articles, case studies and book chapters, and the book titled *Responsible Management: Understanding Human Nature, Ethics and Sustainability*. She edited the series "Teaching Ethics Across the Management Curriculum" for the use of faculty all over the world. Kemi worked as director, team lead and mentor in various projects of the Women's Board (ECS). She belongs to BEN-Africa, ABEN, EBEN and ISBEE, and co-developed the UNGC-PRME Anti-Corruption Toolkit.

Pinto-Garay, Javier is Professor of Business Ethics and Catholic Social Teaching at the School of Business and Economics at the Universidad de Los Andes. He has published several articles on Theory of Work. He is currently working on virtue ethics and the common good theory of the firm in employment and fiduciary responsibilities of managers. He holds a B.S. in Philosophy (Universidad de Los Andes), an MSc. in Organizational Bahaviour and RRHH Management (Pontificia Universidad Católica de Chile) and a Ph.D. in Philosophy (University of Navarra).

Racelis, Aliza is Associate Professor at the Virata School of Business of the University of the Philippines. She obtained her Ph.D. in Business Administration from the University of the Philippines in 2010. Her recent publications include: "The Role of Virtues in Business and Management" (a book chapter in *Connoisseur Strategies for Global Business Management*) and "Examining the Global Financial Crisis from a Virtue Theory Lens" (published in *Asia Pacific Social Science Review*). She also wrote *Business Ethics and Social Responsibility*, a high school textbook for Philippine schools.

Rocchi, Marta is Research Fellow at the MCE Research Centre, Pontifical University Santa Croce, Rome, Italy. She obtained her Ph.D. in Economics from the University of Navarra in 2017. Her research interests include business and finance ethics in the perspective of virtue ethics (with a special attention to the work of the philosopher Alasdair MacIntyre), corporate social responsibility and teaching business ethics.

Rodríguez-Lluesma, Carlos is Associate Professor of Organizational Behavior at the Managing People in Organizations Department, IESE Business School, Madrid, Spain. He obtained a Ph.D. in Philosophy from the University of Navarra in 1995 and a Ph.D. in Management Science from Stanford University in 2009. His research interests include teams, consumption ethics and technology in organizations.

Roncella, Andrea is a Ph.D. student at the School of Economics and Business Administration of the University of Navarra, Spain. He obtained a Master's Degree in Economics and Finance at the LUISS Guido Carli, Rome, Italy and has been Research Assistant at the Markets, Culture and Ethics Research Center of the Pontifical University of Santa Croce. His research interests include Ethics and Finance, Financial Markets and the History of Economic Thought.

Roque, Richard is Managing Director of SA Capital Limited, Hong Kong, Director of the HVLI Asia Centre of Virtuous Leadership in China and Chairman Emeritus of Hong Kong Venture Capital and Private Equity Association. He has an MBA from IESE Business School and MSc. Industrial Economics from Centre of Research and Communication (now part of the University of Asia and the Pacific, Manila). He led a team in developing an enterprise course related to the cultivation of virtues for Chinese enterprises and contributed several articles on related topics such as social enterprises for various publications such as Institutional Investor China and *South China Morning Post*.

Scalzo, Germán is Professor of Business Ethics at the Universidad Panamericana, Mexico. He obtained his Ph.D. in Philosophy (Government and Organizational Culture) at the Institute for Business and Humanism, University of Navarra in 2012. His research interests include the history of economic thought, rationality and virtue ethics in business, as well as Catholic Social Teaching.

FOREWORD

Why business needs virtue

Barry Schwartz

EMERITUS PROFESSOR OF PSYCHOLOGY
SWARTHMORE COLLEGE
HAAS SCHOOL OF BUSINESS, UNIVERSITY OF CALIFORNIA AT BERKELEY

It has been almost 250 years since moral philosopher Adam Smith changed the world. Though there were certainly transactions for profit before *The Wealth of Nations*, Smith offered a comprehensive argument for the benefits that would come from the free exchange of goods and services under conditions of competition. Not only would such an arrangement increase wealth and well-being, but it would do so in almost clockwork fashion, without having to rely on the good will, honesty, communal purpose, righteousness or virtue of its participants. As long as providers of goods were free to compete and consumers were free to choose among providers, quality, honesty, integrity and fairness would drive out self-dealing, dishonesty and downright malevolence. As long as laborers were free to offer their services, fair treatment of employees would drive out exploitation. A market system, under suitable conditions, would regulate itself. As Smith famously said, "it is not from the benevolence of the butcher, the brewer, or the baker that we expect our dinner, but from their regard to their own interest" (Smith, 1776/1937, p. 119). Many years later, Smith's sentiment was echoed by economist D. H. Robertson (1956), who asked "What does the economist economize?" His answer: "The economist economizes on love."

Smith's point was not Hobbesian. He did not think that human beings were the sorts of creatures who would ruthlessly exploit one another. Indeed, in Smith's equally important, but less influential and less discussed *Theory of Moral Sentiments*, he argued that human beings possessed a "natural sympathy" towards one another that would serve to restrain them from doing their worst—keep them from exploiting every possible advantage over others. But even so, how wonderful to operate within a system that did not rely on such sympathy or on any other virtues.

We look back on Smith from the perspective of the twenty-first century and wonder how he could have been so wrong, so naïve. As companies scheme to defeat pollution-detection devices, price gouge for life-saving drugs, offer bogus financial products and services, and charge fees for products and services that people don't need and didn't ask for, we wonder how Smith could ever have imagined that an economy could run itself. Economic historian Karl Polanyi (1944) suggested that one misstep was in the separation of the economy from the rest of life. People might be decent, as Smith asserted, with their families and in their communities, but ruthless in the marketplace. Before the explosion of free-market institutional structures, with economic activity integrated into the rest of life, virtue in the home might carry over into the shop. But after the industrial revolution, such carryover became less likely. "Natural sympathy" got turned off when people crossed the threshold of their commercial worlds. In my own work (Schwartz, 1986, 1994), I have suggested a different account. Smith might have been right about human sympathy, but wrong to suppose that it was "natural." Rather, it was the product of a rich institutional structure that taught human beings how to be good people. Over time, I suggested, contact with the market corroded the institutions that provided the constraints on our worst impulses, with nothing left to replace them. So, on this view, Smith's mistake was in taking a historical, contingent truth about human beings to be a universal characteristic of human nature. Since social scientists continue to make this mistake, even in the "enlightened" twenty-first century, we should, perhaps, forgive Smith his myopia.

Whatever the source of Smith's "mistake," the promise of a self-regulating market comprised of citizens behaving honestly and honorably has not been met. What has arisen over time is a complex web of regulations and rights designed to protect people from the worst excesses of those with whom they do business. And beyond the legal constraints on market behavior, there have also arisen efforts to define what it means to do business ethically. Every business school teaches business ethics, an implicit acknowledgement of two things, I believe: legal protection will always be incomplete; and we can't count on people to do the right thing "naturally."

Into this territory comes *Business Ethics: A Virtue Ethics and Common Good Approach*, co-authored and edited by Alejo José G. Sison, Ignacio Ferrero and Gregorio Guitián, with various other scholars as authors or co-authors of individual chapters. The book covers all aspects of the business enterprise: leadership, finance, marketing, production, governance, compliance and human resources, with a chapter on each. What makes the book unusual is that instead of resting its ethical principles on either a utilitarian or a deontological foundation, it relies on a theory of virtue—or rather, several theories of virtue. Its central protagonist is Aristotle, the progenitor of most virtue theories, but there is also substantial attention paid to neo-Aristotelian Alasdair MacIntyre and to the Catholic Social Teachings (CST). Each chapter gives us a picture of what Aristotle, MacIntyre and CST might have to say about the topic, along with a detailed case that illustrates modern business practices, either at their best or at their worst. The authors' beliefs, which they argue forcefully and convincingly, is that no set of laws, deontological rules or utilitarian calculations can substitute for people who do the right thing *because* it's the right thing.

"Do the right thing" is a nice slogan, but it raises a big question. What exactly *is* the "right thing"? It is easy to imagine a corporate CEO who believes that the right thing is to maximize shareholder value. Such a person might be focused single-mindedly on maximizing value and regard ethical niceties like treating employees fairly and treating customers honesty as nuisances to be minimized or avoided all together, unless they contribute to the bottom line. Aristotle's answer to this central question was to emphasize the teleological nature of all human activity. The *telos* of human life is excellence, and the form that excellence takes depends on the activities in which it is pursued. The *telos* of the flute player is to be an excellent musician; the *telos* of the soldier is to be a brave and cunning warrior; the *telos* of the farmer is to produce a bountiful harvest, and so on. What then, is the *telos* of the financier? The marketer? The production manager? What is excellence in these domains?

The gap between the world that Aristotle was writing about and the modern world is so great that there is no easy way to bridge the gap. Thankfully, we don't have to. Alasdair MacIntyre has done it for us. MacIntyre's *After Virtue* (1981) is a tour de force of what I regard as neo-Aristotelian moral philosophy. It is an attempt to apply key Aristotelian ideas about virtue to the modern world. I think it wholly appropriate that MacIntyre's work has such a prominent place in this book. To me, his work is what gives Aristotle's ideas real teeth.

Let's begin by noting the book's title. It is a remarkably revealing foreshadowing of what is to come. What exactly does "after virtue" mean? It means two different things. First, what, MacIntyre wants to inquire, does the world look like after virtue has disappeared, which he thinks it has in modern, liberal societies. Yes, we still have virtue words in our languages, and we still use them in everyday discourse, but the institutions and practices that gave them deep meaning in times past have largely disintegrated. Second, MacIntyre wants to know how we can go after virtue, how we can pursue it. What changes in social life are necessary in order for virtue, in its deep sense, to reappear?

MacIntyre's answer to this second question is that, in part, we may have to return to the Aristotelian world in which excellence was defined with reference to specific activities. Towards this end, MacIntyre introduces the notion of a *practice*, which is:

> any coherent and complex form of socially established cooperative human activity through which goods internal to that form of activity are realized in the course of trying to achieve those standards of excellence which are appropriate to, and partially definitive of, that form of activity, with the result that human powers to achieve excellence, and human conceptions of the ends and goods involved, are systematically extended.
>
> *(p. 175)*

There are several things to note about this definition of a practice. Practices are complex. They are social. They have standards of excellence that are peculiar to them and partly define them. And they develop. The practice of playing basketball is very different in 2017 than it was in 1957. Standards of excellence have changed dramatically. And importantly, those standards of excellence are established by the practitioners themselves. You might say something like "I don't know much about basketball but I know what I like." True enough, perhaps, but should the practitioners—the players—care what you like? Should your likes influence the path that the development of basketball takes? Decidedly, no. The people who buy tickets to basketball games might enjoy slam dunks and fancy passes, but practitioners might well regard them both as mere decorations and ignore the preferences of fans in pursuing the *telos* of basketball. The same can be said of artists. "I don't know much about art, but I know what I like" may be true. And you may even be entitled to your uninformed preferences. But why should the artist care?

Will the artist and the basketball player ignore the desires of patrons and fans? To answer this question, we must introduce another idea from MacIntyre. Practices depend for their existence on institutions. Artists need galleries, auction houses and museums, and perhaps university programs in art appreciation. Basketball players need leagues, arenas and paying customers so that they can earn a livelihood. And importantly, what enables an institution to thrive—even to survive—may be quite different from what enables a practice to flourish. Without the support of fans, basketball players will have to work at other jobs and develop their skills in their spare time. Without art patrons, artists will be baristas who paint late into the night. Institutions make practices possible, and in doing so, may require practitioners to compromise their standards of excellence. A successful institution—one that is in good working order—will insulate practitioners from the daily pressure to survive. They will support the *telos* of the practice and protect the practitioners from the barbarians at the gate. But sometimes, the practitioners will have to do their part to keep the institutions going.

And so, for MacIntyre, virtue is firmly embedded in and inextricable from the activities and structures of daily life. The enemy of virtue is largely to be found in the sacrifice of the practice-specific *telos* to return on investment, and in the sacrifice of practice-supporting institutions to bureaucratic rule following. Reconstructing our practices and institutions is the way to resurrect virtue. Simultaneously, virtue can be a guide to the shape that reconstructed practices take and to the activities of the institutions that support them.

And now, I think we can see why the authors of this book believe that business ethics should be virtue ethics. The marketers must ask, "what is marketing for? Is it to maximize return or to serve human needs." The financiers must ask, "what is financial engineering for? Is it to maximize profit, or to enable enterprises to have the resources they need to conduct their business activities?" The banker must similarly ask about the *telos* of banking, the production manager must ask about the *telos* of industrial production, and so on. The various professions that make up a business enterprise are each charged with defining the standards of excellence that characterize those professions. The institutions (firms) that support those professions are all charged with providing conditions that enable practitioners to pursue this *telos* and avoid conditions that undermine it.

Why virtue rather than rules? Two reasons, I think. First, rules require policing and enforcement. When people are willing to do whatever they can get away with, enforcement becomes cumbersome, expensive and inefficient (their lawyers are better paid and better trained than ours). But second, and more important, rules are a blunt instrument when it comes to judging whether a practice is on track and judging which compromises an institution can demand of practitioners to assure the survival of both the institution and the practice. Aristotle understood that rules were a poor substitute for judgment. In discussing the virtues, he famously pointed out that virtue typically was located as the mean between defective extremes. Courage, for example, is the mean between cowardice and recklessness. But the "mean" is no arithmetic average. What is courage in one situation might be recklessness in another. Aristotle thought that what he called "practical wisdom" (*phronesis*) was what enabled us to find the mean between the extremes. This has led my collaborator Kenneth Sharpe and I to call practical wisdom the master virtue, the virtue without which none of the other virtues is possible (Schwartz & Sharpe, 2011). Rules (laws) are what you fall back on when people lack the skill (judgment) or the will (motivation) to do the right thing without them. Reconstructing the language of virtue as the hallmark of each of the professions on which business enterprises depend spares us from having to depend on the ever-escalating arms race of rules, rule evasion and more rules.

If not rules, then why not utility calculation. On this, I think, Aristotle would be clear. Utility calculation requires a single metric—utility—that can be applied across people, domains of activit, and situations. It demands a common standard of excellence. It assumes trade-offs, often between goods that seem quite distinct (e.g., the productivity of an office worker on a project traded off against the welfare of the children at home who need some time and attention). The idea that every activity has its own *telos* resists the very notion that there is a single dimension on which all things can be arrayed, assessed and compared. This is not to say that compromises will never have to be made. The financial arm of a company may decide that a high-risk financial move that violates the *telos* of its profession is necessary if the company is to stay afloat. But, the fundamental incommensurability of goods makes trade-offs difficult and, in this way, protects the *telos* of the individual practices from being corrupted by the needs other practices. In his book *Spheres of Justice* (1983), political philosopher Michael Walzer points out that a single metric for evaluation creates a kind of tyranny. Walzer quotes the French philosopher Blaise Pascal (1670/1961), who said:

There are different companies—the strong, the handsome, the intelligent, the devout—and each man reigns in his own, not elsewhere. But sometimes they meet, and the strong and the handsome fight for mastery—foolishly, for their mastery is of different kinds. They misunderstand one another, and make the mistake of each aiming at universal dominion. Nothing can win this, not even strength, for it is powerless in the kingdom of the wise...

Tyranny. The following statements therefore are false and tyrannical: "Because I am handsome, so I should command respect." "I am strong, therefore men should love me...

Tyranny is the wish to attain by one means what can only be had by another. (p. 96).

In sum, I believe that virtue ethics is just what business needs, and it especially needs it now, at a time in history that is "after virtue." Introducing virtue ethics to the business practices that surround us all may reinvigorate the language of virtue by providing vivid illustrations of virtue in practice. Is such a transformation of our moral language possible? MacIntyre was pretty pessimistic. But philosopher Jeffrey Stout, in *Ethics After Babel*, took MacIntyre to task for failing to notice the myriad small ways in everyday life in which the language of virtue was attached to virtuous practices. Stout discusses, for example, the efforts parents routinely make to encourage their kids to have high aspirations but simultaneously to be fair, show good sportsmanship and not cheat on the soccer field. There may, in short, still be a set of practices and institutions to use as the raw materials to reconstruct a language of virtue and a set of virtuous practices that foster businesses worthy not only of our patronage, but of our admiration. *Business Ethics: A Virtue Ethics and Common Good Approach* will certainly help in that effort.

References

MacIntyre, A. 1981, *After virtue*, South Bend, IN: University of Notre Dame Press.

Pascal, B. 1670/1961, *Pensees* (Cohen, J.M., trans.), New York: Penguin.

Polanyi, K. 1944, *The great transformation*, New York: Rinehart.

Robertson, D.H. 1956, 'What does the economist economize?', in D.H. Robertson (ed.), *Economic commentaries*, London: Staples.

Schwartz, B. 1986, *The battle for human nature*, New York: Norton

Schwartz, B. 1994, *The costs of living*, New York: Norton.

Schwartz, B. and Sharpe, K. 2011, *Practical wisdom*, New York: Riverhead.

Smith, A. 1753/1976, *The theory of moral sentiments*, Oxford: Clarendon Press.

Smith, A. 1776/1937, *The wealth of nations*, New York: Random House.

Stout, J. 1988, *Ethics after babel*, Princeton, NJ: Princeton University Press.

Walzer, M. 1983, *Spheres of justice*, New York: Basic Books.

EDITORIAL PREFACE

> Business is a vocation, and a noble vocation, provided that those engaged
> in it see themselves challenged by a greater meaning in life; this will enable
> them truly to serve the common good by striving to increase the goods of
> this world and to make them more accessible to all.
>
> Francis, *Evangelii Gaudium*, n. 203

Business for most is a zero–sum game in which one person's gain is necessarily another's loss. But, business can also be carried out for the "common good," such that everyone involved in the organization or deal wins. As a common good, the purpose of business, then, could only be achieved insofar as everyone else achieves his or her own good in harmony with others. Success in business is like success in a team sport: the whole team together wins the match, although each member plays a different role and perhaps only a few score. What's clear is that the team's goal could only be reached if everyone contributes his or her best in carrying out a particular role. In that case, their common purpose requires something more than the mere alignment of selfish, individual interests.

Understood this way, the aim of business cannot be the mere maximization of profits. Strictly speaking, profits cannot be shared; therefore, they cannot be held in common either. Profits in business are like a pie: one's slice diminishes as the number of partakers increases. No doubt, profits play a necessary part for businesses to be sustainable, but they are neither the sole nor the paramount objective. We believe, rather, that the purpose of business is the promotion of the "common good." This means, above all, the development of the virtues, knowledge, skills and meanings through collaborative work and the efficient production of quality goods and services in the market, resulting in profits. Profits come normally as a consequence of excellence in these collective and interrelated activities or pursuits. All businesses that work for the common good turn out to be profitable, although not all profitable businesses contribute to the common good (think of the drug or the arms trade, for instance). Note that virtues, knowledge, skills and meanings are elements that can be shared and their development benefits everyone. That's why in teaching or mentoring others, for example, one does not lose skill or knowledge, but rather increases it.

Thus, businesses serve to attain the ultimate human ideal of *eudaimonia* or flourishing in society, not only by providing the necessary material means for wellbeing, but also by creating opportunities for the practice of all sorts of human excellences or virtues through work.

This textbook is structured in the following manner. It begins with an introductory chapter that explains the virtue and common good focus of the whole volume, as well as the main sources for these teachings, namely, Aristotle, Alasdair MacIntyre and Catholic Social Teaching. A chapter on cross-functional leadership comes next, followed by others on different operational areas in the business firm, such as finance, production, marketing, human resources, legal affairs and corporate governance. The chapter on Confucian virtue ethics traditions brings the book to a close.

Each unit comprises a theoretical explanation of how various virtue ethics sources shed light on a particular business function and an original case or vignettes that illustrate the challenge to practice the virtues and aim for the common good. Helpful summaries of theoretical contributions as well as case discussion guidelines are also included in every chapter.

As a collective work, overlaps and repetitions are inevitable, but this is a small price to pay for the richness of the distinctive voices speaking harmoniously in the virtues and common good key. All the different continents are represented, with authors coming from Africa (Nigeria), Asia (Philippines, China, Macao, Hong Kong), the Americas (Argentina, Chile, Guatemala, Mexico, the United States, Venezuela) and Europe (Germany, Spain, Italy). They bring forward the results of their research and experience not only with huge, multinational companies and industry leaders such as Volkswagen, Primark, Ben & Jerry's (Unilever), and Wells Fargo, but also small and medium enterprises from various sectors, such as Stelac Advisory Services LLC, Adelante Shoe Company, Innobe Consulting, Ethniki Oil Services and Ouro Casino and Hotel.

We'd like to thank all our co-authors for their generous contribution to this ambitious, global project.

We'd also like to express our gratitude to Barry Schwartz, whose work on the virtues we admire and wish to emulate.

Special thanks as well to our editors at Routledge—Natalie Tomlinson, Judith Lorton and Lucy McClune—for their invaluable assistance in putting this whole project together.

Alejo José G. Sison
Ignacio Ferrero
Gregorio Guitián
Pamplona
September 14, 2017

1

VIRTUES AND THE COMMON GOOD IN BUSINESS

Alejo José G. Sison, Ignacio Ferrero and Gregorio Guitián

Learning objectives

In this introductory chapter, we shall:

- Define the meaning and scope of the virtues and the common good in business, in accordance with Aristotle, Catholic Social Teaching (CST) and Alasdair MacIntyre.
- Illustrate how personal virtues enmesh with corporate culture and traditions.

Virtue ethics is one of the three major schools of ethics in business and management, together with utilitarianism and deontology. The virtue ethics tradition is "agent-centered," focusing on what choices and decisions do to individuals, while utilitarianism and deontology are "action-centered." Utilitarianism judges actions based on results or outcomes, preferring situations when benefits outweigh costs, while deontology prescribes actions in conformity with rules or laws. Utilitarian storekeepers would most likely keep a €500 bill (they actually exist!) lying on the floor, happy they're now that much richer, whereas deontological storekeepers would bring it immediately to the police station in accordance with local ordinances, proud that they've done their duty. Virtuous storekeepers, for their part, may hold on to the money for a day, just in case the owner returned, and only afterwards report to the police. Why? Because it's more likely for whoever lost the money to go back to the shop than to proceed to the police station. The last thing virtuous shop owners would do is to keep what doesn't belong to them—that makes them somewhat like thieves. However, they would also think of the best way to return the money to its rightful owner. So, although virtuous shop owners may eventually do the same as their deontological colleagues, the motives are different.

This example may be a bit too simple, but we nevertheless think the virtue ethics tradition is superior to both utilitarianism and deontology. Despite being "agent-centered," that is, asking in first place "what *kind of person do I become* in performing this action?," virtue ethics also considers actions, albeit secondarily. Virtue ethics weighs the consequences of actions (like utilitarianism) as well as their agreement with rules (like deontology). However, for virtue ethics, unlike utilitarianism, there are "exceptionless prohibitions" or actions that should never be done, regardless of consequences, such as killing the innocent; and unlike deontology, rules are to be followed while paying close attention to particular contexts (including results), never for the sake of rules alone. Virtue ethics, then, afford a more holistic and integral account of agents and actions than the alternatives.

In business and management, deontology has been dominant in theory, with the proliferation of organizational codes of conduct, while utilitarianism has been dominant in practice. Virtue ethics, for its part, had all but disappeared among English-speaking academics, until the publication of Anscombe's essay "Modern moral philosophy" in 1958, sparking the beginning of a revival. A recent literature review of business and management journals reveals that virtue ethics articles shot up from one in the decade of the 1980s to close to 80 in the decade ending in 2010, signaling a strong trend (Ferrero and Sison 2014). Aristotelian, MacIntyrean and Catholic Social Teaching-inspired virtue ethics schools have been the most influential, with topics clustering round "virtues in relations between individuals and firms as moral agents," "virtue ethics as a model for the study and teaching of business ethics" and "virtues in moral psychology, decision-making and leadership" (Ferrero and Sison 2014). Empirical and quantitative methods have also been introduced through Positive Organizational Studies (POS) and the notion of "virtuousness," and interest in Confucian virtue ethics has likewise been stoked, strengthening the tradition's universalist claims (Sison, Beabout and Ferrero 2017).

1. Sources for virtue ethics in business

The three main sources for virtue ethics in business are Aristotle, Catholic Social Teaching and Alasdair MacIntyre.

a. Aristotle

"Virtue" comes from the Latin word "*virtus*," which originates from "*vis*," meaning "force," "power" or "strength." "*Virtus*" is the translation of a Greek concept, "*arête*," which stands for "what is best" or "excellence" in human beings. "Virtue" therefore means "what is best in human beings" or "human excellence." To discover the best for human beings, in a typically Aristotelian fashion, we first have to know what human beings are and the aim or goal of human life. This leads us to examine, on the one hand, the "nature" (*physis*) of human beings, that is, their distinctive activity or function (*ergon*), and on the other, their "final end," which ultimately leads to "happiness" or "flourishing" (*eudaimonia*) (*Nicomachean Ethics*, henceforth NE: 1097b–1098a).

We shall now explain some characteristic features of Aristotle's teachings on the virtues: (1) the reference to the "nature" and "final end" of human beings; (2) their presence in a full range of dispositions to action; and (3) the link to "practical wisdom" (*phronesis*).

Virtues refer to the "nature" and "final end" of human beings

Aristotle defines human nature as that of a "political animal" (NE: 1097b; Politics, henceforth Pltcs: 1253a) or a "living creature that uses words" (Pltcs: 1253a, Metaphysics 1037b). Unlike other animals, humans live and thrive in complex, organized structures called cities (*poleis*, the plural form of *polis*). Also, human beings are distinctively capable of rational thought (*logos*), making use of words to communicate with each other. Virtues perfect human beings in their nature as social and rational creatures.

Virtues as "excellences" are anchored on a specific account not only of human nature, but also of its goal or end, happiness or flourishing (*eudaimonia*). Virtues are necessary for and partially constitutive of flourishing. For Aristotle, flourishing is the end or purpose of politics, because it can only be achieved in a political community (NE: 1095a), which represents fully developed human existence (Pltcs: 1252b). This stresses the need for community, with its web of relationships and spheres (familial, educational, religious, economic, civic or political, and so forth). Since flourishing can be attained only with the help of others and together with them, it is a common good.

Flourishing involves "living well and doing well" (NE: 1098a). This requires both material means and virtues. Hence the importance of the economy, concerned with material resources ("external goods" and "goods of the body"), and ethics, particularly the virtues ("goods of the soul") (NE: 1098b; Pltcs: 1323a). There is a proper order between them, however. External, bodily goods are mere conditions for the performance of excellent actions, the goods of the soul (the virtues) (Pltcs: 1324a). Both the economy and ethics are subordinated to politics (NE: 1094a), as they contribute to the supreme good of flourishing. Flourishing is the highest good because we desire it for itself, and whatever other good we desire, we desire it for flourishing's sake.

Virtues apply to a full range of dispositions

Although virtues as "excellences" apply primarily to character, they speak to other dispositions to action such as habits as well (NE: 1103a). A virtuous character comes from the cultivation of virtuous habits. Virtuous habits themselves result from the repeated performance of virtuous actions, and virtuous actions, in turn, arise from virtuous inclinations or tendencies. Inclinations and tendencies are called "virtuous" insofar as they are in accord with human nature and its final end. Therefore, a conscientious reading of Aristotle reveals that virtues as "excellences" designate, apart from character, inclinations and tendencies, actions and habits, and, indeed, even lives as a whole. They are "multi-track dispositions" attributable to a "certain sort of person with a certain complex mindset" (Hursthouse 2013). We shall proceed with how the virtues may be found in each of these capacities or dispositions.

Actions

Aristotelian ethics is premised on a "proper human function" (*ergon*). This consists of "some sort of life of action of the [part of the soul] that has reason" (NE: 1098a). Human excellence resides in fulfilling this function finely and well: "the human good turns out to be the soul's activity that expresses virtue" (NE: 1098a).

How do we account for the moral significance of actions? First, we must distinguish between involuntary and voluntary actions. Involuntary acts occur by force of nature; people are passive subjects (NE: 1110a). Voluntary actions are those that agents perform intentionally and deliberately, receiving praise or blame (NE: 1111a). They proceed from an internal principle, such as an appetite, feeling, desire or will. Only voluntary actions are truly human actions.

Good voluntary actions are virtuous actions. Their moral valence comes from a triple source in a specific order: the object, the agent's end or intention, and the circumstances. First comes the object of the action: what the agent does as a meaningful whole, not just the physical motions. The object principally determines whether an action is good or evil. Certain actions are prohibited because of their object, such as lying, theft, murder or torture (NE: 1110a). They constitute the matter of absolute or "exceptionless" moral prohibitions.

Next comes the agent's intention, which has to be properly oriented towards the agent's final end. An action choiceworthy by its object may become flawed due to the agent's intention. Think of almsgiving just for show. In third place are the circumstances. "Unfavorable" circumstances sometimes render a good action censurable, as when a person gave so much money to charity that he jeopardized his own solvency. However, "favorable" circumstances do not change the moral quality of an action from evil to good. The evil of torturing just one person is not offset by the belief it could save many lives.

The moral goodness, excellence or virtue of human actions requires the integrity of all three—object, intention, and circumstances. Any defect would turn a voluntary human act evil.

Habits

Habits develop from the repetition of voluntary human actions (NE: 1103a). Every action leaves a trace or by-product called "habit": a stable disposition or manner of being, doing, acting or behaving. Habits comprise a second level in the virtues.

Habit-formation or habituation presupposes freedom. Education, the primordial task of legislators, is nothing else but the formation of good habits

(NE: 1103b). Freedom exists on three levels. The first is physical freedom, an openness or capacity for movement. A human being is deprived of physical freedom when bound or imprisoned, for example. Next comes psychological freedom or freedom of choice. Whenever people choose, their sovereign will is the determining factor. They identify with their moral choices, taking responsibility for them. The third level of freedom is moral freedom. Unlike the first two levels, which are "givens" forming part of our natural condition, moral freedom is a conquest. Physical freedom and psychological freedom are "negative freedoms"—freedoms from contrary physical forces and psychological determinants. Moral freedom is a "positive freedom," a freedom to aspire to something superior and greater than our natural condition. People achieve moral freedom when they develop virtues as good habits. Virtuous habits enable people to perform more good actions better, not only improving their "moral skill" but also deriving greater pleasure and satisfaction. It's similar to how pianists improve through practice, eventually becoming "virtuosos," perhaps. As new, improved and reinforced dispositions, habits constitute a "second nature" for human beings.

Both virtues and vices arise from the repetition of actions (NE: 1103b), but only good actions produce virtues. For example, when faced with a terrifying situation, those who have the habit of courage react bravely and confidently, while those with cowardice, fearfully. How are we to distinguish between right and wrong habituation?

First, to acquire proper habituation, "actions should express correct reason" (NE: 1103b). Individual actions whose repetition constitutes a habit should be done in accordance with reason, with what is opportune in each particular case, as expert doctors or navigators do in practice. Second, right habituation shuns excess and defect (NE: 1104a). The stable disposition generated by repeated action is oriented towards a "golden mean," defined with regard to the individual agent. For instance, someone who is temperate in food and drink neither eats and drinks too little nor too much, but just right. Third, proper habituation comes from an individual's experiencing pleasure or pain in the appropriate kind of action (NE: 1104b). The temperate person delights in eating and drinking just right, abhorring both indulgence and want. With respect to a good habit,

> virtue is a state that decides, [consisting] in a mean, the mean relative to us, which is defined by reference to reason, i.e., to the reason by reference to which the intelligent person would define it. It is a mean between two vices, one of excess and one of deficiency.
>
> *(NE: 1107a)*

Character

Although character is constituted by different habits, the whole is greater than the sum of parts. Character displays greater permanence than habits and is more difficult to change. Character provides a more accurate and complete picture of a person than habits, which are limited to single traits. Knowing a person's character, we would be able to predict actions and reactions better.

Just as a habit unifies many different acts, character integrates diverse habits. Habits perfect a person's operational "faculties," and each habit can exist in various stages of development. A person could be not only temperate or brave, but also braver than temperate. Character accounts for a person's various habits and their degree of development. A habit may reinforce or diminish the effect of others in a person's character. For example, a prudent person is more likely to be brave, just or temperate. Character lends a unique, personal touch to an individual's habits.

Aristotle considers character states the proper genus for virtue (NE: 1106a). Virtue is a good state that causes possessors to perform their specific function well (NE: 1106a). Virtues of character are valued both for their instrumental (they enable one to function well) and their absolute worth (they make one a good human being).

The right character state lies in a mean—not a numerical mean, but one relative to agents. Virtue of character is an intermediate state that eschews the superfluous and the deficient (NE: 1106b).

How do we to acquire virtues of character? Since virtue of character lies in the mean, Aristotle admonishes, first, to avoid the more opposed extreme (NE: 1109a). With regard to courage, for example, it would be better to err on rashness (excess) than on cowardice (defect). Second, Aristotle suggests that one avoid the easier extreme, depending on one's natural inclination (NE: 1109b). With pleasures, for instance, most tend towards intemperance rather than insensibility (NE: 1109b).

Virtues of character deal with concrete, contingent actions and feelings (NE: 1109b). Aristotle remits us ultimately to the perception of a virtuous person, who alone is the competent judge. Indeed, having virtue of character is not so much a matter of feeling or acting, as doing so "at the right times, about the right things, towards the right people, for the right end, and in the right way, [that] is, the intermediate and best condition, and this is proper virtue" (NE: 1106b). This can only be achieved heuristically: "this is not one, and is not the same for everyone" (NE: 1106a). People of virtuous character are all virtuous in their own particular ways.

Lifestyles

Lifestyle choice is arguably the most influential factor in how an individual feels, behaves and lives. Virtue as moral excellence may also be manifested in one's all-encompassing lifestyle choice.

Everyone agrees, at least in name, that what we ultimately seek is *"eudaimonia,"* a flourishing life. Whatever we do, we believe it brings us closer to this goal. Flourishing is desirable in itself and everything else becomes choiceworthy because of it. Flourishing represents the definitive form of virtue or moral excellence; it is human nature in its perfect state.

Despite the terminological agreement on flourishing (*eudaimonia*), not every-one coincides in the kind of life it entails. Aristotle explores four different life-styles as candidates. First, he considers one centered on wealth or money (NE: 1096a). Aristotle then shrugs it aside because money is desirable only instru-mentally. The value of money lies in being a means in exchange for some other object, which is the end. Not that Aristotle despises material wealth; albeit "ex-ternal," he still considers money a "good" and acknowledges that certain pros-perity is necessary for flourishing (NE: 1099a–b).

The next contender is a life of pleasure (NE: 1095b). Aristotle attributes this choice to the many without proper education. Neither does this option convince him, for such a life is "completely slavish" and proper to "grazing animals." Not that Aristotle questions the appeal of pleasure, but endowed with reason, humans should aspire for higher things. Similarly, Aristotle ascribes this choice to those in power who behave as slaves of gratification.

The third option is a life of action, a political life that pursues honor (NE: 1095b). This seems reserved to a cultivated few. However, neither does Aristotle agree with it. For although honor is more elevated than pleasure, it

> appears to be too superficial to be what we are seeking, since it seems to de-pend more on those who honor than on the one who is honored, whereas we intuitively believe that the good is something of our own and hard to take from us.
>
> *(NE: 1095b)*

Further, honor is rendered for a reason, and one should investigate the grounds for praise. We seek to be honored not by anyone, but by those who know us; by intelligent people, rather than by the foolish. We seek to be honored for our virtue (NE: 1095b).

For Aristotle, the best life is one of knowledge or study (*theoria*), which repre-sents the highest form of virtue (NE: 1177a). He enumerates some of its features. First, it is self-contained, a life that includes its own end (NE: 1098b). Second, it is pleasant in itself, for being pleased is a condition of the soul included in its own proper activity (NE: 1099a). And third, it is in accordance with reason and sound judgment (NE: 1099a). Reason is man's superior faculty, and a life of knowledge re-volves around the noblest objects, the immutable and eternal realities (NE: 1100b).

Virtue is the stable and controlling element in flourishing (NE: 1100b). Due to its nobility, self-sufficiency, pleasantness and continuity, it as a life inclusive of all good, more proper to gods than human beings (NE: 1177b). A life of virtue encapsulates the advantages of all the other lifestyles.

Practical wisdom (phronesis) lies at the heart of virtues

It is not enough for an action to seem objectively good to a neutral, third-party observer to be truly virtuous in the Aristotelian sense. Such an action may be the result of a natural inclination or a feeling, but not rational choice. Take for instance a baby that resorts to smiling instead of crying to attract the attention of grown-ups. Virtue demands that an action be the outcome of a conscious decision accompanied by the right reasons. Good intentions alone are not sufficient either. Think of rescuers who remove a victim from a car wreck, but cause further harm by not knowing the proper way. Virtue calls for a correct appreciation of the situation and the practical knowledge of how to proceed. It goes beyond theoretical, abstract, general knowledge and rule-following. Thus, all acts of virtue require practical wisdom or prudence, a rational choice accompanied by the right reasons to act in a certain way, given a set of circumstances. Practical wisdom usually comes with age and experience, which afford an appropriate perception of what is humanly salient in varying contexts.

Practical wisdom is not innate; but once gained, it seems to be a natural state. This misleads many to think that it is impossible to acquire virtue, because to become prudent—for example—one must first do prudent actions. Yet, prudent actions could only be done by one who is already prudent! This circularity makes us think that either one is already by nature prudent or one is not. And being incapable by nature of prudent actions, no amount of habituation will ever make one prudent.

Aristotle offers some clarifications that, besides undoing this paradox, also establish the limits of the craft analogy in the virtues. In the crafts, one may produce something that conforms to a certain expertise only in appearance. The object could have been produced "by chance or by following someone else's instructions" (NE: 1105a)—that is, without accompanying knowledge. Furthermore, "the products of a craft determine by their own character whether they have been produced well; and so it suffices that they are in the right state when they have been produced" (NE: 1105b). Craft products have an objective goodness or excellence without reference to the craftsman.

There is no such thing as an objectively virtuous action, independently of the person who performs it. A virtuous act could never be separated from the virtuous habit or from the virtuous person with the habit. There is a feedback loop along the full range of human dispositions that are analogues of virtue. For an action to be virtuous, it has to be performed as a virtuous person would, and this entails: advertence that one is doing a virtuous act; the decision to do the virtuous act for itself; and lastly, the habit—that "firm and unchanging state"—from which the virtuous act proceeds (NE: 1105a). Since virtuous actions do not occur in a void but in concrete situations, practical wisdom will always be necessary.

The insistence on internal, subjective conditions is important. Virtue cannot be what is merely apparent or superficially good (NE: 1106a). Virtue demands integrity, a complete and thorough goodness. Practical wisdom produces an alignment among right thinking and perception, right desire and right action; it creates harmony among reason, sensibility or emotions and behavior. Thus, we distinguish among one who is weak-willed (*akrasia*) and acts against his better judgment, another who simply practices self-control or is continent (*enkrateia*) and a third who possesses temperance or moderation (NE: 1145a–1152a). The first acts contrary to reason, the second experiences desires contrary to his actual behavior, while in the third, desires and behavior are in synch with his character state. Apart from temperance or moderation, the third also displays practical wisdom.

Together with Aristotle (NE: 1145a), medieval schoolmen consider prudence as the charioteer (*auriga*) that guides and the mother (*genitrix*) that begets all other virtues; without it, no other virtue is possible. This is due to a two-step reasoning. First, all virtues essentially involve practical, normative knowledge, like practical wisdom, and second, knowledge is essentially unified, for to evaluate something is to compare it relative to the value of others. There is a unity among the virtues, such that an individual cannot have one moral virtue without the others (Telfer 1990). This is especially true in the case of practical wisdom: without it, one cannot have any other virtue; but with it, one has all the others.

- For Aristotle, virtues are distinctively human excellences found in different operational levels, which are a necessary condition for flourishing.

b. Catholic Social Teaching

Catholic Social Teaching (CST) is the part of moral theology containing official Church doctrine on social issues. Modern CST began with Leo XIII's encyclical or circular on capital and labor, *Rerum Novarum* (RN), published in 1891, and has broadened to include documents from the Second Vatican Council, apart from papal encyclicals, letters, messages and addresses. CST emerges from the contact of Gospel teachings with social problems. Its purpose is "to stimulate greater insight into the authentic requirements of justice as well as greater readiness to act accordingly" (Benedict XVI, *Deus Caritas Est* (DCE) 2005: 28).

Is not CST's goal hampered by its forming part of Catholic Moral Theology, grounded on authority, beliefs and faith-based claims? What is its value for a secular and democratic society, or for a religious one that does not adhere to the Catholic or Christian credo?

First, Catholics account for almost a fifth of the world's population. By sheer numbers, their official beliefs and practices are influential in the global arena. Further, although the Pope is head only of a miniscule state, Vatican City, he is a global moral and spiritual leader. His teachings possess a unique force, because he is not beholden to particular economic, political and ideological interests. He enjoys people's trust.

Second, CST addresses all people of goodwill and "argues on the basis of reason and natural law, namely, on what is in accord with the nature of every human being" (DCE: 28). CST speaks not only to Catholics. It does not "impose on those who do not share the Catholic faith ways of thinking and modes of conduct proper to faith" (DCE: 28); rather, it proposes cogent explanations of social issues, from reason in harmony with faith.

Third, CST proposals are in line with a growing interest in spirituality and management, borne from the recognition of the non-material or spiritual dimension of human beings. It could make valuable contributions, insofar as religion is a form of spirituality, and business ethics inseparable from management.

And fourth, CST adopts an interdisciplinary approach that provides permanent principles rooted in human nature, orienting action amidst burgeoning social and historical change (Compendium of the Social Doctrine of the Church (CSDC): 76–77).

CST presents six core principles to guide social action in accordance with the virtues: human dignity (personalist principle), common good, universal destination of goods, subsidiarity, participation and solidarity. These principles should not be taken in isolation, for they are interrelated, reciprocal and complementary. They comprise an organic unity or body expressing the truth about society; they constitute a universal and permanent normative standard (CSDC: 163). We shall proceed to explain each one.

Human dignity is the basic principle of CST: "individual human beings [possessors of this "sacred dignity"] are the foundation, the cause and the end of every social institution" (John XXIII, *Mater et Magistra* (MeM) 1961: 219, 220). Also known as the "personalist principle," it states that "the person represents the ultimate end of society" (CSDC: 105, 132). Other aspects of personhood besides dignity are the unity of body and soul, openness to Transcendence (human beings are made in God's image and likeness), uniqueness or unrepeatability and freedom (CSDC: 124–148). Dignity refers to the intrinsic worth of every human being, associated with its capacity for reason and autonomy (self-determination) through free choice. Dignity implies the need for consensus and mutual recognition or respect in the community.

The common good principle "stems from the dignity, unity and equality of all people" (CSDC: 164). It is often defined as "the sum total of the social conditions which allow people, either as groups or as individuals, to reach their fulfillment more easily" (Vatican II, *Gaudium et Spes* (GeS) 1965: 26). However, it is not "the simple sum of the particular goods of each subject of a social entity," because "belonging to everyone and to each person, […] it is indivisible and […] only together is it possible to attain it, increase it and safeguard its effectiveness" (CSDC: 164). Hence, it's better understood as "the social and community dimension of the moral good" (CSDC: 164) or "the good of all people and of the whole person" (CSDC: 165). The common good consists of three essential elements: respect for the person; the social well-being and development of the group; and peace, the stability and security of a just order (*Catechism of the Catholic Church*: 107–109). Therefore, the common good is the aim of dignity, bearing in mind the relational nature of human beings. Due to the principle of the common good, individual flourishing can only be achieved jointly with the flourishing of others in the community.

Corollary to the common good is the principle of the "universal destination of goods": "God intended the earth with everything contained in it for the use of all human beings and peoples," ordaining "that all created things would be shared fairly by all mankind under the guidance of justice tempered by charity" (GeS: 69). Yet, this does not imply that everything be at the disposal of all, because rights have to be exercised in an equitable and orderly fashion (CSDC: 173). Hence, the institution of "private property," by which humans stake claim over part of the earth as their own through work (John Paul II, *Centesimus Annus* (CA) 1991: 31), to ensure personal autonomy and safeguard social order. Private property is not absolute but should always have a "social function" (MeM: 430–431), subordinated to the "universal destination of goods" (John Paul II, *Laborem Exercens* (LE) 1981: 14). An offshoot of this is a "preferential option for the poor" and marginalized.

The principle of subsidiarity is best expressed in the following:

> Just as it is gravely wrong to take from individuals what they can accomplish by their own initiative and industry and give it to the community, so also it is an injustice and at the same time a great evil and disturbance of right order to assign to a greater and higher association what lesser and subordinate organizations can do. For every social activity ought of its very nature to furnish help [subsidium] to the members of the body social, and never destroy and absorb them.
>
> *(Pius XI,* Quadragesimo Anno *(QA) 1931: 79)*

Human dignity is best served when higher-order entities, such as the State, provide assistance to the lower-order entities of civil society, instead of absorbing or substituting them. To do otherwise is to supplant freedom, initiative and responsibility: "Subsidiarity respects personal dignity by recognizing in the person a subject who is always capable of giving something to others" (Benedict XVI, *Caritas in Veritate* (CiV) 2009: 57).

Connected to subsidiarity is the principle of participation (Paul VI, *Octogesima Adveniens* (OA) 1971: 22, 46). It imposes on individuals the right and duty to contribute to the cultural, economic, political and social life, with the common good in view (GeS: 75). In politics, participation implies upholding the democratic process, against totalitarian and dictatorial regimes (CSDC: 190–191). Participation in social life and institutions elevates basic dignity to superior levels.

Last but not least is the principle of solidarity, "interdependence" or "socialization" (MeM: 49; GeS: 42; LE: 14–15). It's the awareness of a deep bond in humanity: "the intrinsic social nature of the human person, the equality of all in dignity and rights and the common path of individuals and peoples towards an ever more committed unity" (CSDC: 192). Solidarity is not a mere "feeling of vague compassion or shallow distress" at others' misfortune, but a "firm and persevering determination" to work for the common good (John Paul II, *Sollicitudo Rei Socialis* (SRS) 1987: 38; LE: 8; CA: 57).

Business ethics is a sort of professional ethics and, like all professional ethics, it is an ethics of work. CST also proposes a clear normative indication in this regard. In work understood as any productive activity carried out by human beings, CST distinguishes two outcomes: one, external to agents (the objective dimension), and the other, internal (the subjective dimension). For CST, the objective dimension of work is "the sum of activities, resources, instruments and technologies used by men and women to produce things," while the subjective dimension, "the activity of the human person as a dynamic being capable of performing a variety of actions" (CSDC: 270). CST requires that in work we prioritize the subjective dimension (the knowledge, skills, meanings and virtues people develop) over the objective dimension (the material products and services, including profits) (LE: 6).

- CST principles provide an orientation for virtuous action in society and establish a normative priority among the different outcomes of work.

c. MacIntyre

It may seem strange to consider Alasdair MacIntyre a source for virtues in business, given his solid, long-standing opposition to capitalism since his early work "Marxism and Christianity" (MacIntyre 1995 [1953]). Modern business is fully ensconced in capitalism, and MacIntyre identifies capitalist production with the twin evils of Weberian bureaucracy and modern Enlightenment (Beadle and Moore 2006). Weberian managers prove effective in bureaucracies thanks to the impersonal, mechanical performance of work. They pursue objectives they do not determine and that are, instead, imposed from above. Decision-making is strictly utilitarian. The compartmentalization of life-spheres (typical of liberal societies) gives rise to the belief that performance as a professional manager has no moral bearing on other social roles, such as being a family member or a citizen of the country, for instance. In these non-work-related realms, choices are made through emotivist criteria such as the satisfaction of individual preferences, if not through cost-benefit analysis. Nothing is more hostile to the virtues than the individualism, utilitarianism and emotivism at the foundations of the Enlightenment.

MacIntyre (1995 [1953]) also criticizes capitalism as the cause of worker alienation. Productive activities are chopped-up or decomposed into simple, meaningless units that even machines can do for the sake of productivity and profits. Workers lose sight of the purpose, meaning and context of their labor as a whole; they are reduced to being just another cog in the capitalist wheel. Work loses all personal value.

Despite such ideological hostility, however, a community of scholars still makes use of MacIntyre's fundamental concepts and methods, describing business organizations and providing normative, virtue ethics standards (Moore 2002, 2012; Moore and Beadle 2006). Underlying these studies is the belief that human action is always socially and historically situated, and therefore cannot be correctly interpreted or judged morally from the neutral standpoint of abstract, general notions of "justice as such" or "prudence as such." The same reasoning then applies to the virtues. More than any other contemporary author, MacIntyre bequeaths us with the resources for a much needed historical and sociological account of the virtues, without losing sight of the metaphysical nature of human ends (*teloi*). In this, MacIntyre lends an invaluable service to ethics in general and to virtue ethics in business in particular.

MacIntyre's sociological approach to the virtues goes through three stages (MacIntyre 2007 [1981]: 273). First, he defines practices (e.g., chess-playing) in contrast to institutions (e.g., chess tournaments with cash prizes, thanks to which chess players can earn a living) and establishes the goods internal and the standards inherent to cooperative practices. Without practices, there are no virtues, because there would be no goods internal to the performance of activities. This would be the difference between playing a musical instrument, which has an internal good and qualifies as a practice, and surfing the internet, which lacks an internal good, for instance. Next, MacIntyre examines how individual agents of practices render their various roles compatible as they live out their biographies or life-narratives. That is because practices are always carried out by flesh and blood agents continually called upon to perform a variety of roles (e.g., familial, professional, religious, athletic, civic and so forth), often in conflict with each other. Virtue consists of the successful, hierarchical ordering of roles, practices and goods. This second requirement underscores the social embeddedness of the virtues through the different roles agents play. Third, the fulfillment of practices and roles also ought to contribute to their development, in advancing the "craft" so to speak, for the benefit of the whole community. Consider what Yo-Yo Ma has done for cellists, for example. Virtues push practices, role-playing individuals and entire communities towards shared excellence in time. Virtues are responsible for the continuous progress of traditions towards their goal, end or perfection.

In a recent work "Ethics in the Conflicts of Modernity" (2016), MacIntyre emphasizes that both the goal and the path of ethics as practical reasoning are common goods. Aristotle established the formal conditions of the common good as first, something that we reasonably desire and which perfects us, and second, something that can only be achieved collaboratively. He also identified flourishing (*eudaimonia*) as the common good of the political community, on which all other human goods are premised. CST put forward the common good principle as "the social and community dimension of the moral good" (CSDC: 164) and "the good of all people and of the whole person" (CSDC: 165). Now MacIntyre asserts that properly recognizing, engaging and developing practices is also a common good. He exemplifies this through a series of stories involving a Danish fishing cooperative, a Brazilian favela, a Kentucky farm, a Japanese car factory and the BBC, among others.

The fact is we rely on others even in procuring our own individual goods. None of us could have become the "independent practical reasoners" we are without the help of committed caregiving individuals and communities, especially our families, during our infancy and youth. All the more so when it comes to attempting the superior common goods—"the goods of family, of political society, of workplace, of sports teams, orchestras, and theatre companies" (MacIntyre 2016: 51–52)—which we can only achieve and enjoy as members of these groups. Deliberation about these goods and how to attain them can only take place as shared deliberation within these collectives. As moral agents in search of our own good, we cannot help but act as social and political agents at the same time, unstintingly influencing the common good. Experience in business or the workplace is no different, for "the common goods of those at work together are achieved in producing goods and services that contribute to the life of the community and in becoming excellent at producing them" (MacIntyre 2016: 170).

The virtues we display at work and in business are essentially the same as the ones we practice in other life-spheres, as members of different communities. We perfect our work skills and we perfect ourselves as human beings, developing distinctive human excellences or virtues, while collaborating with each other in firms to produce goods and services for society.

- MacIntyre contributes a sociological account of the virtues and the common good that is sensitive to differences in time and place.

2. Wells Fargo: not all that glitters is gold

Wells Fargo (WF) was founded in 1852. Its present form is the result of a merger between Wells Fargo & Company and Norwest Corporation in 1998, and the acquisition of Wachovia in 2008. Headquartered in San Francisco, California, WF is now a diversified, community-based financial services company with $1.9 trillion in assets. It offers banking services, loans and credits, insurance, investment services, wealth management services and so forth through 8,600 offices, 13,000 ATMs and the internet. WF operates in 42 countries with 273,000 employees. It is the world's second-largest bank by market capitalization and the third largest bank in the US by assets.[1]

WF was among the few institutions that emerged unscathed from the 2007 sub-prime crisis. While other banks were mired in mortgage and trading scandals, WF took pride in its unswerving dedication to help small businesses and families prosper. It portrayed itself as a stalwart bank, a community bank that always puts customers first. Accordingly, WF was seen on Wall Street as a class apart from the risky global investment banks that triggered the mortgage crisis. In 2013, WF CEO, John Stumpf, was named "Banker of the Year" by the trade magazine "The American Banker" and became the industry's highest paid executive (Aspan 2013).

Key to WF's success was the Community Bank. Inherited from Norwest, it was run with a decentralized corporate structure[2] and enjoyed a long history of stellar sales performance. Ever since the 1998 merger, a catchphrase within the company was "Run it like you own it," indicating the degree of freedom among WF businesses not only to determine their own activities, but also to exercise risk and human resources functions, for instance. In 2002, Carrie Tolstedt was named Head of regional banking and promoted to lead the Community Bank in 2007.

When told of her promotion, Tolstedt immediately thought how proud her father would be. She remembered growing up as the local baker's daughter in Kimball, a small village in Nebraska. During those years, she learned from her father how to run a small business, using bits of home-grown finance and marketing, and above all, trying to keep customers happy. Customer satisfaction was going to be her guiding principle at work.

Tolstedt graduated from the University of Nebraska and joined Norwest in 1986. Her job was to oversee branches in Omaha. One of her most important achievements at that time was to increase the bank's "cross-sell ratio," a measure of how many different banking accounts were held on average by customers. Combining products and services, and offering discounts on fees if customers signed up at once, allowed her to raise her numbers dramatically.

Strong financial performance and high levels of customer satisfaction and employee engagement allowed Tolstedt to cement her leadership role within the bank. Nobody was surprised when Tolstedt was named Head of regional banking at WF in 2002 and five years later was promoted to lead the Community Bank.

The WF CEO Stumpf had enormous respect for Tolstedt's intellect, work ethic, acumen and discipline, thinking she was the "most brilliant" Community Banker he had ever met. She came from Main Street to show how to run the business at the WF flagship in Wall Street.

In late 2013, a Los Angeles Times article revealed, however, that not everything was going on well behind the bank's closed doors (Reckard 2013). Let's hear it from some former WF employees:[3]

Scott T. was a teller and service representative in Galesburg, Illinois in 2009. He was supposed to sell six products a day, regardless of whether he had sold 20 on any particular day. A veteran banker taught him to set fake appointments on his diary only to "cancel and rebook" on a different day. Once, he was reprimanded for not selling an old lady a credit card, saying she could use it as an ID in case a teller didn't know her. Customers were routinely forced into online banking, even opening e-mails for them, just to sell an online account. Because of all this, he would often hide in the men's room to cry. He even left work for the emergency room on an occasion, fearing he was having a heart attack.

Angie Payden was a banker in Hudson, Wisconsin, from 2011 to 2014. She recounts suffering extreme stress symptoms and panic attacks because of work. One day, to calm down before selling a customer unneeded services, she drank some hand sanitizer from the bathroom. Since then, she became addicted to hand sanitizer, drinking a bottle a day to soothe her anxiety. By December 2012, it became so bad she had to go on leave and seek treatment, after having been confronted by management for her behavior.

She attributes the extreme stress, the panic attacks and the sanitizer addiction to things the bank forced her to do. She was supposed to open travel checking accounts for customers, convincing them it was unsafe to travel without a separate checking account and debit card. Also, she would coerce customers to open credit card accounts as overdraft protection, even when they were already struggling to keep checking accounts balanced. Often, she would observe management pressuring staff to add credit defense onto new credit applications without the customer's knowledge, leading to more monthly fees. And lastly, bankers would frequently be closing and opening new accounts for customers, with the excuse that there had been fraud on previous accounts.

Far from being isolated cases, testimonies from different states imply that employee harassment due to unrealizable sales goals or unethical sales practices were recurrent and widespread in WF.

Denise C., a teller and banker in Houston, Texas from 2010 to 2016, tells her story. Despite reaching sales goals, she had to review with her boss every single customer relationship daily. She had to explain why clients weren't forced into opening a third, fourth and fifth checking account for Christmas, birthdays, school, pets and so on. In the end, she was so stressed out she developed shingles.

Ashlie Storms, a teller and banker in West Milford, New Jersey, from 2005 to 2016, has a similar tale. Her belief that customers are always right and that they shouldn't be forced into products or services they didn't need put her at odds with bank officers. She would get conference calls from regional presidents and managers coaching her on how to present selling points so customers couldn't refuse. Feeling like a cheat, she started losing sleep and got nauseous every Sunday night in anticipation of the workweek.

Indeed, albeit decentralized in keeping with the corporate culture, WF had its control systems, mainly through the HR, legal and audit functions, in place. There was no lack of codes of conduct or internal channels (hotlines) through which ethical concerns and complaints could be coursed. Yet, all this went to naught, as issues were ignored, downplayed or reported in a fragmentary fashion, preventing any full picture from emerging. When all else failed, WF authorities took recourse to ugly forms of retaliation against those who stood up against orders.

Beginning 2005, Julie Tishkoff, an administrative assistant, repeatedly wrote to HR about abuses she witnessed:[4] employees opening fake accounts, forging client signatures and issuing unsolicited credit cards. After four years of calling out such practices, she was fired in 2009 while her supervisors were promoted to regional presidents. In a similar vein, Christopher Johnson, a newly recruited banker in Malibu, California, said that WF emphasized the importance of its ethics code and the need to report potential wrongdoing through its confidential hotline. But upon reporting that his manager was pressuring him to open accounts for friends and family without their knowledge or consent, he was fired for not being a team player and failing to meet expectations.

Some of these complaints reached all the way to the CEO Stumpf's desk. Through the ethics hotline, Ricky Hansen reported fake accounts being opened, only to be fired for improperly looking up information in the database. Hansen then e-mailed Stumpf in 2011 about what had occurred. The bank's response was to offer to rehire him, albeit in a lower position, earning $30,000 less. Also in 2011, Rasheeda Kamar, a manager in New Milford, Illinois, sent Stumpf an e-mail protesting her termination for falling short of sales targets. She warned that other bankers were reaching their goals dishonestly, moving funds to new accounts to give an appearance of growth when, in fact, deposits did not increase. What's remarkable is that these incidents happened at least two full years before Stumpf acknowledged receiving notice during the Senate inquiries.

When the dust had settled, investigations by independent directors of the WF board listed the following shoddy practices in which the bank had egregiously engaged:[5]

a   Creating sham accounts without authorization or taking advantage of immigrants who spoke little English, older adults with memory problems or inexperienced college students.
b   Charging borrowers higher fees (listed cryptically on mortgage statements as "other charges" or "other fees"), from $95 to $120, for services that cost $50 or less.
c   Abusive cross-selling of unneeded products or services, and setting up unwanted online banking services.
d   Selling unrequested insurance policies from WF partner Prudential Financial. WF employees steered customers to self-service kiosks or a website on which to sign up. Other times, employees signed people up directly for insurance policies without their knowledge.
e   Improperly charging customers for extending interest rates when mortgage paperwork was delayed due to the bank's fault.
f   Sending hundreds of termination notices of former brokers and representatives to the Financial Industry Regulatory Authority (FINRA) with unfair allegations regarding the employees' dismissal. This made it almost impossible for people to relocate in the industry. Employees were sometimes threatened with this measure if they blew the whistle.

As a result of the aforementioned, in September 2016, WF was charged $185 million in fines for opening as many as 1.5 million bank accounts and 560,000 credit cards without authorization (a case in point: a branch manager had a teenage daughter with 24 accounts while her husband had 21). Meanwhile, the bank fired at least 5,300 low-level employees supposedly involved in these shenanigans. None of the higher-ranking officials were ever held accountable.

A view from the top

Despite the pressure-cooker sales culture battering employee morale and leading to ethical breaches, despite mounting customer complaints and labor lawsuits, the WF Board did not consider potentially abusive sales practices a risk until 2014.

That year, directors received reports from the Community Bank, Corporate Risk and Corporate Human Resources that sales practices were being examined, but by early 2015, such incidences had decreased. Meanwhile, the Risk Committee and the Chief Risk Office were trying to centralize and consolidate the resources of Corporate Risk. By 2015, top management reported smugly that corrective measures were taking effect.

But in May 2015, the Los Angeles Attorney's Office filed a lawsuit alleging widespread improper sales practices at WF branches in its jurisdiction. This brought intensified regulatory scrutiny. From that moment on until September 2016, when settlements were brokered, the WF Board regularly addressed sales practice issues during meetings. It even authorized contracting the services of third-party consultants to investigate sales practices and procedures in the Community Bank and to conduct an analysis of customer harm and remediation. Although throughout 2015 and 2016 the Board regularly dealt with the issue, top management failed to report the true breadth and depth of the problem.

The data showed that as sales goals became harder to achieve, allegations and terminations increased and the quality of accounts declined. Numbers for sales integrity-related allegations, on the one hand, and associated terminations and resignations, on the other, steadily increased from mid-2007 until the end of 2013. In May 2016, the Board received termination figures for sales practice violations in the Community Bank: 1,327 in 2014, followed by a 30% drop to 960 in 2015. Yet, in July 2016, around the time of Tolstedt's retirement, terminations for the first five months remained more or less steady at 483 in the Community Bank.

Because of these communications gaps within WF, until as late as 2015, the general perception of the Board was that sales practice abuses were a problem of relatively modest significance. Directors did not believe that such improper practices caused significant "customer harm," narrowly construed in terms of additional fees and penalties. They failed to take into account the risk to the WF brand and, above all, the loss of customer trust.

Case discussion guidelines

It is clear at this point that what was supposed to be a customer-centric bank in fact did not treat its employees any better than its customers. The glitter in its performance—celebrated for years as the nation's best-run bank—was false and undeserved. But why and how did this happen? Who is to blame? Let us take each of these questions in turn.

The study commissioned by independent members of the WF board enumerates the following causes among others, pertaining not only to individual actions but also to elements of corporate structure, dynamic and culture:[6]

1   Sales practices and culture
     The Community Bank's sales culture and performance management system created extreme pressure on employees to sell unwanted or unneeded

products and open unauthorized accounts. The Community Bank identified itself as a sales organization (like department or retail stores) rather than a service-oriented financial institution. Hence, a relentless focus on sales, shorter employee training and higher turnover. The bank insisted on selling as many new accounts as possible to meet performance goals (and receive higher pay) at the expense of customer service.

Employees felt that failure to meet sales goals meant career stagnation or termination. On the other hand, high sales performers were praised, rewarded and held up as models, regardless of methods. Managers explicitly encouraged subordinates to sell unnecessary products to meet sales goals. They led by fear and intimidation.

2   The decentralized corporate structure
WF gave too much autonomy to the Community Bank's senior leadership, who were unwilling to change the sales model or recognize it as the cause of problems.

Decentralized HR, Legal and Audit functions (terminations, hiring, training, coaching, discipline, incentive compensation, performance management, turnover, morale, work environment, claims and litigations) allowed problematic sales and performance management practices to persist. There was no coordinated effort to track, analyze and report on such issues.

Whenever misconduct was identified, offending employees were terminated without further investigations.

3   The leadership style

a   Leaders fostered an atmosphere of unethical behavior. The Community Bank's senior leaders distorted the sales model and performance management system, creating an atmosphere of low quality sales and improper behavior.

b   Leaders lacked oversight and control. Community Bank leaders even resisted and impeded outside scrutiny. They blindly stuck to their unscrupulous practices and model, as well as unrealistic sales goals.

c   Incoherence: "Do what I say but not what I do." Employees exchanged stories about the incoherence between their ethics training—where they were explicitly warned about misconduct—and the reality of their jobs.

During a Senate declaration on September 29, 2016, WF CEO Stumpf admitted to being "fully accountable for all unethical sales practices in our retail banking business" and expressed regret for "not doing more sooner to address the causes of this unacceptable activity." He added that he was "deeply sorry that we failed to fulfill our responsibility to our customers, to our team members and to the American public" (McGrath 2016). Stumpf tendered his resignation as CEO and Chairman on October 12, 2016. On April 7, 2017, WF determined to claw back approximately $28 million of Stumpf's incentive compensation paid in March 2016, under an equity grant made in 2013. Between 2011 and 2015, his overall compensation in cash, stock and other benefits totaled $103 million.

Carrie Tolstedt, Community Bank head since 2007, did not like being criticized or hearing negative information, effectively isolating herself from feedback. She vigorously challenged and resisted scrutiny. She and her team kept information regarding the number of employees terminated for sales violations from the Board. Nevertheless, she had glowing farewell upon her retirement in July 2016. Not only did Stumpf call her a role model for responsible leadership and a standard-bearer of WF culture, but she was also rewarded with more than $27 million during her last three years. Wells Fargo retroactively fired Tolstedt for cause and revoked $47.3 million that they had previously paid her. This brought the total amount of money she had given up to $67 million, or about 54% of her $125 million pay package she initially received when she retired.

As in most corporate scandals, lower and mid-level employees faced the brunt of the punishments, while senior executives were whisked away to safety, with their compensation—in the measure possible—intact. This unabashedly portrayed a toxic corporate culture of "lions hunting zebras," where predatory executives were on a constant lookout for the weakest among customers and employees alike, those who put up the least resistance to their malevolent designs (Cowley 2016c).

In September 2017, two years after the WF scandal erupted on a nationwide scale and a year after former CEO Stumpf's Senate declaration, the aftershocks have grown even stronger (Cohan 2017). WF disclosed that 3.5 million unauthorized customer accounts were actually created since 2009, 70% more than originally reported. Also, 800,000 WF car loan customers were issued insurance without their knowledge, had refunds withheld or had their mortgage conditions changed. Moreover, it was revealed that 528,000 WF clients were fraudulently signed up for a digital payment service and were owed at least a million dollars in refunds. And all this after top officials had already purportedly owed up to their misbehavior.

Guide questions

1   Could more stringent rules in the corporate code or better-designed performance incentives by themselves have avoided WF's problems? Why or why not?
2   How do individual actions influence corporate culture? Cite examples from the WF case, particularly from Stumpf and Tolstedt. Do the errors of top management automatically exonerate low-level employees from their own wrongdoing?
3   Who was responsible for the communication gaps within WF?
4   Is there anything wrong about ambitious sales targets and tying performance incentives to them? How about decentralization? Where might WF have gone wrong in their implementation?

5   Besides financial losses and termination, how was the dignity of WF customers and employees harmed?
6   How would you reformulate WF's corporate purpose in MacIntyrean terms?
7   What concrete measures would you suggest to the WF Board to clean up the mess?
8   How do you analyze Carrie's behavior from the lens of Aristotelian ethics and MacIntyrean ethics?

Notes

1 Wells Fargo 2017, "Wells Fargo today: Company overview—1st quarter 2017." Accessed July 20, 2017.
2 www08.wellsfargomedia.com/assets/pdf/about/corporate/vision-and-values.pdf, Accessed July 20, 2017.
3 Cowley, S., 2016a, "Voices From Wells Fargo: 'I Thought I Was Having a Heart Attack'" *The New York Times.* www.nytimes.com/2016/10/21/business/dealbook/voices-from-wells-fargo-i-thought-i-was-having-a-heart-attack.html, Accessed July 15, 2017.
4 Cowley, S, 2016b, "At Wells Fargo, Complaints About Fraudulent Accounts Since 2005." *The New York Times.* www.nytimes.com/2016/10/12/business/dealbook/at-wells-fargo-complaints-about-fraudulent-accounts-since-2005.html, Accessed July 15, 2017.
5 Independent Directors of the Board of Wells Fargo & Company Sales Practices Investigation Report. April 10, 2017. www08.wellsfargomedia.com/assets/pdf/about/investor-relations/presentations/2017/board-report.pdf, Accessed July 10, 2017.
6 Independent Directors of the Board of Wells Fargo & Company Sales Practices Investigation Report. April 10, 2017. www08.wellsfargomedia.com/assets/pdf/about/investor-relations/presentations/2017/board-report.pdf, Accessed July 10, 2017.

References

Anscombe, G.E.M. 1958, 'Modern moral philosophy', *Philosophy*, 33(124): 1–19.
Aristotle. 1985, *Nicomachean ethics* (Irwin, T., trans.), Indianapolis, IN: Hackett Publishing.
Aristotle. 1990, *The politics* (Everson, S., ed.), Cambridge: Cambridge University Press.
Aspan, M. 2013, 'Wells Fargo's John Stumpf, the 2013 Banker of the Year', *American Banker.* (www.americanbanker.com/news/wells-fargos-john-stumpf-the-2013-banker-of-the-year, Accessed July 20, 2017).
Beadle, R. and Moore, G. 2006, 'MacIntyre on virtue and organization', *Organization Studies*, 27(3): 323–330.
Benedict XVI. 2005, *Encyclical Letter 'Deus caritas est'*, Vatican City: Libreria Editrice Vaticana. (http://w2.vatican.va/content/benedict-xvi/en/encyclicals/documents/hf_ben-xvi_enc_20051225_deus-caritas-est.html, Accessed September 28, 2017).
Benedict XVI. 2009, *Encyclical Letter 'Caritas in veritate'*, Vatican City: Libreria Editrice Vaticana. (http://w2.vatican.va/content/benedict-xvi/en/encyclicals/documents/hf_ben-xvi_enc_20090629_caritas-in-veritate.html, Accessed September 28, 2017).
Catechism of the Catholic Church. 2000, 2nd ed. Washington, DC: United States Catholic Conference.
Cohan, W.D. 2017, 'Wells Fargo should focus on its actual misbehavior, not on perceptions', *The New York Times*, September 5.

Cowley, S. 2016a, 'Voices from Wells Fargo: "I Thought I Was Having a Heart Attack"', *The New York Times*. (www.nytimes.com/2016/10/21/business/dealbook/voices-from-wells-fargo-i-thought-i-was-having-a-heart-attack.html, Accessed July 15, 2017).

Cowley, S. 2016b, 'At Wells Fargo, Complaints about fraudulent accounts since 2005', *The New York Times*. (www.nytimes.com/2016/10/12/business/dealbook/at-wells-fargo-complaints-about-fraudulent-accounts-since-2005.html, Accessed July 15, 2017).

Cowley, S. 2016c, '"Lions hunting zebras": Ex-Wells Fargo Bankers describe abuses', *The New York Times*. (www.nytimes.com/2016/10/21/business/dealbook/lions-hunting-zebras-ex-wells-fargo-bankers-describe-abuses.html, Accessed July 15, 2017).

Ferrero, I. and Sison, A.J.G. 2014, 'A quantitative analysis of authors, schools and themes in virtue ethics articles in business ethics and management journals (1980–2011)', *Business Ethics: A European Review*, 23(4): 375–400.

Hursthouse, R. 2013, 'Virtue ethics', in E.N. Zalta (ed.), *The Stanford encyclopedia of philosophy*, Stanford, CA: Stanford University. (http://plato.stanford.edu/archives/fall2013/entries/ethics-virtue, Accessed September 28, 2017).

Independent Directors of the Board of Wells Fargo & Company Sales Practices Investigation Report. April 10, 2017. (www08.wellsfargomedia.com/assets/pdf/about/investor-relations/presentations/2017/board-report.pdf, Accessed July 10, 2017).

John XXIII. 1961, *Encyclical Letter 'Mater et magistra'*. Città del Vaticano: Tipografi a Poliglotta Vaticana. (http://w2.vatican.va/content/john-xxiii/en/encyclicals/documents/hf_j-xxiii_enc_15051961_mater.html, Accessed September 28, 2017).

John Paul II. 1981, *Encyclical Letter 'Laborem exercens'*. Vatican City: Vatican Polyglot Press, (http://w2.vatican.va/content/john-paul-ii/en/encyclicals/documents/hf_jp-ii_enc_14091981_laborem-exercens.html, Accessed September 28, 2017).

John Paul II. 1987, *Encyclical Letter 'Sollicitudo rei socialis'*. Vatican City: Vatican Polyglot Press. (http://w2.vatican.va/content/john-paul-ii/en/encyclicals/documents/hf_jpii_enc_30121987_sollicitudo-rei-socialis.html, Accessed September 28, 2017).

John Paul II. 1991, *Encyclical Letter 'Centesimus annus'*, Washington DC: United States Catholic Conference. (http://w2.vatican.va/content/john-paul-ii/en/encyclicals/documents/hf_jp-ii_enc_01051991_centesimus-annus.html, Accessed September 28, 2017).

Leo XIII. 1891, *Encyclical Letter 'Rerum novarum'*. (http://w2.vatican.va/content/leo-xiii/en/encyclicals/documents/hf_l-xiii_enc_15051891_rerum-novarum.html, Accessed September 28, 2017).

MacIntyre, A.C. 1995 [1953], *Marxism and christianity*. London: Duckworth.

MacIntyre, A.C. 2007 [1981], *After virtue* (3rd ed.). London: Duckworth.

MacIntyre, A.C. 2016, *Ethics in the conflicts of modernity: An essay on desire, practical reasoning, and narrative*, New York: Cambridge University Press.

McGrath, M. 2016, 'Elizabeth Warren to Wells CEO Stumpf: You should resign and face criminal investigation', *Forbes*. (www.forbes.com/sites/maggiemcgrath/2016/09/20/wells-fargo-ceo-john-stumpf-to-apologize-to-senate-banking-committee/#4cf90b413aab, Accessed July 15, 2017).

Moore, G. 2002, 'On the implications of the practice–institution distinction: MacIntyre and the application of modern virtue ethics to business', *Business Ethics Quarterly*, 12(1): 19–32.

Moore, G. 2012, 'The virtue of governance, the governance of virtue', *Business Ethics Quarterly*, 22(2): 293–318.

Moore, G. and Beadle, R. 2006, 'In search of organizational virtue in business: Agents, goods, practices, institutions and environments', *Organization Studies*, 27(3): 369–389.

Paul VI. 1971, *Apostolic Letter Octogesima adveniens*, Boston: Daughters of St. Paul. (http://w2.vatican.va/content/paul-vi/en/apost_letters/documents/hf_p-vi_apl_19710514_octogesima-adveniens.html, Accessed September 28, 2017).

Pius XI. 1931, *Encyclical Letter 'Quadragesimo anno'*, Boston, MA: St. Paul Editions. (http://w2.vatican.va/content/pius-xi/en/encyclicals/documents/hf_p-xi_enc_19310515_quadragesimo-anno.html, Accessed September 28, 2017).

Pontifical Council for Justice and Peace. 2004, *Compendium of the social doctrine of the church*, Vatican City: Libreria Editrice Vaticana. (www.vatican.va/roman_curia/pontifical_councils/justpeace/documents/rc_pc_justpeace_doc_20060526_compendio-dott-soc_en.html, Accessed September 28, 2017).

Reckard, S. 2013, 'Wells Fargo's pressure-cooker sales culture comes at a cost', *Los Angeles Times*. (www.latimes.com/business/la-fi-wells-fargo-sale-pressure-20131222-story.html, Accessed July 15, 2017).

Sison, A.J.G., Beabout, G.R. and Ferrero, I. (Eds.) 2017, *Handbook of virtue ethics in business and management* (1st ed., Vols. 1–2), Dordrecht: Springer.

Telfer, E. 1990, 'The unity of the moral virtues in Aristotle's "Nicomachean Ethics"', *Proceedings of the Aristotelian Society*, 90: 35–48.

Vatican Council II. 1965, *Pastoral constitution on the Church in the modern world Gaudium et spes*, Vatican City: Vatican Polyglot Press. (www.vatican.va/archive/hist_councils/ii_vatican_council/documents/vat-ii_cons_19651207_gaudium-et-spes_en.html, Accessed September 28, 2017).

Wells Fargo. 2017, 'Wells Fargo today: Company overview – 1st quarter 2017', (www08.wellsfargomedia.com/assets/pdf/about/investor-relations/earnings/first-quarter-2017-earnings-supplement.pdf, Accessed July, 20, 2017).

2

VIRTUES AND THE COMMON GOOD IN LEADERSHIP

Matthias P. Hühn, Marcel Meyer and Aliza Racelis

Learning objectives

In this chapter, we shall:

- Explain the nature of leadership and why ethics is critical both in the behavior of the leader and the study of leadership.
- Explain leadership from the perspective of Aristotle, MacIntyre and Catholic Social Teaching.
- Discuss the virtues that today's leaders need.
- Integrate notions of human dignity and the common good into a framework for virtuous leadership.

Good leadership drives successful firms. Standard texts on leadership tend to focus on the definition of leadership, "the ability to influence a group toward the achievement of a vision or set of goals," leadership styles and what makes a leader effective. While notions of organizational effectiveness and successful leadership are important, this chapter takes off from the observation that theories based on the economistic paradigm have not helped to deter moral damage in firms and economies. In consequence, it attempts to present a framework for leadership that highlights what makes a firm *good* and how *good* leaders are formed in those companies.

Given prominent ethical scandals in virtually every type of organization, the importance of an ethical dimension of leadership seems obvious. After the global financial crisis that began in 2007/2008, practitioners have strong incentives to select for and develop moral leadership in their organizations; likewise, researchers want to study moral leadership in order to understand its origins and outcomes (Brown and Treviño 2006). Business scholars have put a lot of effort in identifying the characteristics of good leaders. However, attempts to discover innate characteristics of potential leaders have fallen out of fashion as leadership has come to be viewed more as a pattern of behavior that can be learned. Leaders govern by a set of "values" that support the vision of the organization. Such values, in turn, are formed through the cultivation of character: leaders must make the effort to habitually incorporate these moral principles in their behavior.

Increasingly, ethical leadership is seen in terms of virtue ethics. Properly handling issues hinges on the leader's capacity to make rational judgments amidst intense pressure and to relate to core values. Hence, the development of leadership virtues affecting both mind and character is important.

It is not enough for leaders to have the intellectual capacity to distinguish between morally good or evil acts. The leader's character is of paramount importance for two reasons. First, motives and acts that influence strategies are the fruits of character. Second, the leader is a role model in both task performance and ethical behavior. The leader is indeed the soul of the organization; and the leader's beliefs, values and behaviors influence the organization's moral environment with consequences even outside the organization (Mendonca and Kanungo 2007).

We examine the leader: why ethics and the virtues are critical and how the leader's character relates to the firm in particular and society in general. This is because good corporate performance needs good leadership.

1. The nature of virtuous leadership

Significant attention has been given to the topic of leader effectiveness. Leadership literature has focused on leaders' personal characteristics, leader-related skills and behaviors. There is also a stream of research on differentiating transformational from transactional leaders. Transactional leaders guide followers towards established goals by clarifying role and task requirements. Transformational leaders inspire followers to transcend self-interests for the good of the organization. Andrea Jung at Avon, Richard Branson of the Virgin Group and Jim McNerney of Boeing are all transformational leaders. They pay attention to the concerns and needs of individual followers; they change followers' awareness of issues by helping them look at old problems in new ways; and they excite and inspire followers to put out extra effort to achieve group goals (Robbins and Judge 2013).

Leadership literature has typically dwelled on mechanisms to minimize agency conflicts—those between managers and shareholders, arising from the separation of ownership and control in the modern corporation. It proposes ways in which managers can credibly commit to return funds to investors and thereby attract external financing. Such is the economistic paradigm of the firm. However, the view of a firm as *communio personarum*—as a communion of persons where each one strives, along with the others, for personal fulfillment—demands other requirements apart from mere efficiency or profitability (John Paul II *Centesimus Annus* (CA) 1991). In particular, a humanistic view of the firm establishes that each organizational member has a duty to avoid actions that impede the flourishing of others and, as far as possible, to promote that flourishing (Tirole 2005; Pontifical Council for Justice and Peace 2012).

Successful business leaders are those who achieve superior financial results, protect the environment and exercise corporate social responsibility. But what drives corporate performance—beyond luck—is the quality of leadership: the goals they set, the strategy they adopt, the speed and effectiveness of execution and, more importantly, their moral quality. Successful business leaders should have integrity in both their business and personal lives. Long-term corporate performance does not improve through regulation alone; it requires good leaders or executives possessing moral excellence, that is, virtue (Bowie 2005; Canals 2010).

Intellectual and moral excellence entails the possession and practice of a host of virtues within a particular sociocultural context. Virtues may be considered as moral capital because they are productive capacities that accumulate and develop in an individual, through proper investments of time, effort and other resources, including financial ones. Unlike human, intellectual, cultural or social capital that perfect the person in just a limited aspect (health, knowledge, aptitude or skill), moral capital is unique in perfecting the human being as a whole person (Sison 2003).

• A focus on the leader's character, more than just on compliance with rules or regulations, may be a better barrier to evil behavior in organizations. Those who lead corporations successfully can and should serve silently and humbly, assuming individual responsibility (Huehn 2008).

2. Virtuous leadership in Aristotle

Classical Aristotelian political theory was concerned with citizens developing themselves spiritually and internally—that is, acquiring the requisite human excellences or virtues. A view of leadership that concentrates on the ethical and political education of corporate rulers transcends the mere economistic view that, over the years, has led to perverse results such as greed, abuse and corruption (Sison 2008).

From an Aristotelian perspective, good leadership is both ethical and effective: a leader would not be virtuous if he were not also effective. To practice a virtue, we have to apply it at the right time, towards the right objects, towards the right people, for the right reason and in the right manner. Virtue ethics assist us in evaluating leadership behavior. To have a virtue is to have a disposition or tendency to perform a virtuous action from one's character. For example, a leader with the virtue of courage would be disposed to act courageously rather than cowardly. A leader without the virtue of courage may act similarly, but for other reasons, such as the desire for fame. When evaluating a leader's virtue, therefore, we use behaviors and dispositions as indicators that they are acting from that virtue. The more virtuous actions we observe, the more we can ascribe a virtue to the leader (Bauman 2015).

Aristotelian ethics places the cultivation of those traits of character conducive to human flourishing or well-being (*eudaimonia*) at center stage. Virtues contribute to a well-ordered society, and social institutions provide the context within which virtues are cultivated and perpetuated. Although Aristotle does not provide an explicit theory of ethical leadership, his account of human excellence developed through the virtues has important implications for leadership. It emphasizes that leadership is, above all, about character, virtuous habits and actions. Business leaders are in special need of virtues and are held to a higher ethical standard due to their power. Business leaders are expected to ethically guide followers in highly competitive situations (Bauman 2015; Preti 2015; Stückelberger 2016).

- Although Aristotle does not provide an explicit theory of ethical leadership, his account of human excellence developed through the virtues emphasizes that leadership is, above all, about character, virtuous habits and actions.

3. Virtuous leadership in MacIntyre

Virtue ethics has seen a revival and development with Alasdair Macintyre's publication of *After Virtue* in 1981. At the heart of MacIntyre's theory is the notion of "practice": a collective human endeavor in which individuals strive for excellence and are bettered in the process, both technically and morally. "Good" management is based on the maintenance of a "practice," as a "good" organization strives for excellence rather than focusing solely on external outcomes such as financial success (Moore 2002).

The development of the leader is a practice partly defined by the moral perspectives of a particular community: being and doing good by influencing others (Remmel 2004/2005). For MacIntyre, there are certain goods internal to practices and the virtues are among them. Leadership is then viewed as a coherent and complex form of a socially established and cooperative activity bearing its own standards of excellence. In excellent enterprises, the achievement of internal goods such as the virtues is an important element of corporate culture and management responsibility.

For MacIntyre, virtues are exhibited through participation in practices. Business leaders are thus charged with responsibility not only over institutions and their members, but also over practices. Since the maintenance of the institution is also a practice, leadership then serves the function of sustaining both practices and institutions. The supreme goal of leadership is to create human communities with specific social and political values in which the virtues can be exercised and learned (O'Malley 2013).

- Leaders need virtues to achieve the internal goods of business practice and to establish standards of excellence.

4. Virtuous leadership in Catholic Social Teaching

There has been a growing interest in the field of spirituality and management, borne from the recognition of the non-material or spiritual dimension of human beings. One of the claims in Catholic Social Teaching (CST) is that all human beings are made in God's image and likeness (*imago Dei*). As such, the human person is invested with dignity, an intrinsic worth or value that distinguishes him from any other creature. But, this dignity needs to be developed, to be elevated to the level of moral excellence—that is, virtue (Sison, Ferrero and Guitián 2016).

An implication of man's being *imago Dei* is his inescapably social nature: each person is given life and nurtured in community, and social relationships are a crucial component of happiness. Because the person can fully discover his true self only through sincere self-giving, a communion of persons is crucial to flourishing. Accordingly, to evaluate prosperity, we must take into account the quality of relationships and the achievement of the common good. Inasmuch as the human being tends by nature to communion, the true good of persons is communion with other persons, not solitude (Hollenbach 2004; Yuengert 2010).

For both the personal good and the common good to be achieved, leaders need education in the virtues. Without the virtues, the goods or objectives that a corporation should seek could not be properly identified. Neither could the rules, procedures and structures it should follow be correctly formulated, interpreted and implemented. The hope is that a regime be created that allows for the satisfaction not only of material, external goods, but also, and more importantly, one that permits organizational members to develop themselves spiritually and internally through human virtues or excellences (Sison 2008).

CST has traditionally endorsed the virtue ethics approach. "This humanism can become a reality if individual men and women and their communities are able to cultivate moral and social virtues in themselves and spread them in society" (Compendium of the Social Doctrine of the Church (CSDC): 19). "These values require, therefore, both the practice of the fundamental principles of social life and the personal exercise of virtue" (CSDC: 197).

CST reflects the human experience of personal fulfillment and entails a wisdom that all people can understand (Guitián 2015b). It articulates a perspective of the human person in God's plan of love, with a conscience, moral norms and virtues in the human community (Hornsby-Smith 2006). Regarding business and the economy, it promotes social virtues such as trust, honesty, reciprocity, a productive work ethic and recognition of human dignity. These are some important virtues that leadership needs.

• CST underscores the importance of recognizing human dignity and fostering the common good in exercising the virtues of leadership.

5. The virtues leaders need to practice

Virtues are acquired by people over time. Any virtue is mastered through repeated, regular practice. Virtue comes with a cost: excellence and expertise come through committed action. Among the ancient Greeks, "ethics" meant character.

In the context of the Rhetoric, Aristotle stated that ethical character comes from three components: *phronesis* (practical wisdom), *arête* (virtue) and *eunoia* (good-will towards others) (Hannah and Avolio 2011).

The excellences identified by Aristotle in the *Nichomachean Ethics* are the foundation for becoming a virtuous person (Aristotle *Nichomachean Ethics*, henceforth NE). Justice, courage, temperance and practical wisdom lead to a fulfilled life. Business leaders need these virtues more because they are held to a higher ethical standard (Bauman 2015).

> It is his disciplined work in close collaboration with others that makes possible the creation of ever more extensive working communities which can be relied upon to transform man's natural and human environments. Important virtues are involved in this process, such as diligence, industriousness, prudence in undertaking reasonable risks, reliability and fidelity in interpersonal relationships, as well as courage in carrying out decisions which are difficult and painful but necessary, both for the overall working of a business and in meeting possible set-backs.
>
> *(John Paul II 1991: 32)*

a. Diligence, professionalism and competence

The economic health of any community depends on the soundness of business organizations. Their activities require not only strong technical skills but also an ability, based on diligence, professionalism and competence to address myriad ethical issues. These issues arise because of the interests at stake in managing such large amounts of money and conflicts in corporate dealings (Boatright 2010). Large international corporations fail as a result of acts of gross professional negligence and fraud. Leadership rooted in ethical and responsible behavior is needed even more than laws and rules (Osiemo 2012).

b. Courage

Moral courage in the workplace supports principled performance, as it compels an individual to do what he or she believes is right, despite unfavorable social or economic consequences. Leaders often have to confront pressures that discourage their expression of ethical concerns. Therefore, they need moral courage. People with moral courage adhere to the spirit and letter of legal standards, even when difficult, and question legal standards that do not reflect ethical standards. Individuals with moral courage are not superhumans. They often experience worry, doubt and even anger when facing ethical issues. Nevertheless, they learn to proceed, moving through and beyond distress to demonstrate moral action (Sekerka, Comer and Godwin 2015).

Courage typically entails taking the pains to find out something one does not know, yet needs to know, to act as one should. The "stubbornness" to discover this is a sign of courage. Courage in seeking the truth is called "due diligence," and courage is also needed in declaring the truth. An accountant must be prepared to resign, if the alternative is to do or cooperate with something contrary to professional principles (Pakaluk and Cheffers 2011).

Individuals typically experience emotions such as worry, loneliness, fear, shock or surprise, distress and hurt (often from a sense of betrayal) in the midst of ethical challenges (Sekerka, Comer and Godwin 2015). Suffering is an aspect of courage. The brave man suffers injury not for its own sake, but as a means to preserve or acquire something better. Injury suffered in fighting for the good confers an intactness closely related to the core of man's life (Pieper 1965).

c. Justice

Leadership in business organizations requires grappling with questions that require justice and practical wisdom, such as deciding, for example, how to allocate funds to different corporate divisions. Justice allows us to recognize and respect the rights of others, as part of our duty to look after their welfare.

> According to its most classic formulation, it [justice] 'consists in the constant and firm will to give their due to God and neighbour'. From a subjective point of view, justice is based on the will to recognize the other as a person, while, from an objective point of view, it constitutes the decisive criteria of morality in the intersubjective and social sphere.
>
> *(CSDC: 197)*

Justice orients the will towards the good of others and the common good, as discerned by reason. The will is shaped by justice and charity to move beyond natural self-love to wider loves, towards the community, one's neighbors and ultimately towards God himself (Porter 2013). A political regime that looks after the common interest in accordance with the principles of justice is a "true" rule (Sison 2008; Bernacchio and Couch 2015).

It is proper to justice to direct man in his relations with others. Justice, therefore, consists in living well together. A distinguishing mark of justice is that some debt is to be paid, constituting a duty or moral obligation. In many languages, words indicating moral obligation are cognates of justice. "Debt," "debit" and "to be indebted" are related words. And so are "owe" and "ought" (Pieper 1965). Justice is a habit whereby a man renders to each one his due with constant and perpetual will.

What is to be gained from being just? Above all, peace. Further, justice is related to forgiveness. When social justice, just world beliefs, restorative justice, procedural justice and distributive justice are emphasized, individuals find forgiveness easier. "True peace is made possible only through forgiveness and reconciliation … Mutual forgiveness must not eliminate the need for justice and still less does it block the path that leads to truth. On the contrary, justice and truth represent the concrete requisites for reconciliation" (CSDC: 517).

d. Temperance and sobriety

The meaning of "temperance" has dwindled to crude "temperateness in eating and drinking," applied chiefly to quantity, while "intemperance" seems to indicate only excess. But, *temperantia* as a cardinal virtue has a wider significance (Pieper 1965). It does not merely refer to consumption.

> Christian spirituality proposes a growth marked by moderation and the capacity to be happy with little. It is a return to that simplicity which allows us to stop and appreciate the small things, to be grateful for the opportunities which life affords us (...). This implies avoiding the dynamic of dominion and the mere accumulation of pleasures (...) it [sobriety] is a way of living life to the full. In reality, those who enjoy more and live better each moment are those who have given up dipping here and there, always on the look-out for what they do not have. (...) Sobriety and humility were not favourably regarded in the last century. And yet, when there is a general breakdown in the exercise of a certain virtue in personal and social life, it ends up causing a number of imbalances, including environmental ones.
>
> *(Francis, Laudato Si (LS) 2015: 222–224)*

e. Veracity or truthfulness; honesty

Is truthfulness a moral virtue? Most would say that it is. We want to be open with friends and expect the same from them; we want children who speak their minds without subterfuge; we want to vote for candidates who are honest and honorable. Tradition sanctions this view. Moral codes, sacred as well as secular, prohibit lying. In legal proceedings, those who testify bind themselves to tell the truth. But, while we say truthfulness is good and lying is bad, sometimes, the way we act suggests otherwise (Mothersill 1996). Economists, ethicists and business sages have persuaded us that honesty is the best policy. Yet, treachery can pay.

Honesty is a moral choice. Businesspeople say that, in the long run, they will do well by doing good. People typically value honesty (honesty as its own reward), have strong beliefs about morality and want to maintain this aspect of their self-concept. If people fail to comply with their internal standards for honesty, they will need to degrade their self-concept, something to which they feel averse. This suggests that to maintain their positive self-concepts, people will comply with internal standards even when doing so involves investments of effort or sacrificing financial gains (Bhide and Stevenson 1990; Mazar, Amir and Ariely 2008).

Honesty represents a person's sincerity (being genuine in interpersonal relations), fairness (avoiding fraud and corruption), greed avoidance (being uninterested in assets that represent monetary wealth and high social status) and modesty (being humble and unassuming) (Effelsberg, Solga and Gurt 2014). A truthful person may be described in eleven traits: he is rightful, honest and true, he controls his words, he is fair, non-violent without excess, he does not fear wrongdoers, but follows those who behave truthfully, he keeps his promises, does not let himself be exploited, is free of corruption and is incorruptible (also described as "unshakable") (Stückelberger 2016). Authentic leadership can be equated with truthful leadership.

f. Humility

Humility is a virtue particularly important for leaders. In CST, humility is closely related to service, since Christ himself taught the apostles that "anyone among you who aspires to greatness must serve the rest" (Mark 10: 43).

> Responsible authority also means authority exercised with those virtues that make it possible to put power into practice as service (patience, modesty, moderation, charity, efforts to share), an authority exercised by persons who are able to accept the common good, and not prestige or the gaining of personal advantage, as the true goal of their work.
>
> *(CSDC: 410)*

This view has influenced Greenleaf's idea of servant leadership. The word humility comes from the Latin *humilitas*, which in turn comes from *humus*, the earth beneath us. Humility has an intrapersonal dimension, the vision the agent has of himself, and an interpersonal or expressed dimension, how he reacts to how others see him and how he sees others. These are not independent dimensions: what characterizes the humble person is self-knowledge and, in particular, the intention with which he appraises or judges himself. Intention is important because humility is practiced for the agent's development or improvement, and service to others. Service implies being available to others in the awareness that one's talents and competence are called to bear fruit for others. Otherwise, it is difficult to be ready to help or assist others. Being available shows love and respect for others. It is a way of recognizing the dignity of clients or colleagues. Moreover, availability entails humility; availability reinforces one's own dignity because it is an act of love that ethically enriches a person (Guitián 2015a).

New theoretical and empirical approaches in psychology and in business ethics have dealt with humility not as a weakness but as a strength, emphasizing its contribution to social cohesion and the creation of trust (Argandoña 2014). Hubris, on the contrary, has been cited as a common reason for leadership failure. One famous example of hubris was Napoleon's Russian campaign of 1812, in which he lost his army and empire. Some symptoms of such hubris are: unbounded confidence given the leader's past successes and the accompanying narcissism, the adulation that feeds that narcissism and callous indifference towards rules governing organizational behavior. Among the managerial behaviors that reflect hubris are making unsound and overpriced corporate acquisitions, pursuing growth for its own sake and knowingly violating standards of conduct. The obsession with the charismatic appeal of leaders contrasts with a growing call for humility. Humility is a marker of a leader's desire to serve. Research provides evidence for the benefits of humility in leadership. Only a humble person can be a good leader, as opposed to one filled with hubris (exaggerated pride, self-confidence or arrogance) (Kroll, Toombs and Wright 2000; Morris, Brotheridge and Urbanski 2005).

g. Prudence

None but the prudent man can be just, brave and temperate, and the good man is good in so far as he is prudent. Prudence is essential to leadership; it is the "charioteer of the virtues" (*auriga virtutum*), the directive virtue. In leading, the mature person ought to be, with due information and with acquired habits, able to dominate what is novel, unexpected or exceptional. Prudence is needed if man is to carry through his impulses and instincts for right acting, if he is to purify his naturally good predispositions and make them into real virtue—that is, into the truly human mode of a "perfected ability" (Pieper 1965).

According to Aristotle, virtue reaches its height with the exercise of the intellectual virtues of prudence and wisdom. An ethical imperative for business is to give individuals opportunities to thoughtfully participate in management and to contemplate the ultimate meaning of things. To the virtue of prudence belongs the task of guiding action through the thickets of particularity. The prudent individual consistently makes the right decisions to further every facet of a good life for him or herself, making sure to maintain health, finances, social relationships and, most importantly of all, moral virtue (Bragues 2006).

Leaders need to exercise prudence, the virtue of discerning the true good in every circumstance and choosing the right means of achieving it. Through prudence, we live up to our vocation as persons, acting in the created world according to our created nature, ordering it towards our own good and the good of society (Yuengert 2010). Prudence is already highly visible within global regulatory discourse. If regulators are prepared to re-engage with classical prudence, they may rediscover a cultural, psychological and ethical prescription for good judgment that protects firms from vulpine leadership, facilitating regard for the longer term (Marshall, Baden and Guidi 2013).

h. Love, kindness and magnanimity

Love, benevolence, caring, mutual respect and readiness to help are important for ethical business. Love seems to be necessary for business, but that needs to be explained (Guitián 2015a). Indeed, the social nature of the human person implies that each of us only achieves fulfillment in relation to others. In CST, charity— the perfection of love—is a key virtue, and Benedict XVI's encyclical *Caritas in veritate* (2009) insists on it as an essential element in business.

Some people are sceptical about love in business, alleging it is only an emotion or feeling, not a virtue, or that economic efficiency and profit making are incompatible with it. Can there be a place for love in the firm? If a firm is a human community, it needs the virtues including love. In particular, gift-love or love of benevolence consists of wishing good to the person loved.

Magnanimity and humility are indispensable characteristics of great leaders. These demand that people do not let their needs or preferences override obligations to others. True leadership is never self-seeking or self-serving; great leaders seek to serve more than to be served. Magnanimity directs leaders to constantly challenge themselves, striving for the greater good of all and helping others also to set high goals (Osiemo 2012).

• Specific virtues are essential to business leadership: diligence, courage, justice, temperance, honesty, humility, prudence and love.

6. Integrating notions of human dignity and the common good into a framework for virtuous leadership

A humanistic view of the firm entails that each of the organization's members promote the flourishing of others. A fundamental commitment to work for human fulfillment is a necessary condition for business success. Such human flourishing necessarily reveals the beauty and the nature of human dignity. Socio-economic life should bring about mutual advantage. The integral development of the self and others requires enormous effort and constant renewal (Barrera 2010; Pontifical Council for Justice and Peace 2012). The idea of dignity as underlying the intrinsic value of human life is central to societal progress. Dignity represents a pillar of our moral and political heritage; the attribution of human dignity was a key factor of social and economic development in the West. The "priceless" aspects of our humanity—including character, virtue, integrity (moral, physical, psychological), knowledge, wisdom, love, trust and forgiveness—seem to flow from and contribute to human dignity (Pirson and Dierksmeier 2016).

In CST, leaders are reminded to treat each employee not as an object of work but as its subject. This is connected with the protection of human rights, respect of dignity and primacy of employees' well-being.

> Business owners and management must not limit themselves to taking into account only the economic objectives of the company, the criteria for economic efficiency and the proper care of "capital" as the sum of the means of production. It is also their duty to respect the dignity of those who work within the company. These workers constitute "the firm's most valuable asset" and the decisive factor of production.
>
> *(CSDC: 344)*

In CST, the most important factor in business is man himself, with his knowledge, competencies, will to work and ability to perceive the needs of other people and to satisfy them (CA: 35). People should be treated with respect for themselves, their dignity and their rights (Marek 2015). Human dignity guarantees each person a right to well-being necessary for his development. The others "also have a claim on our respect and charity… In fact the more deeply we come to understand their ways of thinking through kindness and love, the more easily will we be able to enter into dialogue with them" (CSDC: 43; Sison, Ferrero and Guitián 2016).

It is possible, moreover, for employees—and not only executives or managers—to have a hand in the governance of the firm. Organizational members collectively find an obligation to work for the common good. Great leadership harmonizes collective endeavor. This can be achieved by improving employees' confidence, helping them give meaning to their work, compensation based on internal equity, participative and delegative practices, flexible working time arrangements and a culture of conciliation (Frémeaux and Michelson 2016).

Firms are vital institutions for society. What drives corporate performance is the quality of leadership teams: the goals they set, the strategy they adopt, the speed and effectiveness of execution and, more importantly, the quality of the people and how they engage them. The notion of the firm as an economic organization whose purpose is to maximize market value in the short term is an oversimplification. It opened the door to a game of incentives with adverse effects in the long term. Too often, this game allowed strategies based on opportunism, self-interest and a lack of integrity. Leaders, however, ought to consider the well-being of the people they govern. Leaders are responsible for the big picture and everything in it. Leadership is morality and immorality magnified, which is why we look for moral leaders (Ciulla 2005; Canals 2010).

Increasingly, ethical leadership is seen in terms of virtue ethics. A common tenet of virtue ethics is that rule-based methods for decision-making are insufficient to deal with the moral complexity of organizational life. In many cases, moral judgements cannot be made by rote. Hence, the development of the virtues of leadership is important. Internal goods derived from practices can be contrasted with external goods such as survival, reputation, power, profit or, more generally, success. If leaders endeavor to maintain integrity of character by exercising the virtues, they will humanize business from within (Moore 2005; Robinson 2011).

This chapter has spoken about the various virtues essential to leadership, ranging from professional competence to honesty and humility, capped by magnanimity and love, apart from the cardinal or hinge virtues. The virtue of prudence is the mold and "mother" of all the virtues; it is essential to leadership, the *auriga virtutum*, or the charioteer of the virtues. All virtue is necessarily prudent. Prudence is the cause of the other virtues being virtues. Virtue is a "perfected ability" of man as a spiritual person. Justice, fortitude and temperance, as "abilities" of the whole man, achieve their "perfection" only when they are founded upon prudence, the perfected ability to make right decisions (Pieper 1965; Moore 2005).

7. Volkswagen, the fallen idol

Julia's first two years of working had been great! As one of the few graduates of her MBA class at a middling university, she had made it to one of the 30 DAX companies in Germany.

She had worked hard for it. While studying for the bachelor degree in engineering, she spent the summers interning with consulting firms while most of her friends relaxed. The little money she earned, she invested in a tough, but interesting semester abroad in Mexico, where she met the German manager of the local VW plant.

All her hard work and discipline paid off when, through the connection made in Mexico, she landed a job at VW's headquarters in Wolfsburg, Germany. The first two years were spent in a happy daze because VW, considered one of the best employers in Germany (Absatzwirtschaft 2013), proved to be a wonderful work environment: smart and nice colleagues, a great salary, fantastic benefits, demanding but rewarding work on different technology projects and all of that in a four-day week with enough time for her hobbies.

Julia's friends and family found her exuberance cute and indulged her when she told them at every opportunity how great Volkswagen really was. And there was much to be proud of. VW was the biggest automaker in the world (Schmitt 2016) and has produced iconic models such as the Beetle and the Golf.

Every time she drove her sporty and environmentally friendly VW Passat CC TDI at 120 km/h on the Autobahn, she felt good about her job. Strangely, she felt even better when a Porsche, Audi, Lamborghini or Bentley—all brands belonging to the VW Group—would overtake her on the left lane with speeds clearly over 200 km/h. Contributing to the development of products that are the epitome of quality and technical expertise made her proud. And more so, the fact that Volkswagen took its responsibility towards the environment and society seriously.

VW was a company that put great emphasis on sustainability and CSR: they were one of the first and most generous supporters of the UN Global Compact,[1] whose four main principles of human rights, working standards, environmental protection and combating corruption Julia wholeheartedly supported. When, after her first year, she read in VW's Sustainability Report (2014), "We intend to put our creative powers to good use for the benefit of people and the environment" (p. 14), she thought to her herself, "Yes, we do!" And she remembered arriving at the VW factory in Pamplona in her first year and seeing the huge "Think Blue" on the wall of one of the factory's buildings and the pictures below explaining VW's commitment to being an environmentally friendly enterprise. Her mother had had the first 3-Litre Car: a VW Lupo that took only 3 L of diesel for 100 km (90 miles per gallon). She felt part of something really great and was thankful to her employer that she, an engineer working on engine development, could be part of this endeavor.

Like almost all employees at Volkswagen, Julia, upon joining the company, became a member of the union IG Metall (Tatje 2016a). It appealed to her sense of fairness that all employees, not only factory line workers, supported values such as solidarity and profit-sharing. And the union used its great power—it had as many directors on the board as the shareholders—to the advantage of all. VW paid the best salaries in the industry. Julia therefore was pleased when the lady in HR presented her with both the contract and the union membership application form.

Julia had expected all of this. Before her series of interviews, she had meticulously researched the history of the company. And VW had a rich history. Even though the enterprise was started by the Nazi trade union (Bowler 2015), Julia excused this as a sign of the times. Even then, the purpose of the company was directed towards being socially responsible. Volkswagen translates into "people's car" and its aim was to allow average families to buy a cheap car to travel all over the country. The idea behind the Beetle was the same as Henry Ford's famous Model T, but this time, the unions and the government (which to this day has a major stake in VW) did not intend to make a profit, but to do good. Anyway, the Beetle with its distinctive Porsche-designed shape and noisy but reliable engine in the back was an instant and lasting success. By 1955, roughly one million Beetles had already been sold and it became a symbol for rebuilding the country. Julia still liked to watch the now-classic commercials shown on TV from the 1950s to the 1970s on YouTube featuring this particular car that contributed so much to the success of the company. Was it not impressive that VW, while only producing 1,000 vehicles a month in 1946, now produced 42,000 a day (see Volkswagen Sustainability Report 2015)? After WWII France, Britain and the United States were not interested in VW (Bowler 2015), but today, Germany's biggest corporation by revenue is a truly global company with 121 plants in 31 countries. In Julia's opinion, this remarkable growth was linked to VW's strategy in the 1970s to introduce models like the Passat, Golf, Polo or the Scirocco, which stayed true to the original idea: produce quality cars for everybody. She also thought it was only logical that VW used the proceeds to grow by buying other carmakers such as SEAT and Skoda in 1990 and 1995, respectively. That later acquisitions of luxury brands such as Bentley, Bugatti and Lamborghini, contradicting Volkswagen's very name, did not dampen Julia's enthusiasm for these super cars and her employer.

During her research, Julia also found some things in VW's history that she didn't really like. They were, she thought, aberrations: individual people's moral lapses that VW's unique governance structure sought to prevent.

In 1993, VW had been involved in one of the most notable cases of industrial espionage. Opel, the German division of GM, accused Volkswagen of industrial espionage when Opel's José Ignacio López became a member of VW's managing board responsible for sourcing. López admitted that he had taken critical documents from his old employer to VW. The case, which resulted in a lengthy legal battle, was finally settled in 1997. VW had to pay GM, Opel's owners, $100 million in addition to buying car parts worth at least $1 billion from the competitor over the course of seven years (Meredith 1997). VW paid up but never publicly apologized.

Then there was a corruption scandal that produced headlines in the tabloids as well as in the business press. In early 2005, it became known that VW had a system in which union bosses and members of the managing board were given jewelry for their wives, pocket money and prostitutes while on business trips, and even money for sustaining long-term extramarital relationships (Hawranek, Rao and Röbel 2005). The direct financial damage of five million euros was negligible and only a few people had to resign, among them, the second most powerful member of the managing board, Peter Hartz, whose transgressions included authorizing payments for fictitious services of over $400,000 for the Brazilian girlfriend of one VW's union bosses (Ritter 2005).

The last scandal that Julia found again involved the managing board of the company. There was always a close personal connection between VW and Porsche, since Ferdinand Porsche designed the Beetle, and while VW was weakened by the sex scandal, Porsche took the opportunity to acquire more and more shares in Volkswagen, until they owned over 30% in 2007 and then, in 2008, when they owned over 40% and announced that they intended to take over the much larger company (Hawranek and Kurbjuweit 2013). In January 2009, Porsche owned over 50%, but a few months later, the tide turned at the massively leveraged takeover was aborted, and it quickly became clear that now VW would take over Porsche. In 2012, when VW took over Porsche completely (Topham 2012), Wolfgang Porsche, chairman of the Porsche supervisory board, had eventually been stopped by his cousin, Ferdinand Piëch, who was VW's CEO at the time.

These scandals had been bad news for VW, but the consumers, if indeed they took note of them, still liked what the VW Group produced: mid-2015, they became the world's favorite automaker.

Shortly after that, Dieselgate broke, and Julia's honeymoon at VW ended. It was all over the news. Michael Horn, still CEO of the VW branch in the US at that point, didn't mince words: "We have totally screwed up!" (BBC News YouTube Channel).

Apparently, as VW had admitted on September 22, 2015, after the Environmental Protection Agency (EPA) filed a notice of violation on September 18, 2015, it had used software to manipulate the emissions of 11 million diesel cars around the world to pass emissions tests (Ewing 2015a; Henning 2015; Sanger-Katz and Schwartz 2015). The software recognized when an emission test was run and changed how the engine worked in order to reduce the emission of certain gases (Dwyer 2015). Then, once the car was on the street again, the software would switch off the emission regulator, improving the car's performance (Dwyer 2015). Among the cars affected were all models that used two types of diesel engines, among them Julia's own Passat, but also Audis and Porsches were affected (Ewing 2015a; Ewing and Vlasic 2015a).

The cheating was discovered in the US where the emission limits for diesel cars are stricter than in Europe and Asia. However, it was not the EPA that discovered the fraud. The cheating had been discovered by engineers from West

Virginia University when they tested VW cars and their emissions in real-life scenarios (Dwyer 2015). Ironically, as Julia had read, these tests requested by the International Council on Clean Transportation were meant to show that diesel cars could actually meet the very strict emission parameters set by the US government.

The manipulations, however, were not only relevant for the US market. Investigations into the matter were launched in many other countries and, if true, they could have serious consequences for VW—they might actually threaten the very survival of the company.

At the very least, VW would have to call back millions of cars and fix the software issues. Julia, who herself was involved in an engine development project, was not even sure whether VW had the technology needed to solve that matter effectively. Worst case was that US judges would impose punitive damages that would be so high that VW would go bankrupt.

Volkswagen shares had fallen continuously since reaching a high of 250 euros in March 2015, but after the EPA announcement, Volkswagen's shares dropped from 160 to just under 100 euros in one week.

Share prices were one thing, but when VW's HR department told a major German newspaper that also because of Dieselgate, between 10,000 and 100,000 employees might have to be laid off (Süddeutsche Zeitung 2016), Julia really started worrying. A week later, VW downplayed that first estimate to roughly 30,000 employees (Rauwald 2016), but at that point, morale in VW had already slumped.

Overnight, Julia's whole outlook had changed from positive to negative. Until recently, she thought that the phasing out of combustion engines was a good thing for the environment and that her employer drove the technological change. Now, she wasn't so sure any longer: why did VW alone have to employ a defeat device to reduce nitrogen oxide (NOx) emissions if they were so technologically advanced? And things were certainly more difficult now than before the scandal broke. All those billions that VW had invested in the past into making engines that have lower emissions had not been enough and that meant they had to invest even more! But, with VW's future in question, the costs of borrowing would surely go up and the money needed for research was now going to the payment of fines. And now that Julia thought about it, she realized that VW was lagging behind other car manufacturers when it came to electric cars. Renault-Nissan, since the start of sales through April 2015, had sold 241,714 plug-in cars worldwide. That was a market share of 28%, more than twice as much as Mitsubishi, its nearest competitor, sold (Schaal 2015). VW was nowhere near these figures.

On the contrary, while other carmakers focused on reducing pollution, VW had knowingly, through unleashing tons of extra pollutants in the United States and elsewhere, harmed human health. Pollutants such as nitrogen oxides, typically produced by diesel engines, can be tied to a multitude of respiratory and cardiovascular diseases, as well as to premature deaths (Sanger-Katz and Schwartz 2015). As the New York Times, backed up by research findings, claimed, it was most likely that Volkswagen had damaged public health and might be responsible for up to 106 unnecessary deaths. Now, for Julia, the fact that VW seemed to have consciously accepted to cause physical harm to human beings in order to sell more cars and be more "successful" was a horrible thought. Julia was not unrealistic and she knew that corporate scandals did happen from time to time— she remembered it vaguely from her Business Ethics class. However, Dieselgate appeared to her as a particularly awful scandal. In the Enron scandal, employees had been financially affected. Dieselgate, however, impacted VW employees, shareholders, other companies' employees not only financially; it had also damaged the environment and people's health!

Julia had read that some journalists claimed that VW's corporate culture was to be blamed for the company's misconduct (Stewart 2015; Lamparta 2016; Tatje 2016b). James Strock, who served as the founding Secretary for Environmental Protection for the state of California, compared Dieselgate to the Watergate, indicating that VW, like Richard Nixon, had promoted a corporate culture that enabled unethical behavior (Tatje 2016b). Even worse, this culture was embedded in and supported by a governance structure. And now that Julia, for the first time, looked at VW with something other than enthusiasm, she suddenly had a very different picture of the company. By law, 50% of the members of the board of directors of Volkswagen were employee representatives and the state of Lower Saxony also had one representative on the board. If the representative of the State of Lower Saxony was from a left-leaning party, it meant that the employees had a majority on the board. Julia had always assumed that this governance structure essentially guaranteed that VW would act responsibly. But now, she remembered a few facts from the last scandal: the main actors had all been employee representatives and it had been organized by someone in the HR department, where virtually everyone had to be a union member! Was there a systemic problem at VW?

Was it realistic that only a very limited number of employees from the middle management of the corporation had been aware of what was going on? Julia had to admit that she could not imagine that top management did not know. And even if the all-powerful leaders of VW did not know what was going on in the company's middle management, how could a few middle managers feel that they could make these major decisions? A CEO was clearly not expected to know if a worker stuck used chewing gum under the driver's seat of a VW Fox, but he would certainly be expected to know about software affecting 11,000,000 cars worldwide. Especially someone like Mr. Winterkorn, a trained engineer and eager to control even small details, was unlikely to miss such a detail. He, however, had clearly stated that he was unaware of any wrongdoing on his part (Hakim and Ewing 2015).

Generally, VW's company culture was described as engineer-driven (Stewart 2015), military-like (Zeit Online 2015), a top-down organization (Ewing 2015b), heavily centralized and slow in decision-making (Ewing and Vlasic 2015b). VW's preferred leadership style was often described as autocratic (Stewart 2015), and technical knowledge, combined with a type of hands-on management, was highly valued (Ewing 2015b). In official documents, VW only referred to its CEO as "Prof. Dr. Winterkorn" and employees also used his academic titles. This had been the case for other VW CEOs as well: they got honorary professorships or doctorates that they used. This didn't exactly make them more approachable. Stephan Weil, Prime Minister of Lower Saxony and as an important member of the executive board of VW not without personal responsibility, admitted that VW suffered from a company culture that did not allow criticism (Slavik and Fromm 2016). In detail, he pointed out that VW needed to transform its concept of leadership, teamwork and responsibility. Julia would never have said anything at work, but she now agreed that changes in the management culture were undeniably needed. The scandal had changed her perspective, she suddenly realized! When she had read a Spiegel article about VW's empire, likening the company's to North Korea's management culture (Hawranek and Kurbjuweit 2013), she had been outraged at the unfair accusation. Now, she admitted to herself that there was tremendous pressure to fulfill one goal and that goal was not social or environmental responsibility but growth.

Nobody talked about it, but it was clear to all of her colleagues: *Strategie 2018*, the company's official strategy document, talked about CSR and the environment, but the only goal that really mattered was to become the world's largest carmaker (Freitag 2014).

Cleverness was vastly more appreciated than wisdom, and being smart with a defeat device had caused the crisis. To her great dismay, Julia discovered that she had never felt like this because she had simply assimilated: she had wanted to be part of a team, support the team and its noble goals. And if she had become part of the system, was she also responsible for Dieselgate? Just as this frightening thought took root in her mind, she remembered something else. She once overheard her team leader Frank Frey talking to a colleague who had been with the company a few years longer than Julia, and the topic was emission management. Frank had talked about a fellow engine project team leader and called him a smart operator because he had been paid a bonus for solving the NOx problem! She had never made the connection and now it was so obvious! But that would mean that Frank—that really nice guy, who had supported her, had been excited about developing better engines, bought them all pizza when his second child was born—knew about the cheating software. Was Frank a bad guy? Was she? No, of course not! Growth was important, otherwise other car companies win and then VW would lose.

But on the other hand, Julia deep down had always hoped for a change towards a more caring and less instrumental company environment. Her wish for more compassion, kindness and understanding at work stood in contrast to what was essentially promoted at VW: all business is a fight, and the good guys are the winning guys. To win is to be good. That was the other thing that had bothered her: the culture was essentially testosterone-driven. The last time Julia had checked the annual report of VW, it showed that the percentage of female employees in the group hovered somewhere near the 16% mark—in the engineering projects she had been involved with, she had always been the only woman.

Interestingly, as Julia had learned in her MBA program that, according to research, male and female workers valued different things concerning a work environment. While pay, benefits, authority, status and power were valued by men, women preferred a company culture based on relationships, respect, open communication, fairness, equity, collaboration and work–family balance (Peterson 2004).

In Julia's opinion, the best option to substitute Martin Winterkorn would have been to find a female CEO—an outsider, not the usual long-time veteran from the inner core of VW's management circle. She was convinced that such a move might have been a better alternative to create a healthier corporate culture based on honesty and truthfulness and, also, to win back the confidence of the customers. However, as Julia was convinced, such a radical thought had never even been present at any discussion about a possible successor of Martin Winterkorn, but they had made a woman the member of the managing board responsible for "Integrity and Law."

The Piëch and the Porsche families had always been very influential. Julia had read the autobiography of Ferdinand Piech: *Auto.Biographie*. His limited need for harmony seemed to have helped shape a corporate culture where robustness and toughness were highly regarded. Employees who did not "function properly" had to be terminated; employees executing their tasks well were to be promoted. It was that easy. Black or white. The NY Times had summarized: "Some critics argue that after 20 years under Mr. Piëch and Mr. Winterkorn, Volkswagen had become a place where subordinates were fearful of contradicting their superiors and were afraid to admit failure" (Ewing and Bowley 2015: 3).

Mr. Winterkorn and Mr. Piëch were demigods within the VW group. However, these two gods were feared rather than seen as loving father figures who could be approached. Visits by Martin Winterkorn were not considered a pleasure around the many VW plants throughout the world (Hawranek and Kurbjuweit 2013). His behavior seemed to be governed by only two all-important and equally significant factors: VW's growth rate and VW's quality. His reactions to, in his opinion, unsatisfactory outcomes were known and feared among VW's employees. It was Julia's opinion that Mr. Winterkorn lacked the virtue of temperance in two ways. On the one hand, harsh criticism could uncontrollably burst out of him when something displeased him. On the other hand, his appetite for success and admiration seemed insatiable. This last characteristic seemed to have infected the whole company. Despite an almost worldwide interest in environmental protection and energy conservation, and despite the fact that many other competitors had shifted considerable resources towards developing more sustainable cars, Mr. Winterkorn solely focused on combustion engines. What was more, VW had now not only one or two sport car brands in its portfolio, but five high-end sports car companies: Porsche, Lamborghini, Bugatti, Audi and Bentley. Even though part of Julia loved these cars, she had to admit that she felt certain unease. It just seemed not right to make cars like this.

Mr. Winterkorn had been replaced and she did not personally know the new CEO, but she now thought that maybe the problem was deeper than just a few rotten apples: maybe it was really a culture problem that was aggravated and perpetuated by the governance structure that should have made VW an especially ethical company. What could one person do? What power did even a new CEO have? The overarching power structure had not changed in the last 50 years: the unions had 50% of the members of the supervisory board, the State of Lower Saxony another member and the rest were the owner family Piech-Porsche and some big investors. Julia strongly suspected that every single top manager and supervisory board member agreed with her business school's motto: It is a jungle out there! The goal there has to be the strongest predator—her business school had a leopard next to the motto—and not to be a productive and flourishing member of a community. Julia had always disliked this view of life and business but never felt brave enough to speak up in class. In class, like at VW, she had resigned herself to go with the flow.

Even though VW was the first car company to be found to have used a defeat device, Julia was sure that other car companies did not fully comply with the standards established by the various governments either. What was more, the rumors that cars polluted much more than what was admitted had been around for a long time. Politicians and environmental agencies had probably been aware that the car industry was rather creative when it came to emissions (Higgins 2015). Car companies were too important for a country's economy; and VW, with being the biggest company in Germany and partly owned by the state, probably felt safer from repercussions that other automakers.

The more Julia thought about the whole scandal, the more she believed that responsibility or the lack thereof was the central problem. Because to her great surprise, she herself felt some responsibility. She had not seen a reality that had been right before her eyes all along, maybe because personal responsibility requires personal consequences. Could she go on working at VW and thereby personally supporting a system that aggressively put money before morals but publicly said the opposite? Her conscience had only been activated by the threat of losing her job—a fact that made Julia very uncomfortable. Would she, if things didn't change, speak up against those at the very top? And would it matter? All scandals had happened in the same governance system, and in all scandals, top managers had been involved. Morality cannot be governed by laws—it always came down to individuals and the context. Wasn't law codified morality, and didn't that make laws the dependent variable and not the determinant? Some contexts made it easier for individuals to do the right thing, and VW's culture and governance structure apparently were making it easier to do the wrong thing, as the scandals showed. Julia had really believed in VW's official social and environmental goals, but had suppressed her conscience when she saw VW going against them. Julia had read somewhere that Martin Winterkorn got a company pension of 3,100 euros—per day (Kronenzeitung 2017)! For endangering hundreds of thousands of jobs and harming people and the environment, the consequences were a life of luxury. Julia could not help but wonder whether these payments were not compensation for making illegal and unethical decisions—a kind of risk bonus in case things become public. And that would mean that she had been duped: while she believed in all those statements that VW was committed to the environment, the top managers always only had growth and profitability as a goal and cynically used her enthusiasm. What it all boiled down to, Julia thought, was that responsibility is always personal and that the notion of corporate responsibility diluted people's sense of personal responsibility. She herself had given up her responsibility because her corporation had been one of the first to have a Sustainability Report as part of the Annual Report. And if the corporation rewarded massive lapses of personal responsibility by paying a corporate pension of 90,000 euros per month, there was something wrong with that whole approach to ethics, leadership and corporate governance.

And what about trust? Could the government be trusted? Could companies be trusted? Could corporate management be trusted? Trust, her management professor had told her, can only develop if it goes both ways: up and down the hierarchy. Could VW's leadership trust their employees? She had not openly communicated her concerns to her project leader and, on reflection, she trusted him even less now. What had the new top managers done to signal that they deserved the trust, that they wanted to know about activities that went against the publicly announced stewardship for society and the environment? The New York Times had written that "while Volkswagen cheated behind the scenes, it publicly espoused virtue" (Hakim, Kessler and Ewing 2015: 3). Had this double standard that had been rigidly enforced in the past been challenged by the new top managers? Julia didn't think so: the new CEO was a protégé of the old. Had her employer just sent a few top managers into well-paid retirement and left the ship on the same course? It had worked for them with the past scandals and it had worked out fine economically in this scandal as well: VW had sold even more cars than in 2015.

What to do? Try and find a new employer? Were there employers that put their money where their corporate managers' mouths were? There had to be. Julia decided that she was going to ask around in the chat forum of her MBA class and take it from there.

Case discussion guidelines

1 Describe the governance structure at VW. How is it different from other corporations?

The idea is that students understand that VW has by law 50% of the directors coming from the employees/unions and that the State government also has a seat on the board. The employee participation is common in Germany but very unusual in the United States and most other countries where only the owners are represented at the highest level.

2 How effective have rules and structures been in preventing scandals at VW?

There seem to be two different rules and structures at VW: official and unofficial. Both sets of rules are made by those who are the top of the organization. The official rules could not prevent this or other scandals. The students should describe the unofficial structure (promotion criteria, growth as only goal, internal organization run by the union, extreme pressure for all to join union).

3   Describe the virtues and vices displayed by various actors in the case.

The students should look at the behavior of people that caused the scandals described in the case and connect them with the virtues and vices that the text of the chapter highlights. They should discover that there seems to be an inverted pyramid of virtues: those at the bottom at least believe in working for the common good, the middle managers have given in to the system and the top has no virtues but many vices (greed, arrogance, pimping) on display.

4   Identify the ethical conflicts that Julia discovered after the scandal broke. Why didn't she see these conflicts before?

The main idea behind this question is that students explore the concepts of responsibility, perception and the systemic aspects of morality. Julia knew about the cheating, she knew about the system that gave bonuses to those who were immoral, but she (subconsciously) suppressed that knowledge, probably because she was not prepared to handle the consequences. In the end, an immoral system corrupts everyone. Julia's project leader was already further down the road and admired a fellow team leader for inventing the defeat device and getting a bonus for it.

5   Describe VW's corporate culture. How are leadership and corporate culture connected? Describe the role played by the CEO, Julia's project manager and Julia when it comes to VW's culture and leadership.

Cultures are ways of acting and they are value sets; cultures are also moral systems that influence members' actions. VW's purpose/goal (*telos*) was once focused on giving mobility to the less affluent, and now it is geared towards creating growth. Growth is financially beneficial for all employees, but the top of the company benefits disproportionally. Students should describe the actions at the three levels that promote VW's culture, and they should debate if and how this moral environment can be changed. Goal setting should be part of the debate.

6   What did Julia learn about the importance of character relative to rules and structures at work?

Students should understand that character is something that all humans value because it defines how others and we look at ourselves. By the time most people start their work life, their character is in place. The work environment can either fit with our character, ideally it even helps us become better, or it can damage our character. Official rules and structures are at best speed bumps, because just like drivers with bad intentions buy cars that can handle speed bumps, managers simply ignore them. When official rules are abrogated by unofficial rules and structures, they create a strong dynamic to be unethical.

Note

1 www.unglobalcompact.org.

References

Absatzwirtschaft. 2013, 'VW ist Deutschlands bester Arbeitgeber', *Absatzwirtschaft*. 18 March. (www.absatzwirtschaft.de/vw-ist-deutschlands-bester-arbeitgeber-14635/, Accessed October 2, 2017).

Argandoña, A. 2014, 'Humility in management', *Journal of Business Ethics*, 132: 63–71.

Aristotle. 1985, *Nicomachean ethics* (Irwin, T., trans.), Indianapolis, IN: Hackett Publishing.

Barrera, A. 2010, 'What does Catholic Social Thought recommend for the economy?: The economic common good as a path to true prosperity', in D.K. Finn (ed.), *The true wealth of nations*, Oxford: Oxford University Press, 13–36.

Bauman, D.C. 2015, 'The drive to virtue: A virtue ethics account of leadership motivation', in A.J.G. Sison, G.R. Beabout and I. Ferrero (eds.), *Handbook of virtue ethics in business and management*, Dordrecht: Springer Science+Business Media.

BBC News YouTube Channel. 2015, 'Volkswagen CEO: "We have totally screwed up"' *BBC* 22 September. (www.youtube.com/watch?v=5uljMgnYcMU, Accessed September 27, 2017).

Benedict XVI. 2005, *Encyclical Letter 'Deus Caritas Est'*, Vatican City: Libreria Editrice Vaticana.

Bernacchio, C. and Couch, R. 2015, 'The virtue of participatory governance: A MacIntyrean alternative to shareholder maximization', *Business Ethics: A European Review*, 24(S2): S130–S143.

Bhide, A. and Stevenson, H.H. 1990, 'Why be honest if honesty doesn't pay?', *Harvard Business Review*, 68(5): 121–129.

Boatright, J.R. 2010, *Finance ethics: Critical issues in theory and practice*, New Jersey: John Wiley & Sons, Inc., 3–20.

Bowie, N.E. 2005, 'Expanding the horizons of leadership', in J.B. Ciulla, T.L. Price, and S.E. Murphy (eds.), *The quest for moral leaders: Essays on leadership ethics*, Cheltenham, UK: Edward Elgar, 144–160.

Bowler, T. 2015, 'Volkswagen: From the Third Reich to emissions scandal', *BBC* 2 October. (www.bbc.com/news/business-34358783, Accessed September 27, 2017).

Bragues, G. 2006, 'Seek the good life, not money: The Aristotelian approach to business ethics', *Journal of Business Ethics*, 67: 341–357.

Brown, M.E. and Treviño, L.K. 2006, 'Ethical leadership: A review and future directions', *Leadership Quarterly*, 17: 595–616.

Canals, J. 2010, *Building respected companies*, Cambridge: Cambridge University Press.

Ciulla, J.B. 2005, 'Introduction', in J.B. Ciulla, T.L. Price and S.E. Murphy (eds.), *The quest for moral leaders: Essays on leadership ethics*, Cheltenham, UK: Edward Elgar, 1–9.

Dwyer, J. 2015, 'Volkswagen's diesel fraud makes critic of secret code a prophet', *The New York Times*, 22 September. (www.nytimes.com/2015/09/23/nyregion/volkswagens-diesel-fraud-makes-critic-of-secret-code-a-prophet.html, Accessed September 27, 2017).

Effelsberg, D., Solga, M. and Gurt, J. 2014, 'Getting followers to transcend their self-interest for the benefit of their company: Testing a core assumption of transformational leadership theory', *Journal of Business Psychology*, 29: 131–143.

Ewing, J. 2015a, 'Volkswagen says 11 million cars worldwide are affected in diesel deception', *The New York Times*, 22 September. (www.nytimes.com/2015/09/23/business/international/volkswagen-diesel-car-scandal.html, Accessed September 27, 2017).

Ewing, J. 2015b, 'Volkswagen C.E.O. Martin Winterkorn resigns amid emissions scandal', *The New York Times*, 23 September. (www.nytimes.com/2015/09/24/business/international/volkswagen-chief-martin-winterkorn-resigns-amid-emissions-scandal.html, Accessed September 27, 2017).

Ewing, J. and Bowley, G. 2015, 'The engineering of Volkswagen's aggressive ambition', *The New York Times*, 13 December. (www.nytimes.com/2015/12/14/business/the-engineering-of-volkswagens-aggressive-ambition.html, Accessed September 27, 2017).

Ewing, J. and Vlasic, B. 2015a, 'German prosecutors investigating Winterkorn, Volkswagen's Ex-C.E.O', *The New York Times*, 28 September. (www.nytimes.com/2015/09/29/business/international/volkswagen-winterkorn-diesel-investigation.html, Accessed September 27, 2017).

Ewing, J. and Vlasic, B. 2015b, 'Volkswagen names Matthias Müller, an insider, as chief executive', *The New York Times*, 25 September. (www.nytimes.com/2015/09/26/business/volkswagen-namesmuller-an-insider-as-chief-executive.html, Accessed September 27, 2017).

Francis. 2015, *Encyclical Letter 'Laudato Si' on care for our common home'*. (http://w2.vatican.va/content/francesco/en/encyclicals/documents/papa-francesco_20150524_enciclica-laudato-si.html, Accessed September 27, 2017).

Freitag, M. 2014, 'Winterkorn verlängert Vertrag bis 2018', *Der Spiegel*, 15 July. (www.spiegel.de/wirtschaft/unternehmen/winterkorn-verlaengert-vertrag-bei-vw-bis-2018-a-981147.html, Accessed September 27, 2017).

Frémeaux, S. and Michelson, G. 2016, 'The common good of the firm and humanistic management: Conscious capitalism and economy of communion', *Journal of Business Ethics*. DOI: 10.1007/s10551-016-3118-6.

Guitián, G. 2015a, 'Service as a bridge between ethical principles and business practice: A catholic social teaching perspective', *Journal of Business Ethics*, 128: 59–72.

Guitián, G. 2015b, 'Service in the catholic social tradition: A crucial virtue for business', in A.J.G. Sison, G.R. Beabout and I. Ferrero (eds.), *Handbook of virtue ethics in business and management*, Dordrecht: Springer Science+Business Media, 177–187.

Hakim, D., Kessler, A.M. and Ewing, J. 2015, 'As Volkswagen pushed to be no. 1, ambitions fueled a scandal', *The New York Times*, 26 September. (www.nytimes.com/2015/09/27/business/as-vw-pushed-to-be-no-1-ambitions-fueled-a-scandal.html?_r=0, Accessed September 27, 2017).

Hakim, D. and Ewing, J. 2015, 'Matthias Müller, in the driver's seat at Volkswagen', *The New York Times*, 1 October. (www.nytimes.com/2015/10/02/business/international/matthias-muller-in-the-drivers-seat-at-volkswagen.html, Accessed September 27, 2017).

Hannah, S.T. and Avolio, B.J. 2011, 'Leader character, ethos, and virtue: Individual and collective considerations', *Leadership Quarterly*, 22: 989–994.

Hawranek, D. and Kurbjuweit, D. 2013, 'Wolfsburger Weltreich', *Der Spiegel*, 19 August. (www.spiegel.de/spiegel/print/d-107728908.html, Accessed September 27, 2017).

Hawranek, D., Rao, P. and Röbel, S. 2005, 'With prostitutes and shady executives, there's no love left in this bug', *Der Spiegel*, 18 July. (www.spiegel.de/international/spiegel/scandal-at-volkswagen-with-prostitutes-and-shady-executives-there-s-no-love-left-in-this-bug-a-365752.html, Accessed September 27, 2017).

Henning, P.J. 2015, 'The potential criminal consequences for Volkswagen', *The New York Times*, 24 September. (www.nytimes.com/2015/09/25/business/dealbook/thepotential-criminal-consequences-for-volkswagen.html, Accessed September 27, 2017).

Higgins, A. 2015, 'Volkswagen scandal highlights European stalling on new emissions tests', *The New York Times*, 28 September. (www.nytimes.com/2015/09/29/world/

europe/volkswagen-scandal-highlights-european-stalling-on-new-emissions-tests. html, Accessed September 27, 2017).

Hollenbach, D. 2004, *The common good and Christian ethics*, Cambridge: Cambridge University Press.

Hornsby-Smith, M. 2006, *An introduction to Catholic Social Thought*, Cambridge: Cambridge University Press.

Huehn, M.P. 2008, 'Unenlightened economism: The antecedents of bad corporate governance and ethical decline', *Journal of Business Ethics*, 81(4): 823–835.

John Paul II. 1991, *Encyclical Letter 'Centessimus annus'*. (http://w2.vatican.va/content/ john-paul-ii/en/encyclicals/documents/hf_jp-ii_enc_01051991_centesimus-annus. html, Accessed September 27, 2017).

Kroll, M.J., Toombs, L.A. and Wright, P. 2000, 'Napoleon's tragic march home from Moscow: Lessons in hubris', *Academy of Management Executive,* 14(1): 117–128.

Kronenzeitung. 2017, '3.100 € VW- Betriebsrente für Winterkorn - pro Tag', *Kronen Zeitung*, 4 January. (www.krone.at/welt/3100-euro-vw-betriebsrente-fuer-winterkorn-pro-tag-plus-17-mio-bonus-story-547104, Accessed September 27, 2017).

Lamparta, D.H. 2016, 'Eine Kultur der Arroganz', *Zeit Online*, 5 September. (www.zeit. de/2016/32/volkswagen-dieselskandal-kosten, Accessed September 27, 2017).

MacIntyre, A. 2007, *After virtue* (3rd ed.), Notre Dame, IN: University of Notre Dame Press.

Marek, A. 2015, 'Leadership in catholic social teaching', *Annales. Ethics in Economic Life*, 18(4): 27–38.

Marshall, A., Baden, D. and Guidi, M. 2013, 'Can an ethical revival of prudence within prudential regulation tackle corporate psychopathy?', *Journal of Business Ethics*, 117: 559–568.

Mazar, N., Amir, O. and Ariely, D. 2008, 'The dishonesty of honest people: A theory of self-concept maintenance', *Journal of Marketing Research*, 45(6): 633–644.

Mendonca, M. and Kanungo, R.N. 2007, *Ethical leadership*, New York: Open University Press.

Meredith, R. 1997, 'VW agrees to pay G.M. $100 million in espionage suit', *The New York Times*, 10 January. (www.nytimes.com/1997/01/10/business/vw-agrees-to-pay-gm-100-million-in-espionage-suit.html, Accessed September 27, 2017).

Moore, G. 2002, 'On the implications of the practice-institution distinction: MacIntyre and the application of modern virtue ethics to business', *Business Ethics Quarterly*, 12(1): 19–32.

Moore, G. 2005, 'Humanizing business: A modern virtue ethics approach', *Business Ethics Quarterly*, 15(2): 237–255.

Morris, J.A., Brotheridge, C.M. and Urbanski, J.C. 2005, 'Bringing humility to leadership: Antecedents and consequences of leader humility', *Human Relations*, 58(10): 1323–1350.

Mothersill, M. 1996, 'Some questions about truthfulness and lying', *Social Research*, 63(3): 913–929.

O'Malley, D.A. 2013, 'Management as a practice', in H. Harris, G. Wijesinghe and S. McKenzie (eds.), *The heart of the good institution: Virtue ethics as a framework for responsible management*, Netherlands: Springer, 35–46.

Osiemo, L.B. 2012, 'Developing responsible leaders: The university at the service of the person', *Journal of Business Ethics*, 108: 131–143.

Pakaluk, M. and Cheffers, M. 2011, *Accounting ethics... And the near collapse of the world's financial system*, Massachusetts: Allen David Press.

Peterson, M. 2004, 'What men and women value at work: Implications for workplace health', *Gender Medicine*, 1(2): 106–124.

Piëch, F. 2004, *Auto. Biographie*, München: Piper Verlag GmbH.

Pieper, J. 1965, *The four cardinal virtues*, New York: Harcourt, Brace & World, Inc.

Pirson, M. and Dierksmeier, C. 2016, 'Human dignity and business', *Business Ethics Quarterly*. DOI: 10.1017/beq.2016.47.

Pontifical Council for Justice and Peace. 2004 (CSDC), Compendium of the Social Doctrine of the Church, Vatican City: Libreria Editrice Vaticana. (www.vatican.va/roman_curia/pontifical_councils/justpeace/documents/rc_pc_justpeace_doc_20060526_compendio-dott-soc_en.html, Accessed September 27, 2017).

Pontifical Council for Justice and Peace. 2012, *Vocation of the Business Leader*. Retrieved 1 December 2016 from Pontifical Council for Justice and Peace. (www.pcgp.it/dati/2012-05/04-999999/Vocation%20ENG2.pdf, Accessed September 27, 2017).

Porter, J. 2013, 'Virtue ethics in the medieval period', in D.C. Russell (ed.), *The Cambridge companion to virtue ethics*, Cambridge: Cambridge University Press.

Preti, A.A. 2015, 'Leadership and moral excellence: Cultivating virtue through moral imagination', in A.J.G. Sison, G.R. Beabout and I. Ferrero (eds.), *Handbook of virtue ethics in business and management*, Dordrecht: Springer Science+Business Media, 973–983.

Rauwald, C. 2016, 'VW said to cut 30,000 jobs, save $3.9 billion in labor pact', *Bloomberg*, 18 November. (www.bloomberg.com/news/articles/2016-11-18/vw-said-to-cut-23-000-jobs-save-3-9-billion-with-labor-pact, Accessed November 18, 2016).

Remmel, M. 2004/2005, 'Developing responsible leaders', *EBS Review*, Winter 2004-Spring 2005: 92–96.

Ritter, J. 2005, 'Sexbelege und Lügengeschichten', *Frankfurter Allgemeine Zeitung*, 16 November. (www.faz.net/aktuell/politik/vw-affaere-sexbelege-und-luegengeschichten-1279720.html, Accessed August 18, 2016).

Robbins, S. and Judge, T. 2013, *Organizational behavior* (15th ed.), New York: Pearson.

Robinson, S. 2011, *Leadership responsibility: Ethical and organizational considerations*, Bern: Peter Lang AG, International Academic Publishers.

Sanger-Katz, M. and Schwartz, J. 2015, 'How many deaths did Volkswagen's deception cause in U.S.?', *The New York Times*, 28 September. (www.nytimes.com/2015/09/29/upshot/how-many-deaths-did-volkswagens-deception-cause-in-us.html?mtrref=undefined&gwh=EB16014338972538594C6BF7ED73337C&gwt=pay, Accessed September 30, 2016).

Schaal, E. 2015, '10 car companies that sell the most electric vehicles', *The Cheat Sheet*, 16 September. (www.cheatsheet.com/automobiles/10-car-companies-that-sell-the-most-electric-vehicles.html/?a=viewall, Accessed September 27, 2016).

Schmitt, B. 2016, 'Despite Dieselgate, Volkswagen is world's largest automaker in first 5 months of 2016', *Forbes*, 29 June. (www.forbes.com/sites/bertelschmitt/2016/06/29/despite-dieselgate-volkswagen-is-worlds-largest-automaker-in-first-5-months/#7705f7314cf6, Accessed October 21, 2016).

Sekerka, L.E., Comer, D.R., and Godwin, L.N. 2015, 'Professional moral courage: Fostering principled performance at work', in A.J.G. Sison, G.R. Beabout and I. Ferrero (eds.), *Handbook of virtue ethics in business and management*, Dordrecht: Springer Science+Business Media, 557–567.

Slavik, A. and Fromm, T. 2016, 'VW-Betriebsratschef droht: "Der Zukunftspakt könnte auch scheitern"', *Süddeutsche Zeitung*, 18 October. (www.sueddeutsche.de/wirtschaft/volkswagen-vw-betriebsratschef-droht-der-zukunftspakt-koennte-auch-scheitern-1.3208800, Accessed October 28, 2016).

Sison, A.J.G. 2003, *The moral capital of leaders: Why virtue matters*, Cheltenham, UK; Northampton, MA: Edward Elgar Publishing.

Sison, A.J.G. 2008, *Corporate governance and ethics: An Aristotelian perspective*, Cheltenham, UK: Edward Elgar Publishing Limited.

Sison, A.J.G., Ferrero, I. and Guitián, G. 2016, 'Human dignity and the dignity of work: Insights from catholic social teaching', *Business Ethics Quarterly*. DOI: 10.1017/beq.2016.18.

Stewart, J.B. 2015, 'Problems at Volkswagen start in the boardroom', *The New York Times*, 25 September. (www.nytimes.com/2015/09/25/business/international/problems-at-volkswagen-start-in-the-boardroom.html, Accessed September 9, 2016).

Stückelberger, C. 2016, 'Global ethics – Scenarios for the future', in C. Stückelberger, W. Fust, and I. Obiora (eds.), *Global ethics for leadership. Values and virtues for life*. Geneva: Globethics.net International Secretariat.

Süddeutsche Zeitung. 2016, 'VW-Personalchef: "Fünfstellige Zahl" an Jobs könnte wegfallen', *Süddeutsche Zeitung*, 28 October. (www.sueddeutsche.de/wirtschaft/autokonzern-vw-personalchef-fuenstellige-zahl-an-jobs-koennte-wegfallen-1.3227534, Accessed November 7, 2016).

Tatje, C. 2016a, 'Unheimlich mächtig', *Zeit Online*, 21 April. (www.zeit.de/2016/16/volkswagen-ig-metall-betriebsrat-unternehmenskultur, Accessed November 10, 2016).

Tatje, C. 2016b, 'Das ist wie im Watergate-Fall', *Zeit Online*, 29 September. (www.zeit.de/2016/39/volkswagen-dieselaffaere-schadensersatzklagen-deutschland, Accessed November 10, 2016).

Tirole, J. 2005, *The theory of corporate finance*, Princeton, NJ: Princeton University Press, 15–73.

Topham, G. 2012, 'Volkswagen swallows Porsche', *The Guardian*, 5 July. (www.theguardian.com/business/2012/jul/05/volkswagen-buys-porsche, Accessed November 1, 2016).

Volkswagen Sustainability Report. 2015. (http://sustainabilityreport2015.volkswagenag.com/group.html, Accessed September 12, 2016).

Volkswagen Sustainability Report. 2014. (http://sustainabilityreport2014.volkswagenag.com/downloads, Accessed September 12, 2016).

Yuengert, A.M. 2010, 'What is "sustainable prosperity for all" in the catholic social tradition?', in D.K. Finn (ed.), *The true wealth of nations*, Oxford: Oxford University Press, 37–62.

Zeit Online. 2015, 'Führungskultur bei VW soll Abgas-Skandal ermöglicht haben', *Zeit Online*, 29 October. (www.zeit.de/wirtschaft/2015-10/volkswagen-aufsichtsrat-stephan-weil-kritikkultur, Accessed October 29, 2015).

3

VIRTUES AND THE COMMON GOOD IN FINANCE

Alejo José G. Sison, Ignacio Ferrero, Gregorio Guitián, Marta Rocchi and Andrea Roncella

Learning objectives

In this chapter, we shall:

- Explain the purpose of finance, identifying the benefits it brings and the harms it occasions when challenges are not properly addressed.
- Present "financialization" as a trend in the economy, together with its opportunities and difficulties.
- Discuss the virtues relevant to financial practices and how they can be lived by individuals in the context of their own biographies and in the face of conflicting professional traditions.

Almost everyone agrees that, thanks to finance, a large segment of the population (including firms) has gained access to credit, buying cars and building homes or shopping malls, for example. Without finance, there would be no viable pensions and insurance systems or long-term infrastructure investments. This has resulted in huge, undeniable improvements in standards of living and peace of mind for many. Likewise, new ways of leveraging capital have been invented, making money more productive and spreading risks more widely and thinly ("hedging"). Moreover, thanks to the ease in acquiring, processing and storing information, new financial intermediaries have cropped up, such as digital wallets (PayPal) and currencies (Bitcoin), lowering transaction costs and providing greater liquidity to markets. Together, these financial developments have contributed to promote entrepreneurship and foster growth through microcredits, for instance, thus also enabling advancement in other socially important areas such as education, healthcare, transport, communication and so forth.

But, in the wake of the "Great Recession," many have come to believe that the harms provoked by finance have outweighed the benefits. This became painfully evident when private sector credit or debt crossed the "tipping point" of 80%–100% of GDP, the level in which the marginal effect of finance on growth turns negative. This has been blamed for the tepid—if at all—growth of the EU, the OECD countries and the global economy in general. The global financial system is now more fragile and volatile, as economies have become more synchronized. The twin specters of debt-deflation and prolonged recession loom large. Without productivity growth, wages have stagnated and jobs have been lost, causing greater wealth inequalities within societies; further, much of the remaining employment is deemed to be of poor quality. And to make things worse, governments, traditionally the ultimate guarantors of social welfare, have been obliged to cut down drastically in public spending, so as to stabilize budgets after expensive stimulus packages and bailouts.

Which of these two contrasting sides represents the true face of finance? Overall, is finance a blessing or a curse for the economy and society at large?

To respond, we first have to consider the purpose of finance. Experts state that the financial system is meant to take care of four major functions: (1) to promote household and corporate savings, (2) to allocate funds to their most productive use, (3) to manage and distribute risks and (4) to facilitate a reliable payment system (Greenwood and Scharfstein 2012). The time factor is crucial in all these operations, which are essentially variants of decisions to pay now and consume later or to pay later and consume now.

Financial institutions promote savings among individuals, families and firms by creating incentives in the form of interests or returns. These funds are then destined to their most productive employment—that is, whatever generates the highest returns or greatest benefits. Such a decision entails evaluating different investment options according to savers' preferences and future requirements, including liquidity. Rates of return reflect the level of risks or the probability of default involved. Take for instance family A, with a combined income of €4,000 monthly and expenses totalling €3,500, thereby yielding a surplus of €500. Instead of hiding that sum under the mattress, it would be better to deposit that amount in an interest-bearing bank account to earn some money. That is possible only if the bank lends those €500 as capital to a micro-entrepreneur, for example, who needs it to put up a hot-dog stand. This businessperson then returns the loan to the bank with interests, and the bank shares part of the proceeds with the depositor.

Finance institutions likewise run payment systems and help configure an overall financial architecture indispensable for the smooth functioning of the economy. Both family A and the hot-dog stand owner could make use of bank services to pay their monthly electricity bills, for example, debiting the corresponding amounts to the power company's account. It is fairly clear that financial institutions carry out a fundamental role in any reasonably developed economy and society. If money is the lifeblood of the economy, finance is the circulatory system that makes sure money goes when and where it's needed.

However, in the past few decades, we have witnessed how finance has come to represent an increasingly bigger share of the economy. Called "financialization," this phenomenon has often been identified as the cause of many global economic and social ills. How true are these allegations?

At its simplest, "financialization" is the characteristic shift of activity in modern, capitalist economies from production to finance. Largely an offshoot of globalization, among its enabling conditions are the end of the "cold war," the spread of deregulation, liberalization and privatization policies advocated by the Washington Consensus (the US government, the World Bank and the International Monetary Fund) and the development of information technologies. These factors gave rise to new entities (venture capital, private equity firms, hedge funds) with products and services created through securitization (mortgage-backed securities and asset-backed securities, for example) and structured finance (collateralized debt obligations, collateralized bond obligations, collateralized mortgage obligations and credit default swaps, among others) that have significantly altered the sectorial landscape. However, despite being closely linked, it is helpful to distinguish "enabling conditions" from financialization itself.

Several indicators have been suggested to measure the degree of financialization in an economy. The most widely used is the size of the financial sector (comprising financial intermediation, real estate, renting and business activities) as a percentage of GDP (Kedrosky and Stangler 2011). This indicates how much finance has gained in importance, influence, activity and profits relative to other sectors. Indeed, it is dangerous when the financial sector becomes inordinately huge and not enough resources are left for other goods (food, manufacturing) and services (education, healthcare). This often means that speculation or rent-seeking have taken over, eventually resulting in harmful bubbles, spurious investments, bogus profits and massive job losses. Excessive financialization does not promote savings, but debt-spending; it does not direct funds to productive uses, but to speculative activities; it conceals and multiplies risks, passing them on to unwary and gullible actors through "duping" (Zingales 2015). Over-financialization destroys confidence, destabilizing payment systems and the whole economy.

On the one hand, the need and the advantages of a financial system are plain. Yet, on the other, the harms brought by excessive financialization are also evident. Granted that financialization is a matter of degrees, how to determine the right proportion? Where lies the golden mean?

First, we have to explain the role of finance in society, particularly with respect to human flourishing (*eudaimonia*). We shall do this by the hand of Aristotle. Second, we will consider financial practices as "goods" embedded in the biographies of financial practitioners and in the traditions of their profession. We shall attempt this making use of indications from MacIntyre and Catholic Social Teaching (CST). Once this theoretical background is set, we could analyze a case that illustrates how the different virtues can be lived in finance.

1. Aristotle and the search for a context and limits in finance

Perhaps Aristotle's main contribution to making virtue possible in finance lies in the creation of a "political" and "eudaimonistic" framework. For Aristotle,

"politics" designates that body of knowledge whose object is happiness or flourishing (*eudaimonia*), the supreme good and final end of human beings (Aristotle
Nichomachean Ethics, henceforth NE: 1094a-b). Since human beings are social
or "political animals" (Aristotle *Politics*, henceforth Pltcs: 1253a), flourishing
can only be attained in fully developed political communities. Flourishing,
however, depends on the availability of both material (external and bodily
goods) and non-material (internal goods of the soul, excellences or virtues) resources (Pltcs: 1324a). Thus, politics rests on two sub-disciplines: "economy"
(*oikonomia*), which takes care of material goods, and "ethics" (*ethike*), which refers to non-material goods. These categories of goods and disciplines rely on
each other. For instance, it would be very difficult to pursue knowledge (an
internal, non-material good) if one did not have any food (an external, material
good). But also, if one spent too much time eating, he would hardly feel inclined
to seek knowledge. Although both material and non-material goods are equally
necessary for flourishing, there is a hierarchical order to be observed. Material
goods ought to be pursued not in themselves, but only insofar as they allow us
to achieve superior, non-material or spiritual goods. For this reason, in the order
of the branches of knowledge, economy is subordinated to ethics, and both, at
the service of politics.

Inasmuch as finance deals with material resources, it fits within the province
of economy. Aristotle distinguishes two main activities in economy, wealth usage (economy proper) and wealth acquisition or production (chrematistics) (Pltcs:
1253b), related to each other as "end" and "means," respectively. Finance belongs
to the latter, as a kind of chrematistics. In both wealth usage and wealth production, there is a proper ("natural") and improper ("non-natural") version, depending on whether they fulfill their purpose. In economy proper, for instance,
shoes used as footwear would be proper, while shoes used as objects of barter
would be improper (Pltcs: 1257a). In chrematistics, money used in exchange for
other goods—such as shoes, for example—would be proper, while money used
to earn interest would be improper—usury—in the primitive economy of Aristotle's time (Pltcs: 1258b).

For Aristotle, finance is "virtuous" when money is used to purchase other
goods necessary for flourishing (*eudaimonia*). Back then, money only had two
functions: as a "store of value" (other goods such as foodstuff usually spoiled) and
as a "unit of exchange and account" (the equivalent of other goods and services
traded). Anything else apart from this was "unnatural" and improper. Hence,
all forms of interests were usurious, because money was not yet understood as a
good possessing value in terms of "opportunity costs" (Henderson 2008).

An emendation has to be introduced, therefore, to Aristotle's teaching, to
make it relevant to far more developed and complex market economies. No
longer are all interests usurious, due to the foregone "opportunity costs" (the
value of alternative uses) of lenders. Interests would only be usurious or abusive if
they far exceeded those opportunity costs. The reference to lending as a perverse
or non-natural use of money is no longer appropriate.

Once finance clears this bar of using money to buy other things (proper chrematistics), we then have to examine whether these other material goods are used rightly (economy proper) and whether they facilitate access to superior, non-material goods (ethics). For example, families could take out a loan from a bank to purchase a home, which in turn provides shelter and stability enabling them to engage in other worthwhile pursuits. Through this chain of events, we can see how finance contributes to the flourishing of the political community (politics). This also paves the way for virtue in finance—as an instance of Aristotelian chrematistics—in view of its end, purpose or objective.

Previously, we saw that financialization refers to the increasing share of finance in the economy. We also learned that there is a point past which financialization may be excessive for the overall good of society. In Aristotelian terms, such occurs when individuals engage in the vice of non-natural chrematistics, because it produces money in a limitless way, as if the need were infinite, without regard to the right amount for flourishing (non-natural chrematistics). The vice of financialization or financialization in excess consists of making money simply for the sake of making more. It has mistaken money, which is a "means" or "instrument," a "good sought for the sake of another," for an "end," a "good sought for itself" (NE: 1096b). This is obviously wrong, for why would we want money, if there was nothing to buy? It is rational to desire money only as a means and never as an end. Money is, by nature, a tool.

From the Aristotelian viewpoint, financialization becomes a vice, not by reason of its object, but because of the agent's intentions or motives. There is nothing wrong about making money so long as it doesn't become an end in itself. Financialization does not belong to the class of intrinsically immoral activities prohibited without exception (NE: 1110a). It becomes a vice when the agent is overcome by an inordinate desire for wealth or greed, accumulating money for itself.

On the other hand, finance as a form of chrematistics can be "virtuous" (proper) if it keeps a "natural" limit. For Aristotle, we only need a finite amount of material resources or money to satisfy our bodily needs (economy proper) and attain flourishing. One could always earn more, although one does not always need more. Having more money does not mean a better life. Certainly, there are material requirements and we should earn perhaps a bit more for incidentals. But beyond this, more money may result in a hindrance than a help. Having too much money can be quite a burden and even detrimental to personal flourishing.

So, how is one to determine the ideal limit for one's financial needs? It's not just a matter of coming up with a formula to arrive at a precise number; although inevitably, one will have to do the maths. It's more a question of looking inside oneself honestly and appealing to a "subjective standard" set by moderation and prudence or practical wisdom. We need to appeal to a "qualified agent account" (Hursthouse 1999) based on the virtues. Acquiring the virtues of moderation and prudence is similar to learning a craft or skill. One needs to put himself as an apprentice at the orders of a master craftsman or teacher of virtue. The apprentice's perception of the standards of excellence in the craft improves to the extent that he pays attention to the master's instructions (who represents the "subjective standard"), although initially he may not understand or agree with them. The same happens in developing the virtues. To refuse is to refuse to learn the craft or to acquire the virtues. Trust in the master or teacher is a *sine qua non* condition to advance and prosper. Only when the apprentice has already successfully embodied the standards of excellence in the craft ("mastery") or in the virtues could he then venture and strike out his own path.

Therefore, the virtues of moderation and prudence are primarily responsible in deciding the right amount of money a person needs to flourish. Moderation refers to "self-control" in pleasures; oftentimes, it lies in the ability to say "no" to desires and wishes. But, saying "no" cannot be arbitrary; it should follow a good reason. And this is what prudence recognizes and provides. Thus, for instance, one realizes that he really doesn't need to spend €2,250,000 on a Bugatti Veyron 16.4 for the thrill of cruising at 431 km/hr, given the speed limits (50 km/hr), traffic conditions (eternally clogged) and daily routines (chauffeur-driven, from home to office and back, for a total distance of 15 kms), living in the flood-prone capital of a developing country.

Besides moderation and prudence, justice and courage are also relevant in determining the right amount of financial resources one needs to flourish. It's not the same to be 50 years old, single and with no plans of marrying, than to be of the same age but married and with 10 kids. The first has significantly fewer economic obligations towards family than the second and would need fewer resources, all things being equal, to lead a good life. Likewise, because of greater obligations, the second will have to exercise more courage and daring in professional pursuits, working harder and perhaps taking more risks.

In typical, circular Aristotelian fashion, therefore, we need the virtues of moderation, prudence or practical wisdom, justice and courage to determine one's subjective standard or limit in money. Virtuous finance is possible so long as one observes the "natural" or proper limit in money according to the cardinal virtues.

For Aristotle, in summary, finance as a kind of chrematistics is not an end in itself. It's nonsense to earn more money simply for the sake of having more. To be virtuous, seeking money has to pursue a different purpose. The immediate end of finance is the use and enjoyment of material resources (economy proper), as a means to the development of non-material or spiritual goods (ethics), with a view to flourishing, the final end of human beings (politics). However, to fulfill these goals, finance has to observe a limit in the amount of material resources. This limit is not so much the result of a mathematical formula, as a "subjective standard" that each one sets for himself as a virtuously "qualified agent." Developing the virtues is like learning a skill or a craft from a master or teacher who embodies the subjective standard of excellence. This standard could only be acquired to the extent one attends to the demands of moderation, justice, courage and prudence. It results from the practice of self-control over wishes and desires, careful attention to duties towards the welfare of others, determination to overcome challenges and difficulties at work, and thoughtful circumspection.

- Finance is a form of wealth-production (*chrematistics*) that should be placed at the service of flourishing (*eudaimonia*). Making more money only for its own sake does not make sense.

2. MacIntyre on financial practices and the lives and traditions of financiers

For MacIntyre, the development of virtues in any field—including finance— always involves a three-step process:

> a first which concerns virtues as qualities necessary to achieve the goods internal to practices; a second which considers them as qualities contributing to the good of a whole life; and a third which related them to the pursuit of a good for human beings the conception of which can only be elaborated and possessed within an ongoing social tradition.
>
> *(MacIntyre 2007 [1981]: 273)*

In the first stage, then, we will identify the practices belonging to finance and their "internal goods," the "external goods" that make their pursuit possible and their modes of institutionalization. Second, we will explain how these goods and practices constitute "the good of a whole life" for individuals through personal biographies or narratives. And third, we will show how these individual narratives, in turn, comprise wider communal traditions, giving "the good life for human beings" its definitive meaning. Only then shall we characterize financial virtues adequately, as instantiations of moderation, courage, justice, prudence and so forth.

Practices

Let us commence with the first of these steps. Initially, in *After Virtue* (MacIntyre 2007 [1981]), MacIntyre spoke of "internal" and "external goods," but in *Whose Justice?, Which Rationality?* (MacIntyre 1988), he changed terminology to "goods of excellence" and "goods of effectiveness" while retaining their original meaning (Miller 1994: 248). In any case, both "internal goods" or "goods of excellence," on the one hand, and "external goods" or "goods of effectiveness," on the other, are designated in reference to practices.

Practices are defined as

> any coherent and complex form of socially established cooperative human activity through which goods internal to that form of activity are realized in the course of trying to achieve those standards of excellence which are appropriate to, and partially definitive of, that form of activity, with the result that human powers to achieve excellence, and human conceptions of the ends and goods involved, are systematically extended.
>
> *(MacIntyre 2007 [1981]: 175)*

Examples of practices are chess, football, farming, architecture and the creation of Aristotelian political communities. They are considered a "universal feature of human cultures" (MacIntyre 1994: 287), denoting activities worthwhile in pursuing. Practices involve two things: goods that cannot be obtained or achieved outside of the cooperative activity ("internal goods") and "standards of excellence" by which the activity could be judged, at least partially. Practices also entail two consequences: the development of distinct human capacities for excellence and an improvement in the understanding of their specific ends or purposes (*teloi*).

Institutions

For their part, "[I]nstitutions are characteristically and necessarily concerned with [...] external goods. They are involved in acquiring money and other material goods; they are structured in terms of power and status, and they distribute money, power and status as rewards" (MacIntyre 2007 [1981]: 194). Institutions refer to the procurement and distribution of goods external to practices, some of which are material, such as money, and others, closely related to the material, like power and status. Institutions are absolutely necessary for they "sustain not only themselves, but also the practices of which they are the bearers. For no practices can survive for any length of time unsustained by institutions" (MacIntyre 2007 [1981]: 194). Thanks to the external, material goods they procure and administer, institutions are essential to the survival of practices (Figure 3.1).

Both institutions and practices, on the one hand, and the external and the internal goods they respectively pursue, on the other, are so intimately related to each other that they form "a single causal order" (MacIntyre 2007 [1981]: 194). Because of this, "the ideals and the creativity of the practice are always vulnerable to the acquisitiveness of the institution, [...] the cooperative care for the common good of the practice is always vulnerable to the competitiveness of the institution" (MacIntyre 2007 [1981]: 194). Due to the dependence of practices on institutions, it could occur that agents seek external goods such as money, status and power in themselves, either forgetting about internal goods altogether or subordinating these to external goods. This leads to the loss of integrity or corruption of practices and institutions (MacIntyre 2007 [1981]: 195). Practices

FIGURE 3.1 The architecture of practices and institutions in organizations.

are distorted and the external goods of institutions invade, rather than support them (MacIntyre 1994: 289).

However, this doesn't mean that institutions are outrightly censurable. Without institutions, neither would there be practices. Further, "the making and sustaining of forms of human community—and therefore of institutions—itself has the characteristics of a practice, and moreover of a practice which stands in a peculiarly close relationship to the exercise of the virtues" (MacIntyre 2007 [1981]: 194). The making and sustaining of institutions, then, also has its own internal goods and standards of excellence (Figure 3.2).

Excessive financialization then is regarded as a vice, from the MacIntyrean angle, because it prioritizes "external goods" over "internal goods" (MacIntyre 2007 [1981]), in a "deficient mode of institutionalization" or "corruption of a practice" (MacIntyre 2007 [1981]). Agents are more concerned with money and power than excellence. The proper order between "external goods" or "goods of effectiveness" and "internal goods" or "goods of excellence" is subverted. Institutions take over practices. Financiers, then, aspire to ever-increasing profits without countenancing how they are attained. Prudent asset management and stable, long-term professional relationships are dismissed.

Adopting a more positive tack, how could we to apply MacIntyre's practice-institution schema to modern finance? As we have seen, modern financiers fulfill four major functions: promoting household and corporate savings, allocating funds, managing and distributing risks and facilitating a payment system (Greenwood and Scharfstein 2012). All comply with the condition of a "coherent and complex form of socially established cooperative activity" (MacIntyre 2007 [1981]: 175). How about the requirement of "internal goods" that could only be achieved in the exercise of such activities? This does not seem to be the case with promoting savings or providing a payment system. Encouraging people to save

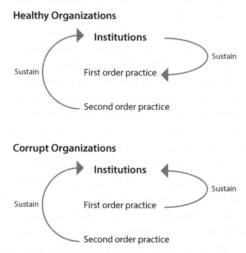

FIGURE 3.2 "Healthy" and "corrupt" organizations.

just for the sake of saving does not make sense, because the rationale lies in investment and future consumption. Saving for its own sake is pure accumulation and devoid of internal goods. Something similar occurs with the setting up of payment systems. This is more of a technical problem to be addressed through the internet and the appropriate software, for instance. Hence the success of MPesa, a mobile phone-based money transfer system that originated in Kenya. There is no internal human good in the mere physical displacement of financial resources. Once again, the purpose of sending money elsewhere is for use in payment, investment and consumption.

It's different with the allocation of funds and the management of risks. In fact, these two functions can be combined, since the distribution of risks is to ensure that agents have the necessary resources for consumption and investment. That is the ultimate aim of risk management. We could then venture an "internal good" for investment consisting of the "best use" of resources, different perhaps from their "most productive or profitable use."

A few clarifications before we proceed. First, we refer to investment rather than consumption because that is the sort of decision a financier makes. The financier is not expected to "use" (in the sense of "consume" or "enjoy") resources for himself, but to invest them on behalf of principals. Often, those resources do not belong to him; he only administers them bearing in mind fiduciary obligations. Second, the "most productive or profitable use" merely indicates obtaining the greatest output for the input, without considering the worthiness of investment objectives or the demands of justice. Yet, we know that investment decisions, as free and rational actions, are morally freighted decisions, and the establishment of moral priorities is something only human beings can do. Therefore, investments should not be guided by the criterion of profit-maximization alone, but by other moral principles as well.

Certainly, profits and productivity are reasonable indicators of investment soundness, but they are not the only ones. Neither should they be the financier's sole or prime objective. Hence, it may not be the best to invest in "weapons of mass destruction," for instance, no matter the financial rewards. In 2016, global military spending was worth $1,711 billion, with an increase of 148% from previous years in critical areas such as North Africa (Statista Research and Analysis 2016). Indeed, it would be very tempting for financiers to have a slice of that pie.

Ethical requirements have to be satisfied first of all. Since practices are social and cooperative activities, special attention has to be given to justice in investment decisions. While prudence dictates that risks be shared and spread, rather than concentrated, among informed and willing partners, justice establishes that there be no free-riders and that those who bear greater risks also enjoy proportional rewards when business prospers. Different savers—such as pension funds and hedge funds—have varying degrees of risk tolerance and time horizons. Financiers should take this into account when choosing—for example—between safe, but low-return sovereign debt from rich countries (for instance, US Treasury bills) and riskier, but high-return opportunities from poor countries, thereby contributing to their development and welfare.

Apart from the internal good consisting of the "best use" of financial resources, investment practice also possesses "standards of excellence." These not only include the skill of finding the "most productive use" or "highest returns," but also, and more importantly, compliance with the different moral virtues. To the extent that financiers live up to these internal standards, they develop different human capacities together with their investment acumen.

The institutions housing financial practices involve all competitive activities dedicated to the acquisition of external goods, such as money, power and status. They include the different ways of capturing funds from deposits, shares or equity, debt and so forth. Power and status can be obtained through various means, as having the biggest market capitalization, the greatest ROI/ROE, the widest operational network, the most advanced technology, the highest profits and so on. However, for financial practices and institutions to be in good order, agents should remember that these external goods are worthwhile only to the extent that they serve the internal good of making the "best investments." Take the case of Wells Fargo bank (Corkery 2016; Corkery and Cowley 2016). It survived the "Great Recession" relatively unscathed to become the biggest in market capitalization, only to succumb shortly after for opening half a million sham credit card accounts in response to unrealistic sales quotas from management. External goods such as market share or sales quotas in Wells Fargo should not to be sought as goals in themselves, for then, they would corrupt both practices and institutions. Also, agents should recall that sustaining financial institutions in itself entails a practice, with the internal good of survival and thriving. Members of top management possess the responsibility of constantly promoting institutions and external goods, but never at the expense of corrupting practices and internal goods. They could always bear in mind how a single rogue trader, Nick Leeson, brought about the collapse in 1995 of Barings, the oldest merchant bank founded in London in 1762 (Rodrigues 2015; Titcomb 2015).

Individual lives

It's time to move on to the second stage and consider how practices and institutions contribute to "the good life as a whole" for individuals through their biographies or narratives (MacIntyre 2007 [1981]: 273).

The unity of our lives is a "narrative unity," expressing continuity not only between our past and present, but also with other people's lives in a common plot. It is a moral unity, a social, systematic quest for the good of flourishing (*eudaimonia*). This type of goal requires a whole life, from beginning to end, not just isolated events. The quest or journey (inquiry) partially constitutes the goal or destination (flourishing).

How can we understand a financier's life as a narrative unity? First, by acknowledging that he inhabits multiple, interrelated roles. Some are of his choosing, such as being a financier in particular firm, while others are not, such as being a son or brother. Both types of roles form part of his identity and give rise to rights and duties. Often, obligations from socially defined roles may go against personal preferences, as when a company superior makes an investment decision contrary to one's proposal. A financier will then have to consider whether to abide by the boss's decision, but not on the basis of personal preferences alone or just because the other is a superior. Rather, he will have to reconsider, insofar as his abilities allow, what is best for the company, transcending particular likes and dislikes, and act accordingly. Even if he were the boss, conflicts could still occur between personal interests (a bigger paycheck) and those of the company, which may incur greater risks and end up in danger of insolvency or bankruptcy. Enron executives egregiously chose to report fraudulent earnings to increase the value of their options at the expense of driving the company off the cliff.

Conflicts may also occur between different roles, as when a financier works overtime to attend to an important client and he is unexpectedly called upon to take care of a sick child. Even within the same family realm, for instance, difficulties too may arise (Sullivan 2016). Couples may decide that the husband, who is a financier, takes care of finances, while the wife takes charge of the home and kids. This division of labor and specialization might make sense at first. But unfortunately, families can break up through separation and divorce, or serious disability and death can suddenly visit the home. Even in successful marriages, the husband may develop Alzheimer's disease. It then becomes extremely burdensome for the wife who has been left out of the financial planning to cope with the new situation. A good financier *qua* husband and father should have contingency plans for these unlikely events to provide for everyone's needs. General guidelines scarcely help. A financier who strives to be virtuous will evaluate priorities and establish order among competing roles and goods to protect everyone's interests. The different life-spheres and roles we inhabit cannot be subject to rigid compartmentalization, since they all form part of a narrative unity.

Traditions

Third, understanding the virtues, with the practices and institutions they entail, within the context of a biography helps us see that flourishing is the object of a communal quest. Referring to productive crafts, MacIntyre suggests that excellence requires not only that there be "a good product, but [that] the craftperson is perfected through and in her or his activity" (MacIntyre 1994: 284). Similarly, a virtuous financier not only ensures, for example, that company performance targets are met, but also that they are met in the proper way—that is, in fair competition, through greater knowledge, skill and effort, without neglecting duties linked to other social roles, with improved cohesion among group members and so forth.

The final step in the characterization of the virtues comprises the advancement of social traditions (MacIntyre 2007 [1981]: 273). Traditions provide an even wider social context than biographies or narratives. They are the means through which practices and institutions are simultaneously shaped and transmitted through generations: "a living tradition then is a historically extended, socially embodied argument, and an argument precisely in part about the goods which constitute that tradition" (MacIntyre 2007 [1981]: 207). Traditions are modes of moral inquiry that develop as a consequence of changing social, historical and cultural milieus. They are the repositories of "standards of excellence," both morally and in terms of skills, to which individuals refer when facing challenges. They are "the best solution so far" that communities have furnished to practical, professional problems.

How relevant are traditions to financiers? Consider a local commercial bank taken over by a much larger and tech-savvy multinational financial organization (Robson 2015). No doubt corporate culture and traditions will change. If a financier is lucky enough to keep his job and position, he will have to confront complicated challenges. Perhaps the new bank now values anonymous, web-based communication with clients more than stable, face-to face long-term personal relationships. Previously, the focus was on customizing financial services to each client's needs; now, it is on meeting quotas set by headquarters based on a menu of standard products. Before, good financial practice meant saying "no" to clients who wanted certain services, such as old ladies who wanted to invest pensions in high-risk technology funds, for example. But now, it consists of glib salesmanship combined with the principle of "caveat emptor." At first, savers knew and had a say on where their money was invested, much of it used in local businesses and projects benefiting the community. At present, funds are allocated to derivatives and other complex financial instruments in offshore centers worldwide.

No doubt these changes will provoke tortured soul-searching in our financier, regarding his professional commitments and his roles as a family man, friend and member of the community. He will have to examine carefully what "being a good financier" meant to him until now and what it will signify in the future. For this, he will need to rely on competing traditions of professionalism to supply him with good reasons to follow one line of action or another. Or he may invent a tradition of his own, in response to evolving circumstances. In any case, he will be able to respond only insofar as he acknowledges his debt to the previous traditions that have sustained him.

MacIntyre affirms that

> no quality can be accounted a virtue except in respect of its being such as to enable the achievement of three distinct kinds of goods: those internal to practices, those which are the goods of an individual life and those which are the goods of the community.
>
> *(MacIntyre 1994: 284)*

First, we defined the distinctive practices and institutions of finance, with their corresponding internal and external goods. Then, we situated them within the narrative unity of an individual's life, with its multiple, often conflicting roles. And only now, after considering those individual lives as followers and innovators of wider social traditions, are we able to fulfill MacIntyre's requirements and render a full account of the virtues.

• The core of financial practice consists of investment and risk management. Excellence in this practice also requires excellence in the different roles individuals inhabit and positive contributions to the development of the profession.

3. Catholic Social Teaching on finance

Due to Aristotelian influence and the widespread, long-standing ethical tradition against usury, the majority of Catholic Social Teachings (CST) texts on finance refer to condemnations of abusive practices. However, CST makes no blanket rejection of financial activities. CST is fully aware that finance is necessary to attain not only economic, but also general, social well-being. Thus, there must be a proper, virtuous way to carry it out. As a first step, finance must operate within the framework of fundamental CST principles. They are premised on the idea that finance constitutes a means or instrument that goes astray when converted into an end in itself.

Already in 1931, Pius XI denounced the tyranny to which the great accumulation and concentration of wealth enabled by finance sometimes leads:

> This dictatorship is being most forcibly exercised by those who, since they hold the money and completely control it, control credit also and rule the lending of money. Hence they regulate the flow, so to speak, of the life-blood whereby the entire economic system lives, and have so firmly in their grasp the soul, as it were, of economic life that no one can breathe against their will.
>
> *(Pius XI* Quadragesimo Anno *(QA) 1931: 106)*

However, Pius XI also acknowledges the need for "expending larger incomes so that opportunity for gainful work may be abundant, provided that this work is applied to producing really useful goods"; he even calls this task "an outstanding exemplification of the virtue of munificence" (QA: 51). This would not be possible in a "finance-free" subsistence economy. Finance, therefore, is essential to increasing incomes and making investments that create employment and produce useful goods.

What are the fundamental CST principles to ensure finance is on track? They are the principles of human dignity, also known as the "personalist principle" (Pontifical Council for Justice and Peace, Compendium of the Social Doctrine of the Church, henceforth CSDC: 105, 132), the common good (CSDC: 164, 165), the universal destination of goods (CSDC: 171), subsidiarity (CSDC: 186), participation (CSDC: 189) and solidarity (CSDC: 192, 193).

The principle of human dignity establishes that "the person represents the ultimate end of society" (CSDC: 105, 132). The common good refers to "the social and community dimension of the moral good" (CSDC: 164), "the good of all people and of the whole person" (CSDC: 165). The universal destination of goods means that "each person must have access to the level of wellbeing necessary for his full development" (CSDC: 172). This occurs when we respect the right to private property and exercise a preferential option for the poor. Subsidiarity implies that "every social activity ought of its very nature to furnish help [*subsidium*] to the members of the body social, and never destroy and absorb them" (QA: 203). It imposes on every individual the right and duty to contribute to the cultural, economic, political and social life (Vatican Council II *Gaudium et Spes* (GeS) 1965: 75), in accordance with the principle of participation. Lastly, the principle of solidarity admonishes us to recognize "the intrinsic social nature of the human person, the equality of all in dignity and rights and the common path of individuals and peoples towards an ever more committed unity" (CSDC: 192).

CST principles apply to finance in two ways. First, they apply negatively, rejecting activities and institutions that have become self-serving or "ends in themselves." But, they could also apply positively, indicating the proper orientation for activities and institutions to contribute to genuine human flourishing.

Let us begin with the first. A self-referential finance does not truly serve human beings or fulfill a social function. It goes against the personalist principle and the common good, only serving the economic interests of the owners of financial capital exclusively. This behavior represents the absolutization of private property, denying the link with the universal destination of goods. It shows no concern for the poor, depriving them of help (*subsidium*). Such financiers neglect their duty to contribute to the community often by evading taxes. They also ignore the interdependence amongst human beings, violating the principles of participation and solidarity.

In 1999, St. John Paul II already warned against the negative consequences when "financial transactions have already greatly exceeded real ones, so much so that the financial sphere has now acquired an autonomy of its own" (John Paul II *Centessimus annus* (CA) 1999). Recently, Pope Francis likewise alerted us that "when money becomes the end and the motive of every activity and of every venture, then the utilitarian perspective and brute logic—which do not respect people—prevail" (Francis 2014). He energetically denounced "the new idolatry of money" (Francis *Evangelii Gaudium* (EG) 2013: 55–56), rejecting a global economic and political system that establishes money, power and possessions as new gods that exercise dominion over everything. Refusing to worship money entails renouncing a "financial system which rules rather than serves," for "money must serve, not rule!" (EG: 57–58). Upholding "absolute autonomy of markets and financial speculation"—as some strains of capitalism, economic liberalism and libertarianism are wont to do—contributes to the "structural causes of inequality" (EG: 202).

CST affirms that "a financial economy that is an end unto itself is destined to contradict its goals," because "it has abandoned its original and essential role of serving the real economy and, ultimately, of contributing to the development of people and the human community" (CSDC: 369). Instead, "the primacy of the spiritual and of ethics needs to be restored, and, with them, the primacy of politics—which is responsible for the common good—over the economy and finance" (Pontifical Council for Justice and Peace 2011: 4).

For CST, excessive financialization is abhorrent because it "commoditizes business" and embraces "short-termism" (Pontifical Council for Justice and Peace 2012: 9). Business, which is a complex human social enterprise, is reduced to the market value of financial assets, and workers cease to count, except when they increase financial value. "Short-termism" is the fixation on huge and immediate profits, while assuming enormous risk burdens in a "casino-style capitalism." As Benedict XVI said,

> [W]ithout doubt, one of the greatest risks for businesses is that they are almost exclusively answerable to their investors, thereby limiting their social value [...] It is becoming increasingly rare for business enterprises to be in the hands of a stable director who feels responsible in the long term, not just the short-term, for the life and results of the company.
>
> *(Benedict XVI* Caritas in Veritate *(CiV) 2009: 40)*

Now we shall examine how CST principles help give the proper orientation to finance. St. John Paul II made it clear that the processes of "globalizing markets and communications do not in themselves possess an ethically negative connotation" (John Paul II 1999).

> Without adequate financial systems, economic growth would not have taken place. Large-scale investments typical of modern market economies would have been impossible without the fundamental role of mediation played by financial markets, which among other things brought about an appreciation of the positive functions of savings in the overall development of the economic and social system.
>
> *(CSDC 368)*

In consonance with human dignity, business owners and managers should not limit themselves to meeting economic objectives only, but acknowledge "also their precise duty to respect concretely the human dignity of those who work within the company," as "the firm's most valuable asset" and "decisive factor of production" (CSDC 344). CST upholds the priority of workers over capital, such that employers are obliged "to consider the welfare of the workers before the increase of profits" (Congregation for the Doctrine of the Faith 1986: 87). This includes the duty to keep capital productive by making investments that consolidate existing jobs and create new ones.

In accordance with the common good, finance ought to recover "its original and essential role of serving the real economy and, ultimately, of contributing to the development of people and the human community" (CSDC 369). The "real vocation" of finance lies in its "social function" of "nourishing markets and financial institutions which are really at the service of the person and are capable of responding to the needs of the common good and universal solidarity" (Pontifical Council for Justice and Peace 2011: 4).

Finance must recognize that private property (land, technology and financial resources) is always subordinated to the universal destination of goods and should not be converted into impediments for the work and development of others (CSDC 282). Private property, acquired primarily through work, must again be placed at the service of work. Financial resources must be put to productive, employment-generating investments.

For St. John Paul II, investment decisions are moral acts and, therefore, opportunities for participation, subsidiarity and solidarity, especially with the poor: "the decision to invest in one place rather than another, in one productive sector rather than another, is always a moral and cultural choice" (CA: 36). Savers and investors should "evaluate the available options not only on the basis of the expected return and the relative risk but also by making a value judgment of the investment projects that those resources would finance" (CSDC 358). Investors and consumers can influence "the presence of correct working conditions in the company as well as the level of protection of the natural environment in which it operates" (CSDC 359). In Third World countries, "the availability of capital and the fact of accepting it as a loan can be considered a contribution to development, something desirable and legitimate in itself" (John Paul II *Sollicitudo Rei Socialis* (SRS) 1987: 19). Unfortunately, financial resources are "often diverted from their proper purpose and used to sustain conflicts, apart from and in opposition to the interests of the countries which ought to benefit from them" (SRS: 21).

It is not enough for financial activities to be congruent with CST principles. They should also become opportunities for the practice of the virtues. St. John Paul II lists among these virtues

> diligence, industriousness, prudence in undertaking reasonable risks, reliability and fidelity in interpersonal relationships as well as courage in carrying out decisions which are difficult and painful but necessary, both for the overall working of a business and in meeting possible set-backs.
>
> *(CA: 32)*

As criteria for determining savings, investments and consumer choices, St. John Paul II includes "the quest for truth, beauty, goodness and communion with others for the sake of common growth" (CA: 36). For his part, Pope Francis states that "economy and finance are dimensions of human activity and can be occasions of encounter, of dialogue, of cooperation, of recognized rights and of services rendered, of dignity affirmed in work" (Francis 2014). He encouraged finance professionals "to always work responsibly, fostering relationships of loyalty, justice, if possible, of fraternity, bravely confronting especially the problems of the weakest and of the poorest," thus exercising solidarity (Francis 2014).

Finance professionals are called, above all, to behave in accordance with justice: never to violate the dignity of man and to always place the human person and the common good at the center of every social project, cognizant that earthly goods are meant for everyone (John Paul II 1999). St. John Paul II recommended that financial operators prepare ethical or professional codes and that international authorities adopt juridical instruments, bearing in mind the interests of the most vulnerable (John Paul II 1999: 2–4). He also reiterated that

> it is not enough to respect local laws or national regulations; what is necessary is a sense of global justice, equal to the responsibilities that are at stake, while acknowledging the structural interdependence of the relations between human beings over and above national boundaries.
>
> *(John Paul II 1999: 4)*

Besides justice, charity is another important virtue in finance. It translates into "the duty to give from one's 'abundance', and sometimes even out of one's needs, in order to provide what is essential for the life of a poor person" (CA: 36). Moderation also ought to be exercised. Apart from promoting savings, "purchasing power must be used in the context of the moral demands of justice and solidarity, and in that of precise social responsibilities" (CSDC 359). Property rights should not be used to justify selfish behaviors. Since finance involves "decisions to buy or sell, to resize, close or to merge a site" (CSDC 344), prudence or practical wisdom must likewise be considered apart from purely commercial criteria.

Another set of CST categories applicable to finance is composed of the subjective and objective dimensions of work. All work gives rise to two kinds of results: one, external, and the other, internal to the agent. CST calls the external results the "objective dimension" of work and the internal results, the "subjective dimension." Work in the objective sense is "the sum of activities, resources, instruments and technologies used by men and women to produce things"; the subjective sense, "the activity of the human person as a dynamic being capable of performing a variety of actions" (CSDC 270).

CST calls for the normative pre-eminence of the subjective dimension of work over the objective dimension. In finance, this means that the knowledge, skills, meanings and, above all, virtues that financiers develop should be given greater value than the external, material products and services, including profits, they generate.

CST initially focuses more on the abuse than on the beneficial use of finance. Yet, this does not mean that financial activities are intrinsically evil. Rather, they need to be carried out in accordance with certain fundamental principles, such as human dignity, the common good, the universal destination of goods, private property, the preferential option for the poor, subsidiarity, participation and solidarity. CST principles perform a dual role. On the one hand, they provide moral grounds for why certain financial practices ought to be rejected, when they become self-serving. On the other hand, they set the right orientation for finance to follow. To the degree that financial activities and institutions satisfy these fundamental principles, the path leading to moral virtues such as justice, charity, moderation and prudence is laid clear. Lastly, CST requires that in financial work, the subjective dimension (results internal to agents) always be given priority over the objective dimension (results external to agents).

• CST acknowledges the usefulness of finance so long as it respects certain fundamental principles and places people before profits.

4. Stelac advisory services and the renewal of financial culture

Carlos Padula was born in 1960 in Caracas, Venezuela to an Italian family with successful businesses in agriculture, hospitals and jewelry. Upon finishing university, he worked in the financial sector, taking on managerial responsibilities early in his career. At the age of 32, he was appointed Executive Vice President, overseeing international operations, and Assistant to the CEO of the fifth largest financial institution in the country. At this point, Carlos had already gotten married and had three children.

Soon after, however, serious conflicts arose between shareholders and the management of the bank which made Carlos decide to leave. This experience taught him the importance of corporate culture and how it could make people want to change their place of work. Shortly thereafter, he moved with his young family to the United States in search of new opportunities. Carlos would then face the difficulty of restarting a professional career, while struggling to provide for his family.

In the early 1990s, after completing an MBA at Boston University, Carlos started working for Bankers Trust (BT), then the second largest bank in the US. Although his position then was considerably lower than the one he had in Venezuela, he found the environment in BT particularly exciting. The bank was supportive of its workers and encouraged them to innovate. This fostered an atmosphere of camaraderie and growth, which BT alumni remember fondly. But, the situation changed completely when Deutsche Bank (DB) acquired BT. Large derivative transactions at BT went badly awry and the Federal Reserve insisted that it look for a new owner—eventually, DB—to keep afloat. Carlos recalls:

> At the time of the acquisition in 1999, we saw that the culture of the bank was going to change, from one that was entrepreneurial, with a family atmosphere and access to management, to one of management by fear and intimidation. This was reflected by the fact that we could only talk to immediate supervisors and not to others. It became a cold, rigid and bureaucratic culture in which everyone—directors, management, the board—remained at their own level and tried not to get in each other's way. It was the complete opposite of how Bankers Trust was before.

Although the new resulting culture and leadership style did not exactly match Carlos' beliefs, he managed to move up the ranks and became the CEO of Latin

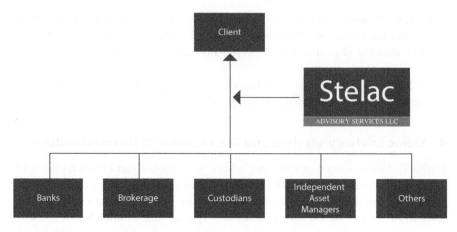

FIGURE 3.3 Stelac within the financial system.

America Private Wealth Management at DB. He tried to create within his division an atmosphere of "joy and freedom, in the sense of allowing people to think out loud, to propose new ideas, to request management for permission for special projects... to transform people into entrepreneurs." But, running the division in stark contrast with the rest of the company created too much friction with other managers and supervisors. In 2007, Carlos realized the differences were too deeply rooted and started looking for other horizons to continue his professional journey.

During the years spent at DB, Carlos had the opportunity to build a strong network of relationships with clients who trusted him deeply and confided in him issues beyond the strictly professional. Upon the suggestion of these clients seeking unbiased financial advice, Carlos set up a "Multi-Family-Office" for ultra-high net-worth individuals. DB tried to convince Carlos to stay, even offering him the possibility of managing a "Multi-Family Office" within DB itself. Nevertheless, after careful consideration, he declined the offer. Former colleagues from BT and DB, tired of financial practices they did not approve of and who believed in Carlos' vision, decided to follow him in this new venture.

Out of this deep desire to provide transparent and straightforward financial advice, Stelac was born in 2007. Carlos and Charlie de Viel Castel were the founders and managing partners, and they were soon joined by Karla Cervoni and Maria Zita La Rosa. Together with two employees, they set up shop at their first office in 598 Madison Ave., New York (Figure 3.3).

What is Stelac?

Stelac is a financial entity involving three different and autonomous components: (1) Stelac Advisory Services LLC, a SEC-registered investment advisor based in New York; (2) Stelac Capital Partners LLC, a private equity fund and late-stage venture capital investment firm; and (3) Stelac Foundation, an initiative committed to community development through the arts and education. Through the foundation, Carlos is able to combine his philanthropic efforts with his love for the arts, being a long-standing patron of the Latin American and Caribbean Collection of the Museum of Modern Art (MOMA) in New York, the Prado Museum in Madrid and the Museum of Contemporary Art of the University of Navarra. The foundation was meant to open a world of giving to his clients and employees, so they can experience the joy of giving back to society.

We shall now proceed to explain the activities of each of these components.

Stelac Advisory Services LLC (henceforth "Stelac") is a "Multi-Family-Office" (MFO) with operations in New York, Miami, Lima, Monterrey, Bogota and Madrid[1]. According to Robert McFall Lamm, Jr., Chief Investment Officer (Figure 3.4),

> essentially, the role of MFOs is to act as an intermediary with other banks and financial institutions to make sure that the client doesn't get scrubbed. [...] Banks focus on making huge profits in the short term, squeezing clients with charges. They don't care about the long term because 'we live in the now'. In MFOs we work for the clients. Our goal is to grow their portfolio smartly, not taking huge risks, because if something bad happens to the clients' portfolio, we also end up paying.

Stelac provides investment advice to non-US clients acting as an independent intermediary with other financial institutions. Its primary task is to consolidate the client's banking relationships and offer expertise on asset allocation, estate planning, family governance and philanthropic endeavors.

Stelac Advisory Services, LLC. is divided into three programs:

i   Investment Supervisor Services (ISS) with two kinds of portfolio management:

   i.a) Individual Portfolio Management
   i.b) Model Portfolio Management

ii Manager of Managers Program (SAS Manager Access Vehicle, Ltd.)
iii Consulting Services

Prior to Stelac Advisory Services	With Stelac Advisory Services
– **Manual** consolidation - time consuming -	- **Systematic** data gathering - time efficient
– **Missing "true"** picture of clients' global asset allocation, performance, risk, and diversification	- **Consolidated** global asset allocation, investment performance attribution and risk assessment
– **Dependent** on the financial institutions' platforms	- **Independent** financial advisor - unbiased approach
– **Complex** communication with several bankers, product specialists and managers - time consuming, conflicting views	- **Simplified** approach on product offering, market views, forecasts - timeefficiency, selective views
– **Push** - Sell (Product pressure)	- **Pull** - Buy (Best of breed)
– **Limited access** to products and investment opportunities	- **Open** access to managers and third party advisors
– **Multiple fee schedules** with banks and managers - higher cost	- **Optimization** of products, services, and fee schedule lower cost

FIGURE 3.4 Advantages of Stelac Advisory Services.

Through Individual ISS, Stelac offers investment advice based on individual client needs. Client goals and objectives, together with a personal investment policy, are established considering the time horizon, risk tolerance and liquidity needs. The client may impose restrictions on certain securities or industry sectors. Stelac investment recommendations include exchange-listed securities, securities traded over-the-counter, foreign issuers corporate debt securities (other than commercial papers), certificate of deposits, municipal securities, US government securities, interests in partnerships and other liquid or illiquid securities such as structured products, currency forward contracts, third-party managers and so forth. ISS fees range from 0.4% to 1% of assets, depending on the asset size and the complexity of the client's profile. Clients can either pay Stelac directly or authorize corresponding deductions from their account (Figure 3.5).

In the Model Portfolio Management ISS, Stelac uses three different model asset allocation portfolios, each with its own investment goal. Although portfolios are managed in accordance with the portfolio's goal, clients nevertheless retain ownership of the securities. Stelac sends monthly reports on the portfolio management to keep clients informed through its proprietary information system (Figure 3.6).

The three portfolios are:

-   "Loss Averse" Portfolio: Designed for investors with low tolerance for losses, it contains substantial cash and fixed-income investments and assumes positive returns in 95% of the investment environments. It has a long-term volatility of 3%–4%.
-   "Moderate Risk" Portfolio: Conceived for investors prepared to take on greater risks. It is the midpoint between the "Loss Averse" and the "Fully Invested" portfolios.
-   "Fully Invested" Portfolio: Planned for more aggressive investors with a perpetual horizon. It is expected to deliver the highest long-term returns, although it may also exhibit substantial losses on occasions. Cash holdings are restricted to zero.

Let us now move on to the "Manager of Managers Program." Stelac is also the investment manager of a hedge fund of funds vehicle named "SAS Manager Access Vehicle Ltd." (henceforth the "Fund"). This was created to allow clients access to a variety of hedge funds without meeting the high minimum investment required. The Fund was launched in 2010 in the Cayman Islands and is available only to non-US investors. Subscriptions require approval from Stelac's Chief Financial Officer and the Fund's independent administrator. Target investments are handled by third-party hedge fund managers who have no relationship with Stelac or any of its employees, officers or owners. Clients are charged no fees while non-advisory clients are charged 0.5% of the net asset value in SAS annually.

Lastly, Stelac also offers Consulting Services, through which clients receive more focused investment advice concerning estate planning, trusts and family

Identification of Investment Goals

– Determine return expectations, risk tolerance and time horizon.

– Incorporate client objectives and liquidity or time constraints.

– Define appropriate asset allocation and investment strategy.

Portfolio Assessment

– Comprehensive review of existing investments.

– Independent and objective analysis of third party products in terms of performance and fees.

– Cost structure across financial institutions are evaluated (custody, transactional and manager fees).

Portfolio Construction

– Recommendations are proposed and a transition plan is established.

– Only the best performing and cost efficient vehicles are employed across all asset classes.

Portfolio Management

– Periodic rebalancing to ensure optimal portfolio.

– Due diligence of current managers and vehicles.

– Tactical investment ideas.

– New products analyzed for suitability.

FIGURE 3.5 Steps in Investment Supervisor Services (ISS) at Stelac.

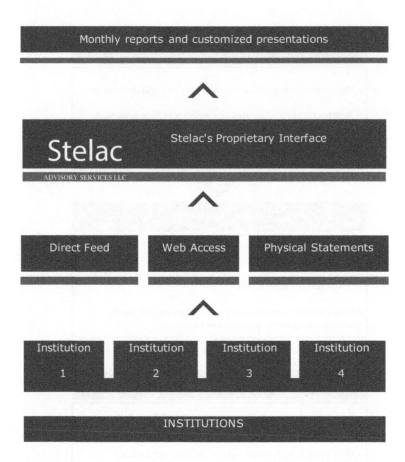

FIGURE 3.6 Stelac IT Services.

The Stelac IT platform provides our clients with a unified secure system, to access their portfolio data and performance analytics. We use proprietary software to build customized reports and presentations according to the client's needs.

Data Aggregation
Portfolio holdings, financial data and transactions are reconciled daily across financial institutions. Clients can see updated snapshots of their portfolio daily, accessible through the Stelac website.

Performance Analytics
Detailed performance attribution is available by asset class, custodian and individual security.

Reporting and Presentations
Our proprietary software generates monthly reports where portfolio data is presented by asset class, entity, financial institution, region and currency. We can also track key variables such as bank fees, third party performance data, and private equity returns.

governance. In carrying out these activities, Stelac avoids the three main conflicts of interest investment advisers in a Multi-Family-Office face, such as operating as adviser and broker-dealer at the same time, having limitless third-party power and pushing their own products to clients. As Carlos clarifies:

> I just want to be an advisor and not execute transactions that could compromise the ethics of the company. Unlike executors of financial institutions who charge fees, Stelac does not receive any payment from investments, so there is no conflict of interest. Broker-dealers do not only receive commissions for asset management but also fees from every investment. Why don't we want that? Because when everything goes fine, you transact correctly, but when the assets are not performing, brokers start to make unsuitable transactions, just for the sake of increasing revenues and their own compensation.

Regarding limited power of attorney and pushing its own products, Carlos adds:

> At Stelac, having limited power of attorney means we can only trade on the client account in the designated bank. We have to ask the bank that if there are instructions from the client to transfer money from the account and this has to be confirmed by the client. We are not allowed to give instructions to transfer money ourselves. There is no temptation for any Stelac employee to execute operations with the money of the client, as is very common in this industry. Lastly, we don't have any product whose sale could benefit the company. So we analyze every vehicle or fund in an objective way. We are unbiased; we don't fall in love with any passive vehicle, manager or financial institution. If a product is not good for the client, we don't buy it. When you have your own product, you are tempted to include that vehicle in your client's portfolio, even if it is not performing.
>
> Most of our competitors have brokerage, they have full third-party power and they have their own products.
>
> Our clients pay us a fixed fee based on total assets and there is no other source of income for the company.

Annual fees range from $30,000 to $250,000, depending on client's profile (asset size and complexity) (Figure 3.7).

Stelac corporate culture

In 2015, Stelac moved to its new headquarters on the 11th floor of 654 Madison Ave., close to Central Park, in the heart of Manhattan. Yet, its original core values of integrity, objectivity and experience remained the same.

Unless he is abroad to meet with clients, Carlos normally arrives at his office at around 9:30 am, having read the papers and analyzed the markets, and tries to

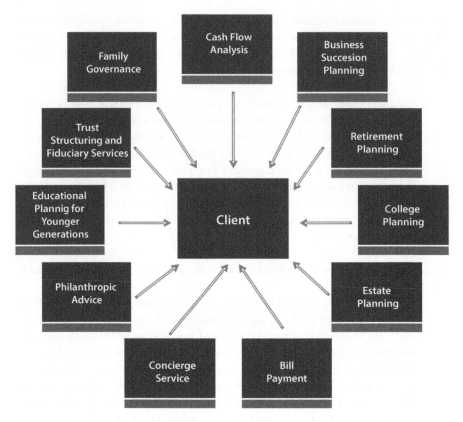

FIGURE 3.7 Stelac's client–centered architecture.

start his day with a smile. As of December 2016, Stelac has 29 employees (21 of them in New York), with an average age of 32 years old, and a very low turnover rate. One of the veterans, Robert McFall Lamn, Jr., explains his journey from DB to Stelac:

> *I made an effort to understand the different business culture* (when BT was taken over by DB), *but I felt pretty uncomfortable. And around the same time when European banks were coming to the US in the 1990s, a new industry was born: the 'MFO' (Multi-Family-Office).*

Indeed, there's a huge difference between Stelac corporate culture and that often found in comparable financial institutions in the US, in what Carlos generically calls "Corporate America." By this, he refers to the way business is conducted in the US, the kind of work culture found even in European institutions operating there, such as DB.

There is no secret about the fierce competition among financial institutions to hire the best people. In "Corporate America," the "best" is commonly understood as those who can bring in the most revenues to the company the fastest. Companies find it particularly important to identify people who are aggressive and money-driven. This means institutions compete against each other in offering the highest salaries and the largest bonuses, generally linked to company revenues. In consequence, the turnover of this kind of employees is very quick, since they move from one institution to another, in search of the highest bidder. For Carlos, on the other hand, the relevant drivers of performance are different:

> In this business it's important that clients are taken care of by the same team, that they feel confident with the people and that they identify with the office. If there is a lot of turnover, they feel uncomfortable and unsafe. For this reason I choose young people, fresh out of university, who could immediately absorb and appreciate the culture of the company. Later, it becomes more difficult. We do not only evaluate their financial capabilities but also their background and human qualities.

Moreover, whereas in "Corporate America," employment relationships are determined above all and almost exclusively by the letter of the contract, Stelac tries to build strong relationships with workers in the spirit and even beyond the contract. This is a direct consequence of the way it chooses employees:

> we don't only look at the potential financial success people could bring to the organization, but also at their personal human qualities. In most cases, we have managed to help employees identify areas of improvement, not only in the professional field.

Due to his unfortunate experience in Deutsche Bank, Carlos only knows too well the difficulties of working in a culture of fear where one can only talk to immediate supervisors and not to others. That's why he prefers a "flat" organization for Stelac: *"Of course there are rules and supervision of activities, but there is no huge distance between the boss and others. We are all members of the same cast or team."*

Stelac workers usually meet at 1:30 pm to have lunch together at the office. Sometimes Carlos manages to come and join them. Thanks to these moments, Stelac staff could share their personal stories with Carlos who, on the other hand, shows genuine interest for them, beyond his role as CEO. Thus, Carlos gains a deeper knowledge of his employees, their passions, difficulties, families and other details of their personal life.

> During the interviews, even though we cannot ask personal questions, something personal usually emerges. So, we realize that we can help our new employees. Everyone in this company creates friendships and they help each other, and they also come to management, sharing their personal life. By helping them, we create a loyal attitude, an environment of family and joy that is difficult for them to find in other places; and when they

speak with their friends outside that maybe earn more money they don't want to sacrifice what they have, they work with joy.

Stelac is perceived to be a place where everyone is fully appreciated as a human being. Friendship and attention to personal needs, fragility and joys abound. This creates an atmosphere of trust that is transmitted to Stelac clients, making them feel at ease.

Carlos is deeply concerned about the continuing education and formation of employees, although this may mean letting go of some momentarily—even helping them finance their studies—with the hope of getting them back later. *"In Stelac we believe that management is responsible for each and every person. We are not supposed to lose any single person who forms part and can contribute to this company. Everyone has a reason for being here."* Stelac invests in its people seriously.

Jean Paul, one of the youngest members of the Stelac research team, wrote to his colleagues on the day he left to pursue a master's degree:

> As I think back on these years and what Stelac has meant for me—perhaps many of you agree—I realize that what was most important for me was that in the financial industry and in a difficult city like New York, we have all been part of a place where we have loved and been loved. When I come to work in the morning, I look forward to seeing all of you and hearing about your life outside of work and getting to know you better. [...] Here at Stelac, we are each from different ethnic, cultural, educational, and spiritual backgrounds. But we love each other not in spite of these differences, but because of these differences. In using the word love, I do not just mean in loving people, but also loving the projects we are a part of. To do things well and to really achieve excellence, the first pillar should be love and the second technique. We often imagine ourselves creating companies, leading teams of people, starting all sorts of projects, and so forth. But, in reality, much of what our life will consist of is not these life-shattering projects, but little things and by doing these little things with great love, we can achieve big results and make a strong impact in the world. [...] So in a way, Stelac is trying to redefine what financial services means both externally and internally and we each have had a part in making this impact. Sure, many of the projects we are involved in seem so insignificant when compared to the impact that can be had by a Goldman Sachs or a McKinsey, but by performing our work with utmost professionalism, dedication, but most of all love, we will each help steer this ship through tough waters. Everything we do is important and has meaning, when done with great love.

In seeking to provide a family-friendly work atmosphere, Stelac offers a stark contrast to "Corporate America," where there is hardly any time for family and friends due to the intense, cut-throat competition among workers. Taking time out for these concerns is perceived to be a sign of weakness. According to Carlos, such a practice *"creates an imbalance in people's lives. They don't even want to leave on time because that may signal a lack of commitment to the institution. Instead, they struggle to be the last ones to leave the office."*

The situation cannot be more different in Stelac:

> Office hours are until 5:00 pm and we ask employees to finish everything that they have to do before 7:00 pm. Otherwise, we encourage them to come earlier in the morning. We think everyone should have time for personal matters after 7:00 pm.

Specific arrangements can be made for workers with special needs, such as pregnant women or those with young children. The firm understands that workers need to keep a balance between their family responsibilities and professional duties. Carlos discloses that *"we have even set up an office in their houses, so that if sometimes they need to stay at home, they don't have to come to the office. Interestingly, female employees with this arrangement even work harder and happier."*

How does Carlos see Stelac evolving in the middle to the long term? He definitely has some unresolved issues and struggles with doubts. He is aware that the size of Stelac could be an obstacle to the legitimate aspirations for professional growth among employees, as only a few can pursue their career paths within the firm. On the other hand, neither would he like to just let go of good people whom he has so painstakingly trained and developed. Hence the dilemma: either Stelac keeps on growing, with the risks this entails for its corporate culture, or it loses its employees in search of greener pastures, both professionally and financially.

Guide questions

1 How does a financial wealth management firm such as Stelac contribute to the common good of society in Aristotelian terms—that is, integral human flourishing, as opposed to purely private and individual goods?

2 Are Stelac operations and policies in keeping with CST principles (human dignity, the universal destination of goods, subsidiarity, participation, solidarity)? If so, identify potential conflicts.

3 Can Carlos Padula's understanding of his work as a financial advisor be framed in terms of a MacIntyrean practice? What are its specific internal goods? How do they relate to the external goods of institutions?

4 Identify different conflicts Carlos Padula had to face between his profession and his other roles as a family man, as an employee and as a founding partner and CEO of Stelac. How did he navigate them? Did his actions exemplify human excellences or virtues?

5 What innovations did Carlos Padula and Stelac introduce to wealth management in general and MFOs in particular? Perform a SWOT analysis of

Stelac, with a special focus on corporate culture, and compare it with "Corporate America."

6   Are you in favor of keeping Stelac as a boutique firm or would you like it to grow to a different dimension?

Note

1   The following information is taken from Stelac Advisory Services LCC (2016) *Part 2A of Form ADV: Firm Brochure*. New York, NY.

References

Aristotle. 1985, *Nicomachean ethics* (Irwin, T., trans.), Indianapolis, IN: Hackett Publishing.

Aristotle. 1990, *The politics* (Everson, S., ed.), Cambridge: Cambridge University Press.

Benedict XVI. 2009, *Encyclical Letter 'Caritas in veritate'*, Vatican City: Libreria Editrice Vaticana.

Congregation for the Doctrine of the Faith. 1986, 'Instruction on Christian freedom and liberation', *Libertatis conscientia*. (www.vatican.va/roman_curia/congregations/cfaith/documents/rc_con_cfaith_doc_19860322_freedom-liberation_en.html, Accessed September 27, 2017).

Corkery, M. 2016, 'Wells Fargo fined for fraudulently opening accounts for customers', *The New York Times*, 8 September.

Corkery, M. and Cowley, S. 2016, 'Wells Fargo warned workers against sham accounts, but 'they needed a paycheck'', *The New York Times*, 16 September.

Francis. 2013, *Apostolic Exhortation Evangelii gaudium*, Vatican City: Libreria Editrice Vaticana.

Francis. 2014, 'Address to the World Congress of Accountants', 14 November. (https://w2.vatican.va/content/francesco/en/speeches/2014/november/documents/papa-francesco_20141114_congresso-mondiale-commercialisti.html, Accessed September 27, 2017).

Greenwood, R. and Scharfstein, D. 2012, 'How to make finance work', *Harvard Business Review*, March, 104–110.

Henderson, D.R. 2008, 'Opportunity cost', *The concise encyclopedia of economics, library of economics and liberty*. (www.econlib.org/library/Enc/OpportunityCost.html, Accessed October 31, 2016).

Hursthouse, R. 1999, *On virtue ethics*, Oxford: Oxford University Press.

John Paul II. 1987, *Encyclical Letter 'Sollicitudo rei socialis'*. (http://w2.vatican.va/content/john-paul-ii/en/encyclicals/documents/hf_jp-ii_enc_30121987_sollicitudo-rei-socialis.html, Accessed September 27, 2017).

John Paul II. 1991, *Encyclical Letter 'Centessimus annus'*. (http://w2.vatican.va/content/john-paul-ii/en/encyclicals/documents/hf_jp-ii_enc_01051991_centesimus-annus.html, Accessed September 27, 2017).

John Paul II. 1999, 'Speech to the Centesimus Annus–Pro Pontifice Foundation', 11 September. (https://w2.vatican.va/content/john-paul-ii/en/speeches/1999/september/documents/hf_jp-ii_spe_11091999_centesimus-annus.html, Accessed September 27, 2017).

Kedrosky, P. and Stangler, D. 2011, 'Financialization and its entrepreneurial consequences', *Kauffman Foundation Research Series: Firm formation and economic growth*. (www.kauffman.org/what-we-do/research/firm-formation-and-growth-series/financialization-and-its-entrepreneurial-consequences, Accessed September 27, 2017).

MacIntyre, A. 1988, *Whose justice? Which rationality?* Notre Dame, IN: University of Notre Dame Press.

MacIntyre, A. 1994, 'A partial response to my critics', in J. Horton and S. Mendus (eds.), *After MacIntyre. Critical perspectives on the work of Alasdair MacIntyre*, Notre Dame, IN: University of Notre Dame Press.

MacIntyre, A. 2007 [1981], *After virtue* (3rd ed.), London: Duckworth.

Miller, D. 1994, 'Virtues, practices and justice', in J. Horton and S. Mendus (eds.), *After MacIntyre. Critical perspectives on the work of Alasdair MacIntyre*, Notre Dame, IN: University of Notre Dame Press.

Pius XI. 1931, *Encyclical Letter 'Quadragesimo anno'*, Boston, MA: St. Paul Editions. (http://w2.vatican.va/content/pius-xi/en/encyclicals/documents/hf_p-xi_enc_19310515_quadragesimo-anno.html, Accessed September 27, 2017).

Pontifical Council for Justice and Peace. 2004, *Compendium of the social doctrine of the church*, Vatican City: Libreria Editrice Vaticana.

Pontifical Council for Justice and Peace. 2011, *Toward reforming the international financial and monetary systems in the context of global public authority*. (www.vatican.va/roman_curia/pontifical_councils/justpeace/documents/rc_pc_justpeace_doc_20111024_nota_en.html, Accessed September 27, 2017).

Pontifical Council for Justice and Peace. 2012, *Vocation of the business leader. A reflection*, Rome/St. Paul, MN: Pontifical Council for Justice and Peace and John A. Ryan Institute for Catholic Social Thought of the Center for Catholic Studies at the University of St. Thomas, MN, USA.

Robson, A. 2015, 'Constancy and integrity: (Un)measurable virtues?', *Business Ethics: A European Review*, 24(2): 115–129.

Rodrigues, J. 2015, 'Barings collapse at 20: How rogue trader Nick Leeson broke the bank', *The Guardian*. 24 February. (www.theguardian.com/business/from-the-archive-blog/2015/feb/24/nick-leeson-barings-bank-1995-20-archive, Accessed October 31, 2016).

Statista Research and Analysis. 2016, 'Statistics and facts about defense spending and arms trade'. (www.statista.com/topics/1696/defense-and-arms/, Accessed October 31, 2016).

Sullivan, P. 2016, 'Making financial management both spouses' job', *The New York Times*, 7 October.

Titcomb, J. 2015, 'Barings: The collapse that erased 232 years of history', *The Telegraph*. (www.telegraph.co.uk/finance/newsbysector/banksandfinance/11427501/Barings-the-collapse-that-erased-232-years-of-history.html, Accessed September 27, 2017).

Vatican Council II. 1965, 'Pastoral Constitution on the Church in the modern world', *Gaudium et Spes*. (www.vatican.va/archive/hist_councils/ii_vatican_council/documents/vat-ii_const_19651207_gaudium-et-spes_en.html, Accessed September 27, 2017).

Zingales, L. 2015, 'Does finance benefit society?', *NBER*, working paper 20894 (www.nber.org/papers/w20894, Accessed September 27, 2017).

4

VIRTUES AND THE COMMON GOOD IN PRODUCTION

Germán Scalzo

Learning objectives

In this chapter, we shall:

- Reflect on the nature of production and the conceptual differences between action and production.
- Explore the purpose of the business firm as a community of people, as well as the issues that arise therefrom related to the virtue of justice and property rights.
- Draw attention to the issues concerning production and the environment that emerged with modernity and industrialization.

Nature has endowed living beings with the functions needed to survive in their environment. However, human beings go beyond biology and turn to culture to satisfy their needs. Instead of adapting to the environment, human beings adapt the environment to themselves. Because of this, human beings in production seek what they consider to be a certain kind of good. "Good is ascribed [...] both to what benefits human beings as such and to what benefits human beings in particular roles within particular contexts of practice" (MacIntyre 2012 [1999]: 65).

The economist J.M. Keynes noted that,

> [f]rom the earliest times of which we have record–back, say, to two thousand years before Christ–down to the beginning of the eighteenth century, there was no very great change in the standard of life of the average man living in the civilized centers of the earth.
>
> *(Keynes 1972: 359)*

However, the birth of modern "political economy" involved a radical change in the understanding of human beings' relationship with nature. Since Bacon and Descartes, knowledge is no longer the discovery of truth or the pursuit of the good life, but the unbridled domination of nature. As a consequence, economic production has been considered largely independent of politics and morality.

Production has become an impersonal and uncontrolled process. The current production paradigm—guided by the maximization principle—requires an incessant multiplication of wants and ever-shorter cycles, transforming not just production and work, but also property and society itself. At the same time, human beings and nature have turned into means in support of the machinery of production and consumption. Although thanks to industrial production, humanity has reached an unprecedented state of material well-being, it has become increasingly difficult for societies to share wealth equitably and preserve nature for future generations.

In what follows, I will present the Aristotelian view of production as subordinate to ethics and politics, and how that view shifted in modernity. I will also briefly show the evolution of organization theory, from a technical account of the firm to a comprehensive idea of cooperative work, thanks to intrinsic and transcendent motivations. Finally, I will explain how Catholic Social Teaching (CST) has consistently called for a moral order of production, emphasizing human dignity and service to the common good.

1. An Aristotelian view of production and its contribution to human flourishing

In a broad sense, to produce comes down to giving rise to something, which is not limited to reproducing a fixed pattern of behavior, but rather involves a kind of mastery. Because human action is free, human beings, unlike others, can produce in so many different ways. This possibility frees man from his environment, allowing him to build his world largely thanks to his capacity to produce freely and rationally. Human production thus involves deciding or having control over action, which is why it is an intentional process. The end of human production is not mere survival, but rather a certain type of life that is social rather than individual. Human production, in this sense, is political; it is a dimension of life in common. Economic production emerges with a view on meeting the common need (Koehn 1992) and involves a division of tasks and functions. Cooperation for the satisfaction of needs requires collaborative work, which is performed by firms as intermediate institutions.

There is a close relationship between action and knowledge, that is, human action transcends the mere satisfaction of immediate vital needs—as is the case with other animals—to deal with activities aimed at a certain representation of the good life; and this is what Aristotle calls *praxis* (Vigo 2007: 110). Only people who possess a certain rational representation of what a good life means are capable of *praxis*. Aristotelian ethics is premised on a proper human function that expresses reason. Human excellence or virtue resides in rightly fulfilling this function in accordance with reason (Sison 2015: 242).

Aristotle classifies the different kinds of human knowledge in accordance with the related activity. He then identifies three kinds of human activity, including contemplation (*theoria*), action (*praxis*) and production (*poiesis*). The different kinds of knowledge correspond with the different uses of reason. Theoretical reason (*sophia*) speculates on something and its aim is the contemplation of truth; practical reason (*phronesis*) deals with human action and it has a moral dimension, i.e., it enables man to reflect on his actions so that they are organized towards their own perfection; and technical reason (*techne*) is aimed at an external end or result (Met. II 2 and VII 1).

The difference between action or *praxis* and production or *poiesis* lies in two kinds of teleologies: "[f]or while making has an end other than itself, action cannot; for good action itself is its end" (Aristotle *Nichomachean Ethics* (NE): 1140b). The ancient Greek world placed these two realms in drastic opposition, both internal and external, since production was an activity for slaves, while practical-ethical knowledge that governs action was reserved for free men. Although Aristotle considers action and production as mutually exclusive (Arendt 1958; NE: 1178b), they must not be understood as two conflicting rationalities; rather, the proper subordination between them should be recognized (Murphy 1993).

There is some ambiguity in the term *techne*, alternatively translated as "art" or "craftsmanship," since it refers to both manual or industrial arts and to instrumental methods—used by people who are skilled at something—in order to achieve ends. Sison highlights that:

> [o]ur modern idea of work as productive activity is linked above all to *poiesis*. In *poiesis*, as in the practice of the crafts, what is important is the external object produced, for which there is a codifiable set of rules or instructions. A master craftsman is one who has perfectly embodied this set of rules in his productive activity, displaying extraordinary skill.
>
> *(Sison 2016: 105)*

For Aristotle, *techne* (art or artistry) is the excellence in *poiesis*, a kind of virtue that leads to technical excellence, instead of directly to the morally good (as *praxis* does). Virtue in *praxis* is strictly directed towards the good, whereas *techne* is ambivalent and can be used badly. *Techne* provides the most efficient means of achieving proposed ends, whether good or bad (NE 1140a). In order for *techne* to be a virtue, it must be subordinated to *phronesis* (Murphy 1993: 106), which is the excellence in *praxis*. *Phronesis*, as a moral and intellectual virtue, includes and perfects *techne* (NE: 1141a, 1141b, 1142a, 1143b, 1153a). Ultimately, both excellences are internal to the subject or agent, and ends cannot be relegated to mere mechanical causality because "in all arts and sciences both the end and the means should be equally within our control" (Pltcs. 1331b).

Aristotle does not develop human production in detail, but he considers the family as the natural unit of production, which ensures survival and supplies goods to the city, the only self-sufficient community (Aristotle *The Politics* (Pltcs): 1253a). The organization of family life or household management (*economy*) is essential for the common good of the *polis* (Pltcs: 1260b). Economy is a subordinate discipline of politics that takes care of material goods and consists of wealth use and enjoyment (Martínez Echevarría 2011; Ferrero and Sison 2017), starting "in the bare of needs of life, and continuing in existence for the sake of a good life" (Pltcs: 1252b). It does not lack an ethical dimension, but is rather an "ethics of private life" (Berthoud 2002), a prior and fundamental instance of public life or politics. "Through the organization of family life, as the Greek word *oikos-nomos* indicates, Aristotle describes the set of private activities of production and consumption that ensure the reproduction and preservation of things and people in a space of common life" (Berthoud 2002: 60).

Every family is comprised of members, the relationships among them and a variety of instruments (Pltcs: 1253b). According to Aristotle, there is a natural kind of acquisition (*chrematistics*) that pursues useful things, according to human needs, and is not endless (Meikle 1995) because "the amount of property which is needed for a good life is not unlimited" (Pltcs: 1256b). Wealth-production (*chrematistics*) is not an abstract process, but it is at the service of flourishing (*eudaimonia*) (Pltcs: 1253b). However, there is also a *bad chrematistics* that has no end (Pltcs: 1257a) and involves exchange for the sake of money. Thus, human production can only be understood as a rational and ethical action if it provides useful things for the good life. Since money is not an end in itself, but rather always a means, when production is organized for the sake of money (*bad chrematistics*), it loses its proper end and becomes an endless process to accumulate wealth of a "spurious kind" (Pltcs: 1257b), tending towards the worst type of acquisition: usury (Pltcs: 1258b). Aristotle does not condemn exchange—as Plato does (see Berthoud 2002)—because it is good for the unity of the *polis* (Pltcs: 1133a). However, modern economics changed the Aristotelian understanding of production by removing its proper end in order to become an instrument in the attainment of maximum wealth.

• Production should not be a mere technical and impersonal process guided by the maximization principle, but rather a human activity involving a kind of mastery. It certainly includes a technical dimension, which is, however, subordinate to praxis, since its end is to provide useful things in accordance with the good life. The end of production should never merely be money.

2. Modern production and MacIntyre's critique

Adam Smith's proposal in the late seventeenth century was built on three basic elements: the private accumulation of wealth, the market as a process of resource allocation and a streamlining of production. Economic activity is constituted as a "gigantic and powerful instrument—the whole collection of means of production that in a sense are considered synonymous with 'capital'—" (John Paul II, *Laborem Exercens* (LE) 1981: 12) within which the modern business firm occupies a central place. The firm resulted in a new way of organizing not just production and work, but also property and society itself.

The Industrial Revolution and the consolidation of factories or "places of production" were made possible thanks to the division of labor, which Smith illustrated with his famous example of the pin factory (Smith 1979, Book I, Ch. 1.) The social division of labor emerged with the appearance of cities. However, the division of labor within the business firm is different; it aims to maximize efficiency and, ultimately, profit. Another important difference is that whereas the social division of labor relies on the natural socialization of men, the technical division of labor does the opposite: it promotes the isolation of individuals in very simple mechanical tasks. Accordingly, wealth and progress emerge from the mechanical interaction of individuals—that is, a model based on machines rather than on persons. This new paradigm relies on the accumulation of capital, since its productivity replaced the fertility of the land.

Indeed, the expansion of a technical division of labor hugely developed manufacturing and mass production but, at the same time, caused serious conflict between social classes. Marx was one of the fiercest critics of modern factories. According to him, in each historical epoch, a ruling class oppressed the rest, thanks to the ownership of the means of production. To end this dialectic of domination, he proposed that the State should own the means of production (communism).

In mainstream economic theory at the beginning of the twentieth century, however, production was considered an amoral realm characterized by three elements: utility, compartmentalization and an independent external objective, understood in a mechanistic way (Ferrero and Calderón 2013: 532). This is the underlying principle in the first models of productive organization, mainly developed by engineers with the purpose of maximizing the input-output relation. Taylor's "scientific management" (1911) focused on mechanical work is paradigmatic of this trend.

However, this mechanical dimension was surpassed in the 1930s with the consideration of psychological and sociological factors. Mayo (1933) and Roethlisberger's Hawthorne experiments became the turning point towards a richer conception of organizations. This looks beyond the objective realm of production to include the subjective dimension, that is to say, not just extrinsic—external—but also intrinsic—internal—motivation, learning and human relationships. Since then, organizational authors have suggested that, "the external utility of production is bound together with a deep meaning of internal utility, understood as the ability of work to enrich employees and managers through practical knowledge" (Ferrero and Calderón 2013: 534).

After the Second World War, a series of scientific developments related to information processing emerged, such as Cybernetics and the Theory of Information. Since then, information has occupied a privileged place within organizations. Daniel Bell's seminal work (1973) shows a shift from the Industrial to the Post-Industrial Society, characterized by the pre-eminence of a service economy over a manufacturing one. However, the "novel and central feature of post-industrial society is the codification of theoretical knowledge and the new relation of science and technology" (Bell 1973: xiv), giving prominence to a theory of value based on knowledge instead of labor. According to Bell, the "information age" is not founded on a mechanical, but rather on an intellectual technology that transcends the boundaries of space and time.

Cybernetics (Wiener 1949) is the science that studies the control or regulation of systems, especially self-regulating ones (machines as well as organisms). Weiner's model explains human action as a continuous feedback process of social interaction. Cybernetics was applied to organizational theory by Pérez López (1991, 1993). Pérez-López developed the implications of cybernetics not only for organizational theory but also for a theory of action (1991: 43), giving rise to three different types of organizations (1993). Besides the mechanistic and the psychosociological models, he introduced the humanistic one.

The most characteristic feature of this model is the so-called "transcendent motivation," which allows the person to go outside herself to serve or cooperate with others (Ferrero and Calderón 2013: 536).

Not all developments in organizational theory are encouraging, however. MacIntyre, for one, posits a pessimistic view of the business corporation or firm (MacIntyre 2015). His critique of capitalism is framed in a broader critique of modernity in general, and especially emotivism as "the doctrine that all evaluative judgments and more specifically all moral judgments are *nothing but* expressions of preference, expressions of attitude or feeling, insofar as they are moral or evaluative in character" (MacIntyre 2007: 11–12; Moore 2008: 484). Nevertheless, he makes a positive contribution to the understanding of production within organizations through the idea of "practice."

A practice is

> any coherent and complex form of socially established cooperative human activity during which goods internal to that form of activity are realized because of trying to achieve those standards of excellence which are appropriate to, and partially definitive of, that form of activity.
>
> *(MacIntyre 2007: 187)*

Furthermore, a practice "is never just a set of technical skills" (MacIntyre 2007: 193), but it "involves standards of excellence and obedience to rules as well as the achievement of goods" (MacIntyre 2007: 31). Human work, as a practice, has a dual dimension; it includes external goods, also called "goods of effectiveness," and internal ones or "goods of excellence" (MacIntyre 1988: 32).

External goods, when achieved, are always an individual's property, whereas the achievement of internal goods—virtues—is a good for the community that participates in the practice (MacIntyre 2007: 190). Virtue is necessary to achieve the goods internal to practices, as well as to keep a tradition alive. Tradition is built through the historical and social development of human identity in communities. These social and historical relationships, which influence practices, link virtues with the tradition of a community (MacIntyre 2007: 221). A living tradition continues a not-yet-completed narrative in dialogue with the goods that a community produces and achieves.

Although internal goods such as virtues are the cornerstone of MacIntyre's theory, he is aware that virtues need institutions to survive. For him, the institutional is the realm of external goods—"they are involved in acquiring money and other material goods; they are structured in terms of power and status, and they distribute money, power and status as rewards" (MacIntyre 2007: 194).

Having made this distinction between internal and external realms, MacIntyre turns to managerial effectiveness, referring to it as a "moral fiction" (MacIntyre 2007: 76). This is because it orders means to ends in a bureaucratic, purportedly value-free way—as described by Max Weber: "[m]anagers themselves and most writers about management conceive of themselves as morally neutral characters whose skills enable them to devise the most efficient means of achieving whatever end is proposed" (MacIntyre 2007: 74). MacIntyre's image of the manager is clearly of someone who "treats ends as given, as outside his scope; his concern is with technique, with effectiveness in transforming raw materials into final products, unskilled labor into skilled labor, investment into profits" (MacIntyre 2007: 30). The manager is not concerned with ethics, but rather uses terms such as "good," "right" or "excellence" as manipulative means of persuasion, corrupting practices and treating workers as mere means on the way to fulfilling his interests (Knight 2017: 3, 6).

The key point here is whether the sustenance of institutions may be considered as a practice that contributes to human flourishing and the common good. For MacIntyre, "the common goods of those at work together are achieved in producing goods and services that contribute to the life of the community and in becoming excellent at producing them" (MacIntyre 2016: 170).

MaIntyre's conceptual framework emphasizes the prioritization of internal over external goods in decision-making, to recover the ethical dimension of human activity and for organizations to become "essentially moral spaces" (Beadle and Moore 2011: 103). That means business organizations should pursue both "the excellence of the product or service and the perfection of the practitioners in the process" (Moore 2012: 366). This dual perfection is not only desirable, but also absolutely necessary when considering the ethics of production:

> [o]ne who works skillfully and conscientiously according to standards of excellence is acting virtuously. But in acting this way a craftsman makes a product, which is supposed to be a good product. A virtuoso creator of a product that is useless in all respects cannot be credited with virtuous craftsmanship.
>
> *(Hartman 2011: 8)*

• After the Industrial Revolution, factories became the center of production. The modern division of labor contributed to the development of manufacturing and mass production, isolating individuals in the performance of simple mechanical tasks. More recently, holistic considerations of human motivation have enriched human work. Despite MacIntyre's pessimism regarding modern productive organizations, he makes space for ethics through the subordination of institutional–external goods—to the internal goods of practice such as the virtues, to promote the common good.

3. Catholic Social Teaching on production

The emergence of Catholic Social Teaching (CST) is related to the defense of workers in late modernity, in the face of capitalism's progress. *Rerum Novarum's* subtitle, "On capital and labor," expresses the idea that social life needed to be interpreted in light of something "new":

> …[i]n the vast expansion of industrial pursuits and the marvelous discoveries of science; in the changed nations between masters and workmen; in the enormous fortunes of some few individuals, and the utter poverty of the masses; the increased self-reliance and closer mutual combination of the working classes; as also, finally, in the prevailing moral degeneracy.
>
> *(Leo XIII Rerum novarum (RN) 1891: 1)*

Indeed, industrialization had serious consequences for the working class and the concentration of capital in the hands of a few (Benedict XVI, *Deus Caritas Est* (DCE) 2005: 26) threatened social order and peace. Leo XIII believed that the solution was not to choose between private or collective property, but to provide a robust understanding of human work as a personal, human action (Crespo 2013: 125) that takes priority over capital (LE 12).

CST is not against material progress, but it claims that any progress should be human, which is to say that

> [t]he fundamental finality of (this) production is not the mere increase of products nor profit or control but rather the service of man, and indeed of the whole man with regard for the full range of his material needs and the demands of his intellectual, moral, spiritual, and religious life.
>
> *(Vatican II, Gaudium et Spes (GeS): 64)*

John Paul II insisted on the proper relationship between capital and work:

> the error of early capitalism can be repeated wherever man is in a way treated on the same level as the whole complex of the material means of production, as an instrument and not in accordance with the true dignity of his work.
>
> *(LE: 7)*

This opposes liberal capitalism, which considers the accumulation of capital to be the purpose of production (LE: 8).

In the *Centesimus Annus,* John Paul II continued to reflect on this subordination, highlighting the current importance of "the possession of know-how, technology and skill" (CA: 31). He also advocated that "people work with each other, sharing in a 'community of work'" (Ibid), for "goods cannot be adequately produced through the work of an isolated individual; they require the cooperation of many people in working towards a common goal" (Ibid). This personalistic approach is, at once, individual and social: "[i]t is his disciplined work in close collaboration with others that makes possible the creation of ever more extensive working communities which can be relied upon to transform man's natural and human environments" (CA: 32).

Production definitely has a technical side—related to the objective dimension of work—but it also has a moral or subjective dimension that takes precedence (LE: 5–7, 10), giving way to the development of virtues. The "subjective dimension" of work makes reference to "all the internal results, consisting of knowledge, skills, attitudes, meanings, habits and virtues that workers develop in their collaborative entrepreneurial activities" (Sison 2016: 95). John Paul II has emphasized this distinction (LE), as well as the importance of the subjective over the objective dimension:

> human activity (action) is simultaneously *transitive* and *intransitive*. It is transitive insofar as it tends *beyond the subject*, seeks an expression and effect in the external world, and is objectified in some product. It is intransitive, on the other hand, insofar as it *remains in the* subject, determines the subject's essentially human *fieri*. In acting, we not only perform actions, but we also become ourselves through those actions—we fulfill ourselves in them.
>
> *(Wojtyla 1993: 265–266)*

Since the subjective dimension is more important,

> the purpose of a business firm is not simply to make a profit, but is to be found in its very existence as a *community of persons* who in various ways are endeavoring to satisfy their basic needs, and who form a particular group *at the service of the whole of society.*
>
> *(CA: 35, emphasis added)*

CST offers orientation in accordance with the truth of man. It sustains that there are no perfect or "finished" models for organizing social life, but "models that are real and truly effective can only arise within the framework of different historical situations, through the efforts of all those who responsibly confront concrete problems in all their social, economic, political and cultural aspects, as these interact with one another" (CA: 43). Hence, CST

> has always maintained that justice must be applied to every phase of economic activity, because this is always concerned with man and his needs. Locating resources, financing, production, consumption and all the other

phases in the economic cycle inevitably have moral implications. Thus every economic decision has a moral consequence.

(Benedict XVI, Caritas in Veritate *(CiV) 2009: 37)*

Moreover, John Paul II warns of the "danger of treating work as a special kind of 'merchandise,' or as an impersonal 'force' needed for production" (Ibid). He also points to the ecological problem as a consequence of industrialization. In *Sollicitudo rei socialis,* he observes that "[a] true concept of development cannot ignore the use of the elements of nature, the renewability of resources and the consequences of haphazard industrialization" (SRS 34).

Similarly, Benedict XVI advocates the protection of the environment through a personalistic perspective, in line with "human ecology" (CA: 38). "It is contrary to authentic development to view nature as something more important than the human person" (CiV: 48). What's more,

[t]he book of nature is one and indivisible: it takes in not only the environment but also [,] human development. Our duties towards the environment are linked to our duties towards the human person, considered in himself and in relation to others.

(CiV: 51)

The 2015 publication of Pope Francis's *Laudato Si'* rallied public opinion on the topic of ecology. He situates the ecological problem on a humanistic plane:

[h]uman beings too are creatures of this world, enjoying a right to life and happiness, and endowed with unique dignity. So we cannot fail to consider the effects on people's lives of environmental deterioration, current models of development and the throwaway culture.

(LS: 43)

An ecological culture is "a distinctive way of looking at things, a way of thinking, policies, an educational program, a lifestyle and a spirituality which together generate resistance to the assault of the technocratic paradigm" (LS: 111). According to Francis, *integral ecology* (LS: 137) demands "an integrated approach to combating poverty, restoring dignity to the excluded, and at the same time protecting nature" (LS: 139) for present and future generations (LS: 22).

Man is not just the subject and maker, but also "the true purpose of the whole process of production" (LE: 7). Production should be at the service of humanity in a global scale, since:

an interdependent world not only makes us more conscious of the negative effects of certain lifestyles and models of production and consumption which affect us all; more importantly, it motivates us to ensure that solutions are proposed from a global perspective.

(LS: 164)

An example consists of

> favoring forms of industrial production with maximum energy efficiency
> and diminished use of raw materials, removing from the market products
> which are less energy efficient or more polluting, improving transport sys-
> tems, and encouraging the construction and repair of buildings aimed at
> reducing their energy consumption and levels of pollution.
>
> *(LS: 180)*

Thus, we underscore the importance of cooperative work for true integral human
development (CiV: 4) and the role of business in achieving the common good

> through the production of useful goods and services. In seeking to produce
> goods and services according to plans aimed at efficiency and at satisfying the
> interests of the different parties involved, businesses create wealth for all of
> society [...] creating opportunities for meeting, cooperating and the enhance-
> ment of the abilities of the people involved. In a business undertaking, there-
> fore, the economic dimension is the condition for attaining not only economic
> goals, but also social and moral goals, which are all pursued together.
>
> *(CSDC: 338)*

- The industrialization process promoted the accumulation of capital, with
  serious consequences for the working class and for the environment. The
  purpose of production cannot be the mere accumulation of capital; it is,
  rather, the promotion of human work as a personal action requiring the
  cooperation of many towards a common good. Although production has
  a technical side—related to the objective dimension of work—its moral or
  subjective dimensions take precedence.

I began this chapter showing how production currently is organized towards the
satisfaction of individual and partial interests to the detriment of the common
good. This has terrible consequences for the environment, as well as for most
workers, who are unable to flourish. After decades of understanding development exclusively as material well-being, some business theorists have started to
highlight the importance of understanding deeper human motivations. Thus, the
cooperative dimension of work has emerged.

CST defends human dignity and the priority of workers over capital and other
external goods, highlighting the need for virtues to attain the common good and
integral development. For this to happen, development should be respectful of
nature and guarantee that this gift is accessible to all.

4. Adelante Shoe Co. and the promotion of artisanry

> Shoes are not my passion. Harnessing the potential of a million individual
> decisions to improve our world, however, gets me fired up.
>
> *Peter Sacco*[1]

Adelante Shoe Co. is a social enterprise that offers handcrafted shoes made by producers in Guatemala. Adelante is a Spanish word meaning "onwards" and the company certainly embodies that sentiment both literally, by providing comfortable shoes, and figuratively, by attempting to revolutionize the market of socially responsible consumer goods.

It was founded by a Massachusetts native, Peter Sacco, in 2016. Sacco is a young entrepreneur who, while working in Guatemala, established connections with local artisan shoemakers. Impressed by their work and with an eye for a business opportunity, he set out to create a socially responsible company that would market stylish, artisan shoes for US consumers. The company's goal was to make it easy for the average consumer in the US to "walk the talk" by purchasing shoes that are responsibly crafted and sold.

The artisan sector all over Latin America represents a challenge for economics and society at large. Most artisans come from very poor families that have traditionally been marginalized and live in precarious rural areas beyond the reach of modern power structures and services. They live and operate in an informal subsistence economy, without access to basic banking and business platforms. Mostly working from home, from a young age, their children are taught the family trade (whether as cobblers, weavers, clay makers and so forth.) in the form of a natural apprenticeship. Adelante's initiative respects artisans' production process. Besides encouraging artisans to keep production in their homes, Adelante avoids implementing a manufacturing mentality with monotonous, repetitive tasks and instead gives them control over the whole process.

However, with this kind of craftsmanship, very few artisans are able to sell their products at fair prices, corresponding to the work and time required for their production. Bartering is common and encouraged in this informal system. Adelante helps artisans to overcome this limitation by providing resources that guarantee the integrity of the production process, as well as support in terms of budgeting and business organization (for instance, they ensure artisans will not run out of raw materials due to the fluctuating market conditions and sales).

This model highlights the meaning of artisans' trade as it is continually improved and, in turn, improves artisans themselves, in terms of skills and virtues. Predictability and stability in business allows them to focus on the development of their trade, keeping the tradition alive while making room for innovation. Although it may sound simple, this model has enormous implications for the way we conceive of socially responsible business, as Adelante's founder states

> we want to change the way business is done by treating our craftsmen as partners and paying them fairly for work well done. We are always on the lookout for people who take our mission to heart and are fired up to make meaningful change.[2]

This startup employs a finance and business development officer, a chief marketing officer and a marketing content manager. Besides the business team, the artisans themselves can be found on the web page (www.adelanteshoes.com).

Adelante's mission is to "make it absolutely effortless to choose a socially responsible pair of shoes without compromising on quality, style or price." The firm is based on a sustainable business model, driven by the desire to uproot entrenched, exploitative production processes, generating systemic social change instead through business. Although Adelante shoes are of great quality, Sacco remarks that, *"the shoes are a vehicle for a simple, powerful idea that can change the world: if business shifts its objective from profit maximization to responsible profit, the private sector can become an unparalleled force for good."*[3]

Adelante's goal is to transform the way consumers buy, giving them the possibility of making a social contribution while enjoying a superior product:

> Our shoes are a superior quality and we never want to use our social impact model as a crutch. Instead we want our product to speak for itself; customers see the quality and value of our shoes and are sold on it, the social impact is added value to the consumer and more importantly, the craftsmen.[4]

In creating this company, Sacco also found a way to promote responsible leadership. When asked what that leadership means, he answered, *"It means choosing partnership rather than exploitation, and transparency over opacity. It means recognizing that treating foreign workers with respect is more than ethical—it is laying the groundwork for future peace and stability in an increasingly globalized world."*[5] Besides maintaining artisan integrity, offering very high-quality products, treating producers with dignity and seeking to make a positive impact in the communities, Adelante is also focused on social inclusion.

Thanks to an agreement with "Serigrafía de la Gringa," a screen-printing social business that works in prisons to provide employment and rehabilitation services, Adelante also contributes to social inclusion. They screen-print their shoe bags in a maximum-security prison for men (mostly former gang members) in Guatemala, and shoe boxes in a Guatemalan women's prison, allowing prisoners to generate income through legitimate employment. By offering an honest job to prisoners, the potential social impact is vast:

> If the gang leader continues to lead with this new mindset, he might inspire those around him to change their mindsets as well, potentially 're-branding' the gang's image altogether—moving away from extortion and towards the production of high quality goods.[6]

One of Adelante's most innovative measures corresponds to a new social impact model based on a methodology developed with the help of professors at Tufts University. The "Living Well Line" balances development best practices with community input to define the cost of living well in a community, taking into account regional differences in living standards. Producers come to an agreement with the company on the amount they need to feasibly provide for themselves

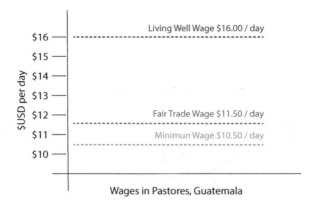

FIGURE 4.1   The living well line.

and their families. This compensation model is flexible in that it reconsiders wages periodically and provides emergency funds in case of need. The *Living Well Line* pays craftsmen a fair price for their impressive work.

The minimum wage in Pastores, Guatemala (where the artisans live) is $10.50/day; fair trade comes in at only $1.00 more or $11.50/day. The *Living Well* wage comes in at $16.00/day, one and a half times the minimum wage. This salary is directly negotiated with the artisans, who are profoundly aware of the resources required in the production process, and is based on what it actually costs to live well in their communities. Since there are no intermediaries, payments enable craftsmen to invest in the betterment of their families. That parameter is determined by cross-checking Guatemala-specific data from the World Bank's Living Standard Measurement Study with in-person craftsman interviews (Figure 4.1).

They also want their model to be financially transparent, making the internal cost structure public, as shown in Figure 4.2.

In addition to the individual impact of a Living Well Wage, Sacco firmly believes that the best way to promote local development is to reinforce producers in their own communities:

> I submit that the best way to galvanize upward mobility in any country is to pay workers enough to consume the goods and services that they define as necessary to live well. That's why Adelante craftsmen play an integral role in defining their own wage in Guatemala and beyond.[7]

Production and trade are at the heart of Adelante's business model, promoting their development through an integral production chain, the Living Well Line, social inclusion measures, showing leadership and innovative ways of contributing to the common good. In this way, Adelante attempts to complement existing business models with an alternative approach that strengthens and organically matures the informal sector, which is key for developing economies.

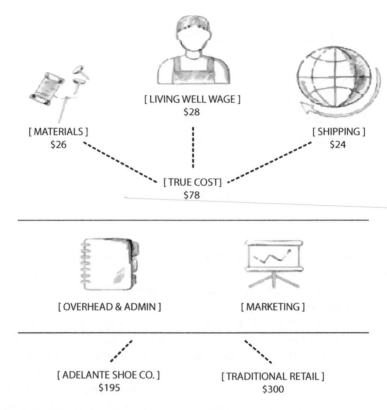

[LIVING WELL WAGE]
$28

[MATERIALS]
$26

[SHIPPING]
$24

[TRUE COST]
$78

[OVERHEAD & ADMIN]

[MARKETING]

[ADELANTE SHOE CO.]
$195

[TRADITIONAL RETAIL]
$300

FIGURE 4.2 The innovation management office.

Guide questions

1 How is the Adelante business model different from conventional ones?
2 Do you think the "Living Well Line" is a realistic compensation mechanism? What obstacles and challenges might its implementation face?
3 Can you identify the objective and subjective dimensions of work in the Adelante proposal? How can producers develop internal goods?
4 How is a fair price related to the common good? Do you think the best thing that business can do for the community is to offer goods at the minimum price?
5 Is the quality of the product important for this business model? Why?
6 How does the "Living Well Line" challenge the maximization of profit? How can business firms be persuaded to promote the common good over the maximization principle?

Notes

1 Retrieved from blog entry "The Big Idea," https://adelanteshoes.com/blogs/news/the-big-idea, accessed September 27, 2017.
2 Retrieved from Adelante web page: "The Adelante Founders Club," https://adelanteshoes.com/pages/the-adelante-founders-club, accessed September 27, 2017.

3 Retrieved from blog entry "The Big Idea" (by Peter Sacco), https://adelanteshoes. com/blogs/news/the-big-idea, accessed September 27, 2017.
4 Retrieved from blog entry "Quality and Social Impact Are Not Exclusive" (by Michael Pelzer), https://adelanteshoes.com/blogs/news/quality-and-social-impact- are-not-exclusive, accessed September 27, 2017.
5 Retrieved from blog entry "A Deeper Connection" (by Peter Sacco), https://adelan- teshoes.com/blogs/news/a-deeper-connection, accessed September 27, 2017.
6 Retrieved from blog entry "Gangs, Shoe Bags, and Prison Reform" (by Bob Mott), https://adelanteshoes.com/blogs/news/gangs-shoe-bags-and-prison-reform,accessed September 27, 2017.
7 Retrieved from blog entry "The Big Idea" (by Peter Sacco), https://adelanteshoes. com/blogs/news/the-big-idea, accessed September 27, 2017.

References

Arendt H. 1958, *The human condition*, Chicago, IL: University of Chicago Press.
Aristotle. 1985, *Nicomachean ethics* (Irwin, T., trans.), Indianapolis, IN: Hackett Publishing.
Aristotle. 1990, *The politics* (Everson, S., ed.), Cambridge: Cambridge University Press.
Beadle, R. and Moore, G. 2011, 'MacIntyre: Neo-Aristotelianism and organization the- ory', *Research in the Sociology of Organizations*, 32: 85–121.
Bell, D. 1973, *The coming of post-industrial society*, New York: Basic Books.
Benedict XVI. 2005, *Encyclical Letter 'Deus caritas est' (on Christian love)*, Vatican City: Libreria Editrice Vaticana (DCE). (http://w2.vatican.va/content/benedict-xvi/en/ encyclicals/documents/hf_ben-xvi_enc_20051225_deus-caritas-est.html, Accessed September 27, 2017).
Benedict XVI. 2009, *Encyclical Letter 'Caritas in veritate'*, Vatican City: Libreria Editrice Vaticana (CIV).
Berthoud, A. 2002, *Essais de philosophie économique. Platon, Aristotle, Hobbes, A. Smith, Marx*, Arras-Lille: Presses Universitaires du Septentrion.
Crespo, R. 2013, *Philosophy of the economy. An Aristotelian approach*, New York: Springer.
Ferrero, I. and Calderón, R. 2014, 'The ethical dimension of industrial mass production: the role of transitive motivation', *Markets & Morality*, 16/2: 529–541.
Ferrero, I. and Sison, A. 2017, 'Aristotle and MacIntyre on the virtues in finance', in A.J.G. Sison, G. Beabout and I. Ferrero, I. (eds.), *Handbook of virtue ethics in business and management*, Dordrecht: Springer.
Francis. 2015, *Encyclical Letter 'Laudato Si' on care for uur common home'*. (http://w2.vatican. va/content/francesco/en/encyclicals/documents/papa-francesco_20150524_enciclica- laudato-si.html, Accessed September 27, 2017).
Hartman, E. 2011, 'Virtue, profit, and the separation thesis: An Aristotelian view', *Journal of Business Ethics*, 99: 5–17.
John Paul II. 1981, *Encyclical Letter 'Laborem exercens'*, Vatican City: Typis Poliglottis Vaticanis. (http://w2.vatican.va/content/john-paul-ii/en/encyclicals/documents/hf_ jp-ii_enc_14091981_laborem-exercens.html, Accessed September 27, 2017).
John Paul II. 1987, *Encyclical Letter 'Sollicitudo rei socialis'*. (http://w2.vatican.va/content/ john-paul-ii/en/encyclicals/documents/hf_jp-ii_enc_30121987_sollicitudo-rei- socialis.html, Accessed September 27, 2017).
John Paul II. 1991, *Encyclical Letter 'Centesimus annus'*. Vatican City: Libreria Editrice Vaticana. (http://w2.vatican.va/content/john-paul-ii/en/encyclicals/documents/hf_ jp-ii_enc_01051991_centesimus-annus.html, Accessed September 27, 2017).
Keynes, J.M. 1972, 'Economic possibilities for our grandchildren', in *Essays in persuasion*, New York: W. W. Norton & Co., 358–373.

Knight, K. 2017, 'MacIntyre's critique of management', in A.J.G. Sison, G. Beabout and I. Ferrero (eds.), *Handbook of virtue ethics in business and management*. Dordrecht: Springer.

Koehn, D. 1992, 'Toward an ethic of exchange', *Business Ethics Quarterly*, 2(3): 341–355.

Leo XIII. 1891, *Encyclical Letter 'Rerum novarum'*. (http://w2.vatican.va/content/leo-xiii/en/encyclicals/documents/hf_l-xiii_enc_15051891_rerum-novarum.html, Accessed September 27, 2017).

MacIntyre, A. 1988, *Whose justice? Which rationality?* Notre Dame, IN: University of Notre Dame Press.

MacIntyre, A. 2007 [1981], *After virtue* (3rd ed.), London: Duckworth.

MacIntyre, A. 2012 [1999], *Dependent rational animals: Why human beings need the virtues*, Chicago and La Salle, IL: Open Court.

MacIntyre A. 2015, 'The irrelevance of ethics', in A. Bielskis, K. Knight (eds.), *Virtue and economy*, London: Ashgate.

MacIntyre, A. 2016, *Ethics in the conflicts of modernity. An essay on desire, PR, and narrative*, Cambridge: Cambridge University Press.

Martínez Echevarría, M.A. 2011, 'Aristotle on technique and chrematistics', *Empresa y Humanismo*, XIV(2): 69–88.

Mayo, E. 1933, *The human problems of an industrial civilization*, New York: Macmillan.

Meikle, S. 1995, *Aristotle's economic thought*, Oxford: Oxford University Press.

Moore, G. 2008, 'Re-imagining the morality of management: A modern virtue ethics approach', *Business Ethics Quarterly*, 18(4): 483–511.

Moore, G. 2012, 'Virtue in business: Alliance boots and an empirical exploration of MacIntyre's conceptual framework', *Organization Studies*, 33(3): 363–387.

Murphy, J.B. 1993, *The moral economy of labor. Aristotelian themes in economic theory*, New Heaven, CT and London: Yale University Press.

Pérez López, J.A. 1991, *Teoría de la acción humana en las organizaciones. La acción personal*, Madrid: Rialp.

Pérez López, J.A. 1993, *Fundamentos de la dirección de empresas*, Madrid: Rialp.

Sison, A. 2015, *Happiness and virtue ethics in business. The ultimate value proposition*, Cambridge: Cambridge University Press.

Sison, A. 2016, 'Revisiting the common good of the firm', in K. Akrivou and A.J.G. Sison (eds.), *The challenges of capitalism for virtue ethics and the common good*, Cheltenham and Northampton: Edward Elgar, 93–120.

Smith, A. 1979, *An inquiry into the nature and causes of the wealth of nations*, Oxford: Clarendon Press.

Taylor, F. 1911, *The principles of scientific management*, New York: Harper and Row.

Vatican Council II. 1965, 'Pastoral Constitution "*Gaudium et spes*"', Vatican City: Vatican Polyglot Press. (www.vatican.va/archive/hist_councils/ii_vatican_council/documents/vat-ii_const_19651207_gaudium-et-spes_en.html, Accessed September 27, 2017).

Vigo, A. 2007, *Aristóteles. Una introducción*, Santiago: Institutos de Estudios de la Sociedad (IES).

Wiener, N. 1949, *Cybernetics: Or control and communication in the animal and the machine*, Paris: MIT Press.

Wojtyla, K. 1993, 'The problem of the constitution of culture through human praxis', in K. Wojtyla (ed.), *Person and community. Selected essays*, (T. Sandok, trans.). New York: Peter Lang: 263–275.

5

VIRTUES AND THE COMMON GOOD IN MARKETING

Pablo García Ruiz and Carlos Rodríguez Lluesma

Learning objectives

In this chapter, we shall:

- Present the function of marketing, including its intrinsic purpose, typical benefits and common pitfalls.
- Discuss the relationship between marketing and overconsumption.
- Discuss the virtues relevant to marketing and sales practices and how they can aid marketers in the pursuit of the goods pertaining to the marketing practice, their lives as a whole and their professional traditions.

Marketing is the activity, set of institutions and processes for creating, communicating, delivering and exchanging offerings that have value for customers, clients, partners and overall society (American Marketing Association 2016). In our consumerist society, marketing processes, activities and institutions have given rise to an enormous and powerful system. Marketing departments devote increasing resources to discover customer needs and preferences, and have clients participate in the design of products and services. As a result, distribution systems grow ever larger and more efficient, and advertisements and malls have become ubiquitous.

Beyond customer satisfaction and profits, marketing generates both positive and negative effects for society. Regarding benefits (Wilkie and Moore 1999), it promotes products and services, offers choices for consumers, provides a customized fit with customers' needs, facilitates purchases, saves time and promotes efficiency, delivers products and services, provides post-purchase support, enables market learning, brings new items to the market, fosters innovation and development, and engenders a pleasant "approach" environment for the buyer.

The marketing and sales profession, however, has long been plagued with criticisms concerning crooked intentions, manipulation, fraud, lies and, generally, questionable behavior. Regardless of whether they are justified, salespersons have been heavily and regularly criticized. Marketing allegedly promotes, creating a cycle of overwork and overspending through artificial needs and wants, and fosters resource depletion and global warming. The marketing of violent video games and music to children, the impact of the fashion and beauty industry on the body image and self-esteem of teenagers and poor dietary choices due to sugar-laden and high-fat foods have also been sources of concern. How food is marketed shapes children's preferences and eating behavior. Breakfast cereals, fast food, carbonated beverages and snacks are heavily promoted. Children are exposed to extensive marketing, yet the advertised diet is largely inconsistent with public health recommendations.

Marketing and advertising, however, may also exert a positive influence. For example, the outdoor clothing company Patagonia has long been known for its dedication to protecting the environment—a passion it has extensively shared with customers (Mish and Miller 2014). The "Footprint Chronicles" in Patagonia's website allows customers to track the environmental impact of each product and to know the pros and cons of each production step, including the sustainability of distribution channels. Effective brand-building and storytelling promote consumer identification with sustainability. A hiking enthusiast who purchases outdoor clothing and gear from Patagonia may thus feel she has made the choice that best preserves nature. Providing customers with personally meaningful options can increase not only brand loyalty but also customer satisfaction and positive value commitments.

Marketing activities may affect customers and society positively or negatively. Marketing ethics should seek the causes of this ambivalence to promote benefits and minimize harms. In this chapter, we address, in first place, marketing as an economic activity, its purpose and consequences for the firm, customers and society. Building on the distinction between economy and chrematistics proposed by Aristotle, we discuss the risks of a marketing for the sole purpose of wealth creation, as well as the ethical arguments to orient it towards the greater good. Next, we focus on the virtues of marketing decision makers. Norms and incentives based on cost-benefit analyses do not suffice to foster excellence and the common good. Rather, a strong and upright character is needed. Next, we build on Alasdair MacIntyre's ideas on moral development, practices and institutions to explore how marketers may develop virtues. Since professions become part of people's identities, the values that orient personal aspirations influence how work is performed. These subjective values and aspirations, however, call for objective principles to act as limits and guides. For this reason, we put forward Catholic Social Teaching (CST) principles and their repercussions on marketing ethics.

1. An Aristotelian view of marketing and its contribution to human flourishing (*eudaimonia*)

Aristotle introduced a distinction between "wealth usage" (economics) and "wealth acquisition" (chrematistic) (Politics, henceforth Pltcs: 1253b). Both are related to each other as the "end" and "means." Chrematistics is subordinated to economics because wealth acquisition is just a means for wealth usage for a good life. The ethical account of both wealth creation and wealth usage will depend on how they serve human flourishing (*eudaimonia*). We now explore the consequences of this distinction with respect to marketing.

a. Means and ends in marketing

Virtually every definition of marketing incorporates a distinction between content and goals. "Content" refers to business activities designed to plan, price, promote and distribute products and services. "Goals" can be described as value creation for customers and profit for firms.

Content and goals are related. Firms try to know their customers, their needs, desires, purchasing habits and power, and this knowledge guides the portfolio of products and services offered, prices, distribution channels, promotions and advertising. Success depends on determining the needs and wants of target markets and delivering satisfaction more effectively than competitors. The goals of firms may vary from mere survival to the more daring, such as dramatic sales growth, broadening the product portfolio or opening new markets. These objectives will depend, on the one hand, on management ambition and, on the other hand, on external pressures by competitors and financial markets. Both ambition and pressure push companies to go beyond customers' present needs and wants to obtain ever-increasing profits.

From an Aristotelian perspective, profits should be considered a means to stay in business to satisfy customers' needs and desires better. However, when firms see profits as ends in themselves, economic activities become an inappropriate form of chrematistics. The temptation to put organizational goals ahead of customers by creating artificial needs becomes permanent.

On many occasions, the good of the firm overlaps with the good of the customer. On other occasions, however, the firm seeks its own interest at the expense of the customer or society. For this reason, some scholars have proposed the concept of "societal marketing," where firms seek profits in a way that preserves or enhances the well-being of consumers and society (Kotler and Keller 2009; Mick et al. 2012). We now turn to the different kinds of goods that marketing affords.

b. Kinds of goods

Marketing ethics requires understanding the role business plays in providing the goods and services that a community needs to flourish (Gaski 2013). Salespeople must consider how products affect consumers, how they help people live a good life. Aristotle distinguished between useful, pleasant and honest goods. Some goods—such as bitter medicines that help us manage a cold—benefit people despite their unpleasantness. Other goods are pleasant, such as reading poetry or listening to music. Honest goods are goods that are neither pleasant nor useful for the agent. Examples include playing with one's child even though one may be tired or accompanying a sick relative. Agents perform such actions not because they obtain pleasure or utility but because they are the right thing to do.

Consumer goods usually fall into one of these categories: useful or pleasant. On occasion, some products—e.g., safety belts—will prove uncomfortable but offer a real service. Other products—e.g., going to the movies or eating a cake— will provide more pleasure than usefulness. Ethical criticism becomes salient when firms launch useless and unpleasant products into the market, such as bitter drugs with no real effect. Criticism also arises when the product is pleasant and attractive but harms the health of consumers, such as alcohol or tobacco. These products may be pleasant or useful, but they are not truly good for those who consume them without moderation. For this reason, firms need to consider the third kind of good in Aristotle's taxonomy: honest goods. Firms should take into account what people appreciate not only in terms of usefulness or pleasure but also in terms of values, to offer products that help customers live with what they care about, as the environment in the Patagonia case.

c. Selling goods (or evils)

Choosing a product portfolio involves moral decisions on the part of firms. Firms must consider to what extent they offer not only useful and pleasant but also honest goods and services. Some products—e.g., child pornography or untested medical drugs—are forbidden by government precisely because they hurt consumers and overall society. Other products may not by forbidden, but firms know they may harm consumers. For example, firms in gambling and betting aim to entertain consumers, but may also generate an addiction among the vulnerable, such as minors and those with psychological problems. The consumption of these products and services calls for strict regulation and clear information to protect individuals.

Clear and straightforward information helps consumers balance asymmetric power in commercial exchanges. Asymmetric power in marketing appears in several ways. First, regular consumers—unlike specialists—find it difficult to assess the quality of products (e.g., the durability of a sport shoe sole). Advertising tends to emphasize the attractive features of products and to conceal or gloss over limitations and disadvantages. It is not infrequent to find out soon after a purchase that a printer cannot print on both sides of the paper or that a car does not just consume, but guzzles, gas. Even worse is when firms take advantage of people's ignorance and manipulate them into forced consumption. Some "termite inspectors" place bugs in consumers' houses and threaten frightened residents of an imminent collapse, unless their homes are immediately disinfected. Although customers also sometimes take advantage of firms—for example, abusing liberal return policies— power lies with firms for the most part. A basic ethical demand is that information be truthful and complete with regard to factors relevant to the purchase.

Planned obsolescence also draws widespread criticism. A mobile phone that can last ten years or more dies after three or four years because of a programmed breakdown. In North America, over 100 million cell phones and 300 million personal computers end up in landfills each year, resulting in tremendous environmental damage owing to lead, mercury and toxic glass.

Product obsolescence may result from a hidden programming of weaknesses, but it may also stem from rapid change of technology or fashion, or from a product's low quality. Low quality does not deserve straightforward moral condemnation. It depends on the extent to which low-quality products contribute to people's good. Simple models of cell phones, for example, may provide communication services to those who cannot afford smartphones. Sometimes, the most useful feature for a consumer may be simplicity itself, as most capabilities of high-end products go unused.

Consumer good and firm profits may also clash with regard to prices. Usually, it is the market that sets prices, as broad competition and access to relevant information help consumers assess competing products. However, competition may not always occur. Consequently, clients pay a hefty price, not justified by R&D investments (as is the case with drugs) or political reasons (e.g., higher groceries prices owing to the protection of local farmers for the sake of food sovereignty). The expanding practice of so-called "dynamic pricing," setting prices according to real-time demand, raises ethical concerns. From air flights to theater seats and hotel rooms, prices vary as the date approaches. Alternatively, as in the case of Uber rides, prices adjust to the state of the traffic and weather conditions. Prices may double or triple (air tickets, Uber rides) or amount to a fraction of its value (theater or baseball tickets). Some customers feel this situation is unfair and complain, while others just accept it.

The price of a product may reflect several of its features. Firms obtain high margins for their products in competitive markets because they add value to their clients. Consumers accept their value proposition and show their approval by paying the price. Whole Foods provides a powerful example of skillfully managing pricing. In line with their "Whole Foods, Whole People, Whole Planet" motto, this grocery chain grew rapidly through a very clear positioning strategy, demonstrating that consumers consider social and environmental impacts as part of the value equation (Mish and Miller 2014). Cheaper products may be found elsewhere, but some customers consider that the global value (useful, pleasant and honest) offered by Whole Foods is worth their money. Comprehensive moral thinking must take into account the full effects of a company's products on society or the environment, from production to recycling, as well as the desirability of operations that might reinforce good or bad consumer habits (Goodpaster 2011). Since the market tends to promote consumerism, people can easily get caught up in a whirlwind of needless buying and spending (Abela 2007).

Marketing should constantly consider not only "what is good for business" but also "what is good for people." Clear rules and moral principles are undoubtedly important. Marketing must strive towards customers' well-being and not take advantage of power asymmetries to maximize profits. However, this principle does not make clear what the well-being of customers is or how it is to be harmonized with reasonable profits. Sometimes, resorting to general rules or universal ethical principles does not solve marketing problems. People agree that lying is immoral in advertising, but there are many ways to present a product or service (puffery or celebrity associations) that do not involve straightforward deceit. No set of rules could cover all the ways in which product claims can be presented.

d. The need for virtues

Aristotelian virtue ethics emphasizes that ethical norms and principles be applied according to the particulars of the case (Aristotle Nicomachean Ethics, henceforth NE: 1138b, 21–23). If marketing is to be considered ethical, it depends on marketers possessing sufficient virtues to discern and do what is best, striking a balance between consumers' well-being and the firm's goals. Prudence (i.e., "practical wisdom") is the virtue that helps one assess circumstances adequately and decide what to do. Prudence is not the mere application of a general rule; it involves discerning the salient aspects in a situation to respond appropriately.

Along with prudence, virtues such as honesty, fairness, trustworthiness, respect and empathy seem essential to marketing professionals, as they ease commercial exchanges (Murphy 1999). According to the American Marketing Association Statement of Ethics (2016), the collective conception of what people find desirable, important and morally proper for marketing activities includes honesty, responsibility, fairness, respect, transparency and citizenship. However, for these firms to behave according to these values, employees must internalize them. Firms are just, respectful and truthful not only because they proclaim codes of conduct but also—and precisely—because their employees behave justly, respectfully and truthfully towards consumers. It is not only a matter of complying with the law, with established rules, to avoid suits but also a matter of achieving excellence in dealing with clients. Virtues are concrete aspects of such excellence.

Honesty means conveying accurate and complete information to customers, being truthful and forthright in dealings with them. A salesperson should present a company's market offer in the best light, but not lead a customer to think that the product's price or performance is better than it is (Weber 2014). A salesperson targeting an uninformed customer to sell an overstocked, soon to be out-of-date product at full price falls short of being honest. Salespeople sometimes disguise a lack of honesty behind tricks and ambiguity. For example, some salespersons use technical jargon to sell the customer a higher-end product than the one needed. Such a sale would also be unfair.

Fairness means selling and pricing products at a level commensurate with the benefits. Salespersons who balance the needs of the buyer with the interests of the seller act fairly and are worthy of their customers' trust.

Trustworthiness implies integrity, i.e., acceptance of the consequences of decisions and strategies, and fulfillment of obligations without monitoring. A trustworthy person avoids deception and betrayal.

Respect addresses the esteem or consideration salespeople owe all customers, regardless of background, social class, opinions or preferences. Respect leads to decisions such as altering products to meet cultural needs or changing a commercial message that discriminates against a minority, even though this may imply a lesser margin.

Empathy implies knowing how to listen and accepting and assimilating customers' needs and concerns to offer the most adequate good or service. A salesperson may be empathetic when she refrains from selling products to consumers who cannot afford them.

These virtues, though diverse, show strong connections among them. A firm that withdraws harmful products (e.g., packaged food, pharmaceutical drugs) from global markets when initial signs of human or environmental problems occur shows respect for clients, honesty and trustworthiness, as did Johnson & Johnson in withdrawing Tylenol or unlike Nestlé with its infant formula crisis in Africa.[1] Understanding the plight of others does not require managers to be soft-hearted. Tough decisions are often necessary, and trade-offs inevitable. This includes determining what constitutes a reasonable level of customer satisfaction and how it could be obtained in a particular case.

Virtues in marketing help establish long-lasting and satisfactory exchanges with customers. The importance of these virtues for relational marketing is difficult to exaggerate because enduring relationships cannot be built or sustained without a solid moral foundation. Even in the case of one-time transactions, such as the purchase of a trip or a second-hand car, virtues are important. On such occasions, when the buyer may not have acquainted himself with the seller or may not expect to deal with him again in the future, trust in salespeople hinges on their reputation. The rise of electronic commerce has exponentially boosted the importance of reputation. One's reputation as a salesperson accrues over a long series of honest, fair, respectful and empathic transactions. Knowledge of the salesperson's character eases the consumer into purchasing. In contrast, when customers perceive that a firm—or, more specifically, its salespeople—does not behave with fairness, honesty, empathy and respect, they conclude it is not trustworthy, despite trust-generating commercials.

- Marketing is an economic activity that aims to satisfy (end) the client's needs and wants while contributing to the continuity and flourishing of the firm (means). When the order of ends and means is subverted, marketing turns into a chrematistic activity that hinders rather than favors the clients' and the firm's flourishing.

2. Cultivating virtues in marketing: practices, lives and the traditions of marketers

Among the different versions of virtue ethics, Alasdair MacIntyre's (2007) provides a clear framework to think about the ethical dimension of marketing. To the question, "How can people acquire and develop virtues?", he responds that virtues are acquired and developed within practices. Ethics can be taught, whereas ethical conduct cannot; it must be practiced. All the theoretical knowledge in the world about ethics will not make you a virtuous marketer unless you practice, just as all the theoretical knowledge in the world about music will not make one a good pianist unless one practices.

a. Marketing as a practice

Marketing can be regarded as a practice (in the MacIntyrean sense) insofar as it is a cooperative activity through which internal goods are realized in the course of trying to achieve specific standards of excellence. Before, we defined marketing as the set of activities and processes for creating, communicating, delivering and exchanging offerings with value for customers, partners and overall society. There are good and bad marketers, and the distinction between them rests not on personal preference, but on the degree to which they achieve the standards of excellence in the profession. To create value for consumers and meet the firm's demands, the *modus operandi* of marketing is the pursuit of a deep understanding and orchestration of consumers' intentions, needs and decisions. Marketers help crystallize clients' needs, educate about alternative offers and customize the firm's offering when feasible. Salespeople work to facilitate the entire transaction, payment and product delivery or project completion. During this process, a sales professional will provide support and services to ensure customer satisfaction and a continuing relationship. In most firms, marketers specialize in creating good products, promoting them, placing them at their customers' convenience and deciding on the best price. In doing so, professionals develop specific skills and abilities: some are technical skills, others are moral.

Some people excel in marketing practice. To illustrate, Steve Jobs became an extraordinary exemplar for marketers. He imagined, designed and commercialized new products such as the iPod, iPhone and iPad, which have enjoyed overwhelming success. Millions of people have integrated these gadgets into their lives, reaping sizeable benefits in terms of communication, entertainment, social mobility and social relation capabilities, among others. Another well-known example is Zara, the fast fashion company. Because of its intelligent information and distribution systems, the firm is able to deliver accessible and trendy garments to customers all over the world.

Marketing's purpose does not consist in merely satisfying consumers through existing goods and services. As one marketer put it, "If we were to wait for demand bells to go off, we'd be out of business in two years, and I'd be out of a job long before that. No, we've got to identify unmet needs ourselves, which is why we have research" (Applbaum 2004: 37). Consumers have a set of needs that they often cannot clearly articulate. Marketers think it is their job to determine those needs and make people perceive some products as the proper solution to those new needs. Is it ethical to be a good marketer?

Virtue ethics offers some ideas to answer this question. MacIntyre distinguishes between goods internal and external to practices. Internal goods are the skills (technical or moral), experiences and abilities one achieves by engaging in a practice. In consumer marketing, internal goods could be summarized as the capacity to create value for customers, partners and overall society through the creation, promotion, distribution and exchange of products and services. External goods are the rewards—money, fame and power, among others—obtained through the exercise of a practice. To be able to "add value" to customers, partners and overall society, marketing needs institutions to provide much-needed resources. Problems arise, MacIntyre holds, when the urge to acquire external goods ends up corrupting and hollowing out the capacity to gain internal goods. Next, we turn to how virtues can be developed in such a context.

b. Value creation and the development of virtues

Marketing aims to create value for (a) customers, (b) firms and (c) society through the design, production, distribution and sale of goods and services. Value creation refers not only to what is useful or pleasant for customers, but also to honest goods. Excellent marketers are those who excel at selling goods that are truly good (useful, pleasant and/or honest) and at serving people in search of a good life (Goodpaster 2011). By engaging in value-creation practices, marketers can improve as professionals and as moral agents, because they acquire and develop specific virtues while searching for professional excellence.

Virtues develop through the exercise of actions adequate to the circumstances at hand. As Aristotle (NE: 1103a14b -1103b125) notes, "we become just by performing just acts, temperate by performing temperate ones, brave by performing brave ones." Moral virtues are learned in practice. A marketer will develop the virtue of empathy if he or she repeatedly engages in the exercise of listening and understanding each customer's viewpoint. Similarly, she will become trustworthy if she regularly avoids lying to or taking advantage of her customers, and honors the commitments to them.

However, to act in a virtuous fashion, more is needed than simply bringing general principles to bear in a case; practitioners must assess what circumstances demand. To illustrate, the virtue of honesty leads to not lying about, for example, the specifications of a product or the risks of its misuse. However, being honest does not require us to reveal all the details of its manufacturing or design. Honesty consists in disclosing to customers or stakeholders that which they have a right to know. Determining what is to be communicated in each case requires practical wisdom—that is, the ability to distinguish the important from the insignificant, the necessary from the futile, and the helpful from the harmful. Therefore, telling the truth counts as virtuous action only inasmuch as it is told by who should tell it, to whom it is adequate, at the right moment and for the right motives.

Virtues are not acquired one by one in a disconnected fashion. To be honest, a marketer should be simultaneously wise and just, courageous and moderate. One can comprehend the situation but that will not suffice. One must have the courage to go on trying until she succeeds. One must have endurance and moderation to abide by what is right. Courage, endurance and moderation are moral qualities associated with good judgment. Only thus will a marketer not get carried away by the urge to close a sale or to show off her knowledge.

Discernment may be acquired through trial and error or through the experience of others. Virtue ethics emphasizes the importance of role models. Ordinarily, virtues are discovered by witnessing and imitating behavior. To become virtuous, one must see others practicing the virtues one wishes to acquire. New employees often imitate the behavior of senior or experienced managers, and that way, a more virtue-oriented culture is reinforced (Murphy 1999). To acquire virtues, marketers need to know not only the organization's mission, vision and value statements but also see top managers and senior employees act as role models. Absent this virtuous example, the organizational climate may veer towards incoherence or cynicism (Hartman 2013). This occurs, for example, when a firm states that respecting the client is of paramount importance but, in practice, allows (or celebrates) misleading customers or abusive commercials because they pay off financially.

Virtue ethics aims not merely to prevent unethical behavior but to encourage excellence in action. Rather than providing a set of rules or prohibitions, virtue ethics offers ideals towards which marketers may strive. Such exemplars appeal not only to effectiveness, but also to affection and emotion. Anita Roddick, founder of natural cosmetics company The Body Shop, provides a case in point. Roddick contended that improving the world by caring not only for its workforce and customers, but also for its communities and the environment constituted the main purpose of business. She articulated an ideal of excellence upon which to evaluate her integrity and that of her company's marketing strategies (Hartman and Beck-Dudley 1999). Roddick set out to offer clients cosmetics to beautify and care for the body. Concurrently, however, she wanted to "make a difference" with respect to the cosmetic industry and the beauty culture of her time. A passionate supporter of natural beauty, she focused on increasing women's self-esteem. She wanted customers and employees to develop a social consciousness so that they would see in The Body Shop an ally in the creation of a more just society. The success of The Body Shop should contribute to a cultural and social change in her employees' and customers' lives. Learning from good exemplars like Roddick, many marketers have developed their own professional skills and moral wisdom.

c. The corrupting power of institutions

Marketers need the support of their organizations. Good ideas do not suffice. They need funding, teamwork, design, production, distribution and promotion, among other factors. Even marketing geniuses such as Anita Roddick and Steve Jobs need an organization to host and sustain their initiatives. However, the organization has economic, political and social goals of its own. In particular, firms need profits to provide a return to shareholders and compete in the market. The risk of the practice-organization relationship is that the search for profits crowds out excellence in practice. Abbott's subsidiary in India provides a rather dramatic illustration. According to a piece in *The New York Times* (August 11, 2016), the company's overly aggressive sales policies spurred public protests by more than 250 Abbott drug representatives. To win customers in India's chaotic and highly competitive drug market, some Abbott managers instructed employees to push their products at all cost, in violation of Indian law, professional medical standards and the company's own ethical guidelines. In one of the most common practices, Abbott managers told sales staff to hold "health camps," where representatives would perform tests on patients for doctors to prescribe Abbott drugs. These camps typically focused on chronic ailments such as diabetes, thyroid disorders, heart problems and lung disease. Sales personnel did the testing at no charge, and doctors increased their business by advertising free check-ups. In return, doctors were expected to prescribe the drug maker's products. This initiative had sales personnel performing screening tests, practicing medicine without a license. In addition, Indian medical ethics regulations prohibit *quid pro quo*. Abbott's Indian public affairs director stated that the "health camps" were just "disease aware-ness education programs" and that company policies did not allow them to be conducted in exchange for an obligation to prescribe Abbott products. How-ever, former employees accused sales managers of "exerting immense pressure" on them to do more screenings and promote Abbott drugs among doctors and patients. Some employees tried to resist the pressure out of respect for national rules and company policies, but they were eventually dismissed or forced to re-sign. Evidently, this leadership style counts as an example of malpractice, since the pressure to boost sales trumps reasonable commercial and medical practice. Owing to an "inhuman and unnatural pressure to sell," one sales representative committed suicide. This shows clearly how a firm's priorities may push employ-ees to act against professional standards and abandon the search for excellence, harming other employees, customers and the society in which the firm operates.

Organizational influence on practices, however, does not always need to be negative. In fact, it supports practices by providing the resources that practition-ers need to carry out practices well and improve standards of excellence. How-ever, the paths towards value creation and excellence do not come ready made. Virtue ethics turns to moral traditions as sources of inspiration.

d. Moral traditions in marketing

A tradition is a set of values, norms, ways of doing and meanings proper to a community that are shared and handed down from generation to generation. Inasmuch as organizations behave as communities, they also become sites in which traditions arise and are passed on. Value declarations—and, especially, mission statements—constitute a clear illustration through which an organiza-tion expresses its identity, purpose and values. *Levi Strauss & Co.*, the denim textile company, provides a clear illustration. Through a series of mission and aspirations statements, this firm has built and promoted a culture with specific values that have withstood the passage of time, strategies and product changes. Its web page states that

> the culture of Levi Strauss & Co. is fueled by strong values: empathy, originality, integrity, courage, creativity and hard work. Using innovative, sustainable and progressive practices isn't just how we make our jeans and other products, it is a principle we value in all of our work.

Some of these cultural traits refer to technical skills (originality, creativity), while others refer to moral ones (empathy, integrity, courage). Overall, both sets define the internal good of the practices housed in this firm. These skills and virtues define excellence in *Levi Strauss & Co.,* with reference to which management assesses employees.

Virtues relate to the communities and traditions in which actors are embedded. Actors do not start their careers in a void; rather, they find themselves in roles whose content has evolved before, during and after they occupy them. Actors are inducted into the practice of marketing—in college, through trade unions or on the job—starting from a body of established knowledge about their function, and they join firms in which the function of marketing may differ. Those roles and traditions are understandable only in terms of the shared history and values that characterize firms. Traditions regarding "how to add value to customers" play out differently in firms. What may work in one may not in another because practical knowledge (which includes moral knowledge) is contextual. It depends on the particular case and on the tradition within which knowledge has been acquired.

That knowledge and moral virtues are relative to one's life and tradition does not mean that virtue ethics lacks norms and principles. For example, if moderation is the central virtue of consumption, marketers should examine whether they push consumers to overconsume. A marketer who abuses his social or natural environment is far from good.

- Engaging in the practice of marketing, individuals submit themselves to standards of practice to pursue goals internal to that practice (e.g., particular analytical skills and an understanding of consumer behavior), which they have to harmonize with their good *qua* human beings and that of their communities. In doing so, marketers develop virtues.

3. Catholic Social Teaching on marketing

Virtue ethics is contextual. How people pursue goodness and excellence will vary according to the specifics of the case (Aristotle NE: 1138b21–23). Salespeople and marketing managers face different circumstances depending on the industries, firms, products and services. The qualities and competencies needed to become an excellent salesperson vary, depending on whether one sells energy, cars or executive education, for example. This does not mean, however, that virtue ethics is incompatible with universal norms and principles. There may be no universal "one way" to be virtuous, but there are universal norms about what one should avoid in order to become virtuous.

CST provides a set of moral norms and principles to aid in the avoidance of evil, the discernment of good and the search for excellence in one's profession and life. In the first place, CST poses the demand of honoring the Ten Commandments. All salespeople working in the industry of renewable energy, used cars or executive education, for example, may check their acts against the standards of the Commandments. Lying is ethically deplorable conduct even though it may bring profits. Lying is a kind of act that does not lead to excellence as a salesperson or as a human being. The same goes for cheating, stealing, coveting others' possessions or harming third parties. None of these actions should be included in an excellent professional's project or a virtuous salesperson's character.

The Ten Commandments also include positive precepts, particularly that of loving God over all things and neighbors as oneself. CST has developed a set of moral principles to specify those general precepts. For marketing professionals, some relevant CST principles are those on human dignity, the common good, the universal destination of goods, solidarity, subsidiarity and the normative pre-eminence of the subjective over the objective dimension of work (Laczniak, Klein and Murphy 2014).

First is the principle of human dignity. The most basic instruction of CST flows from the idea that all persons have inherent worth regardless of their race, color or creed. Dignity is not "earned"; rather, it is a right accorded to all persons in all circumstances. Dignity demands respect because human life is sacred. This would call into question the selling of dangerous or unsafe products as well as practices such as deceptive advertising or sharing customers' personal data without permission. Respecting customers as human beings also requires marketers to offer them nothing but useful goods and services, rather than taking advantage of their inexperience or weakness or inducing them to spend on things they do not need or that can harm them. As *Centessimus Annus* (n. 36) puts it, in singling out new needs and new means to meet them, marketers must be guided by a comprehensive picture of man that respects all the dimensions of his being and subordinates his material and instinctive dimensions to his interior and spiritual ones. If, in contrast, a direct appeal is made to his instincts, then unhealthy consumer attitudes and lifestyles can be promoted.

Second is the principle of the common good. This principle builds on the idea that persons typically live in a community, and therefore, social norms should contribute to the benefit of the commonwealth. While CST clearly affirms the right to private property, this teaching provides grounds for the notion that all persons have the right to secure the basic necessities of life (e.g., food, shelter and access to education and affordable healthcare). It "stems from the dignity and equality of all people" (Compendium of the Social Doctrine of the Church (CSDC): 164). This principle refers to goods such as sustainability and to duties such as stewardship, which

> captures the responsibility of every party—including corporations—to contribute to the care of the earth. Marketers practicing the common good (sustainability/stewardship) principle would likely develop less environmentally harmful versions of their products, never engage in "greenwashing" and would create reverse channels for the disposal of their products.
>
> *(Laczniak, Klein and Murphy 2014: 107)*

Pope Francis' Enciclycal *Laudato Si'* (n. 22) encourages these initiatives and notes that "a serious consideration of this issue would be one way of counteracting the throwaway culture which affects the entire planet."

The principle of the common good in CST goes beyond environmental concerns. It refers to the conditions that enhance human development in all its dimensions, including the economic, social, cultural and spiritual. In fact, multiple common goods can be pursued in business. Easier and cheaper communication provided by mobile phone manufacturers and network companies, faster and safer transportation offered by airplane makers or operators, noise abatement systems, healthier nutrition, learning software, consumer credit and a plethora of other products can all contribute to goods that benefit all and offer people closer access to full development as human beings (Murphy and Sherry 2014). All these commercial products certainly constitute the common good of a society, especially when all members have access to them.

With the teaching of the universal destination of goods, CST "argues that the proper end of economic activity is the progress of the entire community, especially the poor" (Murphy, Laczniak and Harris 2016: 204). This is a corollary of the principles of human dignity and the common good. Such principles guarantee each person a right to the well-being necessary for development but do not require that everything be at the disposal of all people, as rights must be exercised in an orderly fashion. Hence, the role of private property is to ensure a sphere of autonomy, safeguard social order and avoid the "tragedy of commons," by which what belongs to everyone is sooner or later laid to waste (Sison, Ferrero and Guitián 2016). The right to private property is never viewed as absolute; rather, it is subordinated to the good of the entire community, especially the poor. The centrality of the obligation to help the poor is manifest not only in CST but also in every other major religious doctrine. Business opportunities at the so-called "bottom of the pyramid" pose interesting challenges for firms. When designing and marketing products and services, firms may take into account the needs and purchasing power not only of the affluent, but also of those with scarce resources. Targeting the latter is also a way of conducting business. Examples abound of profitable businesses at the base of the pyramid. Products aimed at this segment are often simpler and cheaper, less innovative or of a lower quality, but sufficiently useful and affordable for the underprivileged. Cell phones, computers and other technological gadgets, shared transport and accommodation, and microcredits have been designed for this particular market.

The principle of subsidiarity encourages personal freedom, initiative and responsibility as manifestations of human dignity. "Subsidiarity respects personal dignity by recognizing in the person a subject who is always capable of giving something to others" (Benedict XVI, *Caritas in Veritate* (CiV) 2009: 57). In close connection with subsidiarity is the idea of participation, which refers to the right and duty to contribute to the cultural, economic, political and social life of the community (Vatican II, *Gaudium et Spes* (GeS) 1965: 75). Participation guarantees, as long as it is carried out with practical wisdom, that workers contribute their genius and creativity—not merely their muscles—to business. To follow the subsidiarity/participation principle, companies must "allow marketing departments, product managers, and salespeople to make decisions at the lowest feasible level in dealing with customers and other stakeholders" (Laczniak, Klein and Murphy 2014: 106–107). It may also include fostering client participation in the design and use of products and services through co-creation processes or simply through suggestions about, for example, recreational activities for large families.

The principle of solidarity "recognizes that all people and social groups are united in a brotherhood that seeks common growth and fulfilment, dependent on one another for the support that we require in community" (CSDC: 192). This principle provides a basis for advocating the ethical responsibilities of rich nations towards poor ones as well as the special ethical obligations of multinational business operating in developing countries. Solidarity ought not to be reduced to vague compassion or shallow distress at the misfortune of others; rather, it should grow into a firm and persevering determination to work in favor of the common good (Sison, Ferrero and Guitián 2016). Thus, for instance, international marketers should develop products that are economically affordable and appropriate for customers in less affluent markets (Laczniak, Klein and Murphy 2014: 107).

The solidarity principle also refers to the impact of marketing activities within the firm. The demand to cooperate towards the common good also applies to that of the firm, which consists in achieving the conditions (whether they be economic, labor related, social, educational or cultural, among others) that foster the professional and human development of members. It includes profits, obviously, but also learning and self-fulfillment opportunities for all employees. How product design and marketing are carried out affects the company as a whole.

CST calls for the normative pre-eminence of the subjective dimension of work over its objective dimension. This principle suggests that managers have a moral obligation to create trusting, nurturing communities in which employees can improve as persons. In marketing, this means that the knowledge, skills and, above all, virtues that marketers develop should be given greater value than the products and services, results and profits.

For CST, work represents a privileged means through which basic human dignity is developed. "Work is for man and not man for work" (John Paul II, *Laborem Exercens* (LE) 1981: 6). All work is dignified insofar as a means to the self-formation or self-transformation of free, rational and dynamic persons (Finn 2012). Through work (by virtue of this subjective dimension), human beings improve themselves and achieve perfection in virtue. This principle clearly applies to marketing. Marketers can develop specific virtues through their profession. The perfection of the product, an increase in market share or the profit obtained may count as criteria for excellence. But, these objective results of work should not be attained at the cost of human dignity, the common good, solidarity or subsidiarity. Marketing is excellent when it incorporates these principles in activities such as designing, pricing, promoting or distributing goods and services. Unlike trash TV, which succeeds by exhibiting the vices of actors and appealing to the lowest passions of the audience, there are other ways of producing TV in accordance with human dignity and the common good. Some local TV channels, for example, have developed a model that focuses on the events that citizens positively value, such as the lighting of streets during Christmas and local celebrations, such as food festivals or sports. Channels have perceived that these broadcasts—proudly joined by local citizens—get the highest ratings. This is not the only way to produce TV programs ethically, however. In fact, CST does not propose any particular model, but it presents TV professionals, as well as marketers, with the chance to reflect on whether their products, services and prices respect human dignity and contribute to the common good.

CST moral teaching focuses more on the misuse than on the positive side of marketing. Yet, this does not mean that marketing activities should be regarded as intrinsically evil. Rather, they may and must be carried out in accordance with certain fundamental principles, such as human dignity, the common good, the universal destination of goods, subsidiarity and solidarity (Klein and Laczniak 2013). On the one hand, CST principles provide moral grounds to reject wrong or abusive marketing practices. On the other hand, they provide an orientation for marketing to excel and serve human individuals and communities.

4. Primark: the hidden costs of low prices[2]

It was 7:30 pm on a winter afternoon. Clouds rolled through the sky in typical Brit fashion as Mr. Marchant left Primark's head office at 41 West Street. A cab waited outside to take him to his return train to London. The top management team meeting had ended later than expected, but the state of the new European and World markets demanded a bold yet precise strategic plan to surmount the challenges that loomed on the horizon.

Marchant had taken charge of the chain after the resignation of its founder, Arthur Ryan, who had steered the firm for over 40 years. Ryan had changed the rules of the retail market in both Ireland and the UK and turned Primark into a wonderful success story. His shoes seemed very hard to fill. Standing at the helm meant taking up considerable responsibilities. Marchant knew that he had to start delivering. Could he do away with Primark's weak spot—that is, the growing criticism over the social, environmental and moral consequences of its business model? Was listening to its critics compatible with keeping prices low and maintaining the high profit levels that ABF (Primark's parent enterprise) had become accustomed to under Ryan's leadership?

While the English countryside slipped before his eyes, Marchant went through all the topics covered during the morning meeting and how they had come to find themselves in their current predicament.

The story: Primark's founding and expansion

The Primark that we now know started in 1935 as a set of bakeries under the name "Associated British Foods" (ABF). After 15 years, it had become the world's largest bakery chain and the largest retail chain in the UK. In 1969, its founder, Willard Garfield Weston, decided to diversify its business and offered Arthur Ryan the chance to establish its first non-food-related retail operation. The first Penneys store was set up in Dublin with this goal in mind. Its success and expansion across Ireland proved so overwhelming that it crossed the Irish Sea in 1973 to open its first British shop under the Primark name.

The 2008 financial crisis marked a turning point for the company, which, based on its price strategy, took advantage of the situation to expand across Europe. In Spain, for example, twice as many clothing items as 10 years earlier were consumed, while spending remained stagnant.

Nowadays, Primark runs 320 stores in 11 European countries and the US, out of which 38 still operate in Ireland under the Penneys brand. These stores account for 25% of ABF's total revenue and 33% of its profits, with the remaining 67% being split between food (27%), sugar (26%), ingredients (11%) and agricultural products (3%).

The retail fashion market

With global sales nearing $2.4 billion in 2016, the retail fashion industry has become one of the largest industries in the world (McKinsey & Co. 2017). A fundamental shift in the industry took place in 1980, with a new manufacturing technique known as "Quick Response" (Lago, Martínez-de-Albéniz, Moscoso and Vall 2014). This strategy, based on the search for a tighter interface between supply and demand, allowed manufacturers to reduce order lead time, spawning the "Fast Fashion" phenomenon (see exhibit 1). In this new model, differentiation came from price and design, branding in the hands of either designers (independent labels) or retailers (private labels).

Independent labels faced low barriers to entry, as anyone could design, produce and sell a clothing line, even if at a small scale, particularly given the surge of online channels. In this model, designers retained tight creative control on the product, while retail activity remained in the hands of third-party vendors.

In contrast, private labels faced high barriers to entry, as the product was created and branded from beginning to end by the firm itself. This approach involves hiring a design team to create a collection and then producing it through the firm's own or hired channels, where the firm ends up managing both distribution and branding. In contrast, independent labels set consumer trends, which allowed them to extract higher rents from their customers. The development of the "Quick Response" and "Fast Fashion" models diminished the risks of producing such items, allowing private labels to expand and compete with independent labels and thereby increasing market share.

The key to success: the Primark model

The Primark model had enjoyed raving success because of low prices based on (a) its streamlined supply line and focus on fast-turnover items, (b) low operations costs (shunning advertising and relying on word of mouth and social media), (c) and focus on large showrooms to encourage large volume shopping.

a   Fast turnover

In line with most of competitors, Primark followed a private label strategy. Unlike firms such as Zara or H&M, however, which privileged quality or general affordability, Primark based business strategy on its ability to set the lowest prices in the industry while reaping hefty profits through high sale volumes. To do so, Primark keeps costs to a minimum by using artificial materials, unlike its competitors, which use finer ones to achieve product differentiation.

Primark also keeps inventory levels of finished products at very low levels to minimize the need for circulating capital. Little savings at different points of its manufacturing process generate sizeable savings when total volumes are considered, which clearly benefit the firm's profitability and balance sheet. As Jaime Isenwater, an analyst for Deutsche Bank, explains, "With fewer stock keeping units than competitors, and because of the lower average price point, [Primark] can buy much larger volumes from suppliers [and thereby] offer the lowest prices in the market" (Isenwater and Thompson 2010).

Primark's stores order well above the expected sales level and then sell overstock at deeply discounted prices, which can take the total price down to €1 or €2. This allows the company to take advantage of economies of scale and reclaim part of the production costs of surplus items.

b   Communication and marketing: riding the wave

To keep operating costs low, Primark limits advertising to the large shopping bags carried by customers and relies on word of mouth (Mohsin 2009). When, in 2007, Primark decided it would use social media for free advertising, the brand's fans had already created a group on Facebook that boasted of 97,000 members. Primark decided not to go ahead with its own official Facebook account. This support becomes evident in the opening of new stores, when numerous followers gather to mark the occasion.

Free advertising also comes in the form of "YouTubers," who record and publish videos raving about the number of items they have bought at a very low price. This low-cost phenomenon was all the rage during the recent financial crisis, when young consumers competed for the best offer. Celebrities wearing cheap clothes on magazine covers broadcast the message that one can dress in style for a low price. In sum, Primark could ride the wave of free advertising to maintain its sales.

c   Stores: hypermarkets of fashion

While other firms tried to reduce store sizes and move downtown, Primark stuck to a large stores policy to foster high volume sales among customers. Average store area was 2,800 square meters, and plans were in place to reach an average of 3,700 square meters. Relocating to the periphery of cities or to large malls helped keep costs low.

Primark stores bear a closer resemblance to supermarkets than to its competitors' stores, as cashiers are the only staff members around. Nevertheless, Primark succeeds at selling an average of six items per customer, double of what its competitors achieve.

This uncontested business success, however, has come under closer public scrutiny with regard to its social, environmental and moral impact.

A tragic turn of events: the Rana Plaza collapse

Despite favorable financial auditing reports and a sound business model, Primark's manufacturing processes began to raise concerns. News such as the death of 120 Bangladeshi workers in a factory fire severely tarnished Primark's reputation, sparked vocal protest campaigns and prompted conversations of concern within the firm.[3]

Primark's supply chain had been raising eyebrows with NGOs and with the public for a few years with respect to alleged exploitation of workers and use of child labor (Alam 2008). Scepticism about the firm's ability to keep prices low while respecting human rights seemed to be spreading.

Breene O'Donoghue, human resources director for Primark, responded to the criticism with the company's usual line that

> Irrespective of what is on the label, the workers are paid the same. Our factories are shared by 98.3% of our competitors…, [and] we spent more than £3 billion in developing countries last year, so we say we helped over two million people. We would say trade is better than aid.
>
> *(Scally 2010)*

In 2009, several labor irregularities were revealed: nine-year-old Indians working for 60 pennies a day, Bangladeshi workers toiling 80 hours per week at a seven-penny/hour rate and a workshop in Manchester that hosted illegal immigrants working 12 hours per day at a £3.5/hour rate.

Criticism increased in 2012, after a fire in the Tazreen Fashion factory on the outskirts of the capital of Bangladesh, Daca, left 111 workers dead. The factory lacked fire extinguishers, emergency exists turned out to be sealed, and workers were instructed for what proved an excessively long time to remain at the workstations despite billowing smoke. The incident sparked widespread protests among Bangladeshi workers—some evolving into riots against other, similar factories—and the expulsion of some 850 factories from the Bangladesh Garment Manufacturers and Exporters Association. Later, a pact was signed by several hundred North American and European firms to upgrade safety and labor conditions for Bangladeshi workers (Zain Al-Mahmoud 2014).

Everything changed for the Irish Firm when the Rana Plaza, a hotbed of textile manufacturing including Primark, collapsed. An eight-story building, the Rana Plaza hosted banks and apartments but mostly textile operations. On April 24, 2013, a mostly female workforce labored as usual. The day before, some tenants vacated the building because of large cracks on the walls, but textile workers were instructed to report to work as usual. On that nefarious day, the building collapsed, leaving 1,129 dead, 2,515 injured and a host of amputees and crippled Bangladeshi workers.[4] Witnesses spoke of scores of people crying out for help from underneath the rubble. Investigators concluded that the building left much to be desired. Built on what used to be a swamp with low-quality materials and deficient construction, the Rana Plaza began to emit ominous sounds shortly after its inauguration. These factors, together with a dismal lack of maintenance, was a recipe for disaster. The collapse made it to news reports, front pages and magazine covers all over the world. The outcries about exploitation, recklessness and greed placed enormous pressure on textile firms, including Primark, a supplier of which occupied the second floor of the building.

More sources of concern

The fast fashion system has expanded over the last several years. According to a McKinsey & Co. report on The State of the Fashion Industry (McKinsey & Co. 2017), the number of garments produced annually has doubled since 2000, and it exceeded 100 billion for the first time in 2014, which equates to nearly 14 items of clothing for every person on earth. Emerging economies have seen large rises in clothing sales, as more people in such countries have joined the middle class. In five large developing countries—Brazil, China, India, Mexico and Russia—apparel sales grew eight times faster than that in Canada, Germany, the United Kingdom and the United States.

a   Environmental concerns
    This tremendous growth has caused substantial and worrying environmental effects: making clothes typically requires abundant water, chemicals and the emission of significant amounts of greenhouse gases.
        When it comes to disposing of clothing, current technologies cannot reliably turn unwanted apparel into fibers suitable for further manufacturing.

Recycling methods such as shredding or chemical digestion work poorly, and markets sufficiently large to absorb such a volume of material are nowhere to be seen. Consequently, nearly three-fifths of all clothing produced ends up in incinerators or landfills within a year of being made.

A few apparel businesses have begun tackling sustainability challenges on their own. In 2016, H&M launched its *Conscious Collection,* which aimed to encourage customers to recycle by bringing their old clothes (from any brand) and putting them in bins in its stores worldwide. "H&M will recycle them and create new textile fibre, and in return you get vouchers to use at H&M. Everybody wins!" its blog claimed.[5] However, H&M admits that just 0.1% of all clothing collected in such programs is turned into new textile fiber (Wicker 2016).

Some apparel companies, such as The Better Cotton Initiative, I:CO and others, have formed coalitions to tackle environmental and social challenges together. Several initiatives, such as designing garments to be more easily reused or recycled, developing fibers that will lower the environmental effects of garment manufacturing, improving recycling technologies and establishing higher labor and environmental standards for suppliers, have also been implemented.

b   Concerns about consumerism and lifestyles

Primark's success has also fueled concerns about growing consumerism in affluent societies. Fast fashion consumers keep clothing items about half as long as they did 15 years ago. They treat the lowest-priced garments as nearly disposable and discard them after just seven or eight wears (McKinsey & Co. 2017). The eagerness for novelty is paramount. Zara offers 24 new clothing collections every year. H&M offers 12 to 16 and refreshes them weekly. Numerous voices wonder whether we need this amount of clothing and where the limit of consumption lies.

Social agents such as the Ethical Fashion Forum seek to transform social and environmental standards in the fashion industry. Teaching consumers how to live with considerably less is critical. EthicalConsumer.org has launched its Fight-Fast-Fashion Campaign to encourage people to ditch the January sales and instead celebrate the clothes they already own. They are popularizing tips on how to extend the life of one's clothing. They also ask people to think twice before buying, encouraging them to repair, reuse and recycle what they already have.

Popular bloggers and trendsetters, such as Kristiana,[6] say that "we need to get on a different mindset about this disposable fashion idea we are so actively contributing to." She takes Primark as an example of what to avoid: "Buy in smaller quantities, buy what you NEED, buy from local artists, buy second hand or vintage." Nevertheless, as a member of the Millennial generation, she plainly admits that

I still shop more than I would like to, and feel myself getting distracted (and affected emotionally) by things I don't need. It's difficult when you're in the blogging world and you are a young, impressionable woman. It is so easy to get influenced by others and seek self-worth in acquiring the items you see on your favorite people on Instagram.(...) I want to inspire people in their styling choices, but I do not want to make people buy things they didn't know they wanted.

Even a global moral leader such as Pope Francis has voiced concern:

Since the market tends to promote extreme consumerism in an effort to sell its products, people can easily get caught up in a whirlwind of needless buying and spending. Compulsive consumerism is one example of how the techno-economic paradigm affects individuals (...). This paradigm leads people to believe that they are free as long as they have the supposed freedom to consume. But those really free are the minority who wield economic and financial power. Amid this confusion, postmodern humanity has not yet achieved a new self-awareness capable of offering guidance and direction, and this lack of identity is a source of anxiety. We have too many means and only a few insubstantial ends.

(Laudato Si': *n. 203*)

Marchant's ruminations

Marchant wondered how to approach Primark's ethical responsibility. As he said in a recent interview, "[I am] very proud of (...) my customers being able to follow the latest trends without having to spend a lot of money. We're obsessed about prices."[7] Kristiana herself reckoned that Primark "is great in many ways, especially in that it enables less wealthy families access to trendy clothing for almost no money, which is a great thing."[8]

Nonetheless, Marchant did not lose sight of imminent challenges. First, Primark had to rethink how deeply it should monitor its supply chain. The question "what should we do?" encapsulated the more basic "what is enough?" question. How far back into Primark's supply chain should one go? Bangladesh's institutional context made trust difficult, as many labor and building licenses and accreditations proved to be false in the aftermath of the collapse. Should Primark send its own architects, engineers and labor experts to check the whole ecosystem of factories that their garments may traverse in their journey to final consumers?

In addition, while it was true that they could not shrug off their ethical duties, he felt that other players may also have decisive roles in the issue. For example, a piece published in The Economist shortly after the collapse (May 4, 2013) argued that much of the blame lay with Bangladeshi governments, which had made only rudimentary attempts to enforce the national building code, especially against politically well-connected landlords.[9]

Then, Primark's margins posed additional constraints. As an analyst commented, "Primark's relatively low gross margin goes a long way towards proving

[that] it is Primark taking the impact of low prices, not the suppliers" (Critchlow and Baillie 2008). If they decided to go what some vocal critics called "the right way," Primark might be forced to source its garments from other low-cost countries, such as Cambodia or Vietnam. Should they take the high road and wait for their competitors to follow? This was a difficult move that could put them out of business, as margins were not ample.

Finally, there are environmental and moral concerns. Should Primark take the lead in addressing environmental improvements in the production and distribution of clothing? Is a largely diffused consumerist culture really harming young people in developed countries? Is Primark responsible for it? Should they do anything about it? And if so, what?

About to enter Paddington Station, Marchant saw his wife and two children. During his thirty-minute journey, Marchant had sifted through different ideas and exchanges in the meeting, but the hardest leg of the process now stood before him; he had to begin drafting a road map the coming Monday. The risk of Primark's model being out of sync with society in the short term was high. Factors such as rising purchasing power, growing interest in quality, serious social concerns about the environment and a cultural turn towards simpler, less materialistic lifestyles spelled trouble. Compounding these, Marchant worried about how to maintain his pricing strategy while addressing all these challenges.

Guide questions

1 How does Marchant define "value creation" at Primark?
2 What kind of goods (and evils) and virtues (and flaws) is Primark promoting among customers, employees and society?
3 Do you think Primark is promoting integral human and social flourishing? Or, in contrast, does Primark's business model foster rampant consumerism?
4 What initiatives could Marchant take to improve Primark's empathy with customers' concerns and trustworthiness? For instance, should Primark launch its own kind of Conscious Collection? Or should it be transparent about its dealings with contractors and suppliers? To what extent should Marchant take into account complaints from NGOs and civic associations? What are the limits of Primark's reach?
5 Is Primark's model ethically sustainable in terms of CST principles (human dignity, the common good, the universal destination of goods, subsidiarity, solidarity)?

Notes

1 In 1982, in the wake of the death of seven people who had taken cyanide-laced capsules of Extra Strength Tylenol, Johnson & Johnson recalled 31 million bottles of Tylenol capsules from stores and replaced them with tablets. The contrary case is found in Nestlé's handling of its infant formula crisis in Africa. By peddling on the glamour of infant formula—linked with a Western way of life–as opposed to

breastfeeding, Nestlé hooked numerous emerging-economy mothers to their product. Given their financial constraints, mothers would dilute the formula with as much as three times the recommended amount of water, which led to malnutrition. When this situation was brought to public attention, Nestlé, instead of making amendments, sued the publications attacking the company.

2 Based partially on iese m-1249-e case study, 'Primark: £10? Ooh that's expensive!' written by professors Julián Villanueva and José Luis Nueno, with the research assistantship of Julie Ziskind.

3 Reuters: 'At least 120 killed in a factory fire in Bangladesh'. Dacca, 25/11/2012.

4 'Bangladesh building collapse death toll over 800'. *BBC News*. 8 May 2013.

5 www.hm.com/ma/magazine/culture/h-m-inside/2016/03/m_i_a-and-h_m-will-recycle-your-old-clothes (Accessed September 27, 2017).

6 www.styledbykristiana.com/2016/03/consumerism-why-i-avoid-primark.html (Accessed March 17, 2017).

7 www.modaes.es/back-stage/20151116/paul-marchant-primark-estamos-atrayendo-a-nuevos-consumidores-a-la-moda-pero-tambien-llevandonos-de-nuestros-competidores.html (Accessed March 17, 2017).

8 www.styledbykristiana.com/2016/03/consumerism-why-i-avoid-primark.html (Accessed March 14, 2017).

9 www.economist.com/news/leaders/21577067-gruesome-accident-should-make-all-bosses-think-harder-about-what-behaving-responsibly (Accessed September 27, 2017).

References

Abela, A.V. 2007, 'The price of freedom: Consumerism and liberty in secular research and Catholic Teaching', *Journal of Markets and Morality*, 10(1): 7–25.

Alam, K. 2008, 'Fashion Victims II', In *War on Want*. (https://waronwant.org/sites/default/files/Fashion%20Victims%20II.pdf, Accessed November 28, 2017).

American Marketing Association. 2016, 'Dictionary', *Definition of marketing*. (www.ama.org/resources/Pages/Dictionary.aspx?dLetter=M, Accessed November 21, 2016).

American Marketing Association. 2016, 'Statement of ethics', *Ethical values*. (www.ama.org/AboutAMA/Pages/Statement-of-Ethics.aspx, Accessed November 21, 2016).

Applbaum, K. 2004, *The marketing era. From professional practice to global provisioning*, London: Routledge.

Aristotle. 1985, *Nicomachean ethics* (Irwin, T., trans.), Indianapolis: Hackett Publishers.

Aristotle. 1990, *The politics* (Everson, S., ed.), Cambridge: Cambridge University Press.

Critchlow, A. and Baillie, J. 2008, 'Associated British Foods: Primark – low margins could get lower', *Société Générale Cross Asset Research*, 16 October.

Finn, D. 2012, 'Human work in Catholic social thought', *American Journal of Economics and Sociology*, 71(4): 874–885.

Gaski, J.F. 2013, 'To serve man: A marketing manifesto (and an article that should not have been necessary)', *Journal of Public Policy & Marketing*, 32(1): 6–17.

Goodpaster, K.E. 2011, 'Goods that are truly good and services that truly serve: Reflections on "Caritas in Veritate"', *Journal of Business Ethics*, 100(1): 9–16.

Hartman, C.L. and Beck-Dudley, C.L. 1999, 'Marketing strategies and the search for virtue: A case analysis of the body shop', *International Journal of Business Ethics*, 20(3): 249–263.

Hartman, E. 2013, *Virtue in business: Conversations with Aristotle*, Cambridge: Cambridge University Press.

Isenwater, J. and Thompson, H. 2010, 'All about Primark', *Deutsche Bank Global Markets Research*, 13 April.

Klein, T.A. and Laczniak, G.R. 2013, 'Implications of Caritas in Veritate for marketing and business ethics', *Journal of Business Ethics*, 112(4): 641–651.

Kotler, P. and Keller, K. 2009, *Marketing management*, London: Pearson Education Limited.

Laczniak, G.R., Klein, T.A. and Murphy, P.E. 2014, 'Caritas in Veritate. Updating Catholic Social Teaching for responsible marketing strategy', in P.E. Murphy and J.F. Sherry (eds.), *Marketing and the common good: Essays from Notre Dame on societal impact,* London: Routledge, 105–118.

Lago, L., Martínez-de-Albéniz, V., Moscoso, P. and Vall, A. 2014, 'The role of quick response in accelerating sales of fashion goods', in T.M. Choi (ed.), *Analytical modeling research in fashion business*, Springer: Singapore, 51–78.

MacIntyre, A. 2007, *After virtue* (3rd ed.), London: Duckworth.

McKinsey & Co. 2017, *The state of fashion*. (https://images.businessoffashion.com/site/uploads/2016/11/The_State_of_Fashion_2017.pdf, Accessed March 17, 2017).

Mick, D.G., Pettigrew, S., Pechmann, C.C. and Ozanne, J.L. (Eds.) 2012, *Transformative consumer research for personal and collective well-being*, London: Routledge.

Mish, J. and Miller, A. 2014, 'Marketing's contributions to a sustainable society', in P.E. Murphy and J.F. Sherry, (eds.), *Marketing and the common good: Essays from Notre Dame on societal impact,* London: Routledge, 153–174.

Mohsin, S. 2009, 'How Primark thrives in the downturn', *Business Week Online*, 22 April.

Murphy, P.E. 1999, 'Character and virtue ethics in international marketing: An agenda for managers, researchers and educators', *Journal of Business Ethics*, 18(1): 107–124.

Murphy, P.E. and Sherry, J.F. 2014, *Marketing and the common good: Essays from Notre Dame on societal impact*, London: Routledge.

Murphy, P.E., Laczniak, G.R. and Harris, F. 2016, *Ethics in marketing: International cases and perspectives*, London: Routledge.

Scally, D. 2010, 'The true cost of low prices', *The Irish Times*, 16 January.

Sison, A.J.G., Ferrero, I. and Guitián, G. 2016, 'Human dignity and the dignity of work: Insights from Catholic Social Teaching', *Business Ethics Quarterly*, 26(4): 503–528.

Weber, J.A. 2014, 'Ethics in selling', in P.E. Murphy and J.F. Sherry (eds.), *Marketing and the common good: Essays from Notre Dame on societal impact*, London: Routledge, pp. 267–280.

Wicker, A. 2016, 'Fast fashion is creating an environmental crisis', *Newsweek*, 9 January.

Wilkie, W.L. and Moore, E.S. 1999, 'Marketing's contributions to society', *The Journal of Marketing,* 63: 198–218.

Zain Al-Mahmoud, S. 2014, 'Safety groups agree on standards for Bangladesh garment factories', *The Wall Street Journal*, 19 November.

6

VIRTUES AND THE COMMON GOOD IN HUMAN RESOURCE MANAGEMENT

Javier Pinto-Garay and María José Bosch

Learning objectives

In this chapter, we will:

- Explain fostering virtuous work among employees as the guiding moral principle of HR managers.
- Present virtuous work as one that prioritizes excellence and intrinsic motivation over effectiveness and extrinsic motivation, and is, at the same time, meaningful and engaging.
- Show how to create an organizational culture or corporate *ethos* that is supportive of virtuous work.

The behavior of the new generation of employees—the so-called millennials—reflects a new social dilemma about the value and meaning of work. These young professionals do not view their job as a long-term project and their aim is usually not to rise through the company's hierarchy, as it was with the previous generation. Instead, they value horizontal organizations, team work and co-working facilities. This has important consequences on personnel turnover and long-term human capital development.

Another important difference between millennials and other generations is that, in choosing a job, they give priority to work-life balance. According to McCarthy (2016), they give more importance to this balance than to future career opportunities. They measure compensation not only in monetary terms, but also in time for the family, leisure, sports, travel and so on. This poses a challenge for companies to attract and retain talent. To be attractive to this generation, they must change their culture. For Benson (2016), work policies must be more flexible because millennials have broader societal concerns; they want more frequent communication with their boss; they like to research and develop their own ideas; and they expect to work in communities bound together by mutual interests and passion, not structured hierarchies.

Millennials, like any other generation, have a purpose and a way of understanding the meaning of work. For them, it is mostly related with achieving more freedom and having new experiences. The challenge for the HR manager is to achieve a fit between the expectations of these professionals and what the firm demands in terms of efficient production, quality service and good work in general.

HR managers are tasked with overseeing HR practices and aligning them with corporate strategy. Over and beyond this, virtue-oriented HR managers will also try their best to foster virtuous work in the organization. We shall now explain each of these elements.

HR practices refer to basic responsibilities including selection, recruitment, staffing, promotion, dismissal and compensation. Training is also important, but HR managers are not always responsible for this, particularly in small- and mid-sized enterprises (SMEs). Similarly, they may not be responsible for issues related to organizational culture and behavior, labor relations and unions or workplace health and safety.

HR strategies refer to goals involving other departments that have an impact on the whole organization in productivity, business strategy, organizational costs, services and marketing. HR managers add value to the organization when they understand how the business operates and adapt to those conditions. Understanding its financial, strategic, technological and organizational capabilities, they can play a valuable role in strategic discussions (Becker, Huselid and Ulrich 2001). This implies that they should (1) provide the firm with the necessary personnel; (2) provide services for employees; (3) translate business strategies into HR priorities; and (4) synchronize the non-strategic goals such as reducing costs, improving efficiency and seeking better ways of doing things with the rest of the organisation (Ulrich 2013).

There is a moral guiding principle to HR practices and strategic responsibilities. This principle orients standards in HR practices, such as personnel assessment methods (enabling the firm to select the best candidates as regards compliance and accountability), training, reinforcing good behavior, introducing codes of conduct and preventing malpractice (fraud, mobbing, harassment and other illegal behaviors at work). Compensation also has an ethical dimension as firms ought to take employee welfare into account, not only paying market salaries, but also considering personal or family situations. The moral guiding principle in HR likewise refers to the responsibility for virtuous work. HR managerial responsibilities include fostering personnel development, thriving and fulfillment through work.

This chapter will proceed to explain virtuous work and how HR managers can contribute to it as follows:

i   The Aristotelian contribution: action (*praxis*) over production (*poiesis*).
ii MacIntyre's contribution: excellence over effectiveness and intrinsic motivation over extrinsic motivation. "Meaningful work" and "engaging work."
iii CST and a supportive organizational culture or *ethos*.

1. Elements and conditions of virtuous work

Aristotle: action (praxis) over production (poiesis)

Aristotle explains work or any productive activity as *poiesis*, whose end or goal is to bring about an object external to the agent (Aristotle, Physics: 202a13-b29). Think of constructing a house, for instance. For this we need, besides the materials found in nature, such as wood or iron, the work of carpenters. The purpose of the carpenters' activity is to build a house, an external object that exists independently of them. Work as *poiesis* refers primarily to the productive activity carried out by artisans, such as potters, blacksmiths or shoemakers.

Understanding work exclusively as *poiesis*, however, proves very inadequate for modern society. First, because we no longer limit work or production to manual labor as in ancient times. Second, because nowadays, everyone works or is expected to work. Production is not confined anymore to a specific social class of laborers or servants. Third, and most importantly, we have increasingly realized that what adds most value to work is not the physical force expended, but the knowledge employed in production. That knowledge goes far beyond manual or technical skills, hinting at something more abstract, intellectual and creative.

At this stage, introducing the Aristotelian category of *praxis* (action) becomes useful. *Praxis* refers to human activities whose end or goal is internal to agents (Nicomachean Ethics, henceforth NE 1149b). Take the case of someone who, with no ulterior motive, seeks to learn non-Euclidean geometry. That person's activity need not result in any external object or product. What it brings about is new or increased knowledge that remains or is internal to the agent.

We need *praxis*, therefore, to account for the intangible results of human activities, including work or production. *Praxis* alludes to the information, knowledge, skills, habits and so forth that work generates in individuals. Insofar as these are personal attributes or qualities, they are ethically more valuable than the external objects produced through *poiesis*. The results of *praxis* are inseparable from the workers or agents, unlike those of *poiesis*. A better understanding of work as the productive activity in which human beings characteristically engage combines the Aristotelian notions of *poiesis* and *praxis*.

The Aristotelian distinction between poiesis and praxis is useful for HR managers to orient practices more towards personal development than the mere improvement of objects or systems. Indeed, if *praxis* highlights the acquisition of knowledge, experience, skills and habits at work, investments in employee training and education become more important than those in infrastructure and equipment, which are the results of *poiesis*. Better still, improvements in the physical plant matter only to the extent they help employees work better, not the other way around.

- The *praxis/poiesis* distinction affects HR Strategic Responsibilities as well. HR managers are not mere internal workforce suppliers to different departments, but direct contributors to optimum firm performance by developing employee skills, knowledge and attitudes above all.

2. MacIntyre: excellence over effectiveness and intrinsic motivation over extrinsic motivation. "Meaningful work" and "engaging work"

MacIntyre's contribution to ethical HR management hinges on the distinction he makes between "practices" and "institutions" (Macintyre 1981). By "practices," he means complex, social activities that pursue goods or objectives internal to the activities themselves, very much like the Aristotelian *praxis* (MacIntyre 1981). MacIntyrean institutions, on the other hand, seek goods or objectives that are external to activities and could therefore be obtained in more than one way (MacIntyre 1981). They are similar to Aristotle's *poiesis*. Consequently, standards of excellence in practices are internal, those of institutions, external. And while practices are occasions for cooperation or collaboration among agents, institutions encourage competition among them.

Let us illustrate this by means of examples. Study, the cultivation of knowledge for itself, corresponds to a MacIntyrean practice. Knowledge is internal, in the sense that it cannot be separated from the activity of study or learning. Judging the excellence or quality of knowledge, in terms of validity, depth, breadth, scope and so forth, is for the already learned, not the uninitiated. And study or learning does not take place in a void. Rather, students learn not only by themselves, but also through the cooperation of teachers and fellow students. Brick-making, especially on an industrial scale, displays the features of MacIntyrean institutions. Bricks are, of course, external to brick-makers. They could be even made by machines in huge brick factories. In such cases, the objective often is not so much the making of bricks, but the making of money. More important than excellence, then, are effectiveness and efficiency, combined under the managerial notion of "productivity." And among several brick factories, what we expect to find, rather than cooperation, is competition for technologies, markets and profits.

The ethical value of work is promoted insofar as it instantiates a MacIntyrean practice instead of an institution. This ought to be the virtue and common good-oriented HR manager's main concern.

We can see this through the experience of Southwest Airlines. The People Department for Southwest Airlines—a company well known for its good HR practices and also for its very high standards of productivity and efficiency—declares the following corporate mission:

> Recognizing that our people are the competitive advantage, we deliver the resources and services to prepare our people to be winners, to support the growth and profitability of the company, while preserving the values and special culture of Southwest Airlines.
>
> *(O'Reilly and Pfeffer 1995)*

Southwest Airlines offers employees the necessary conditions to perform productive and profitable work, turning every single job into an opportunity for personal development, which is a good of excellence. Excellence, "becoming winners," is achieved when employees improve personally while meeting the productivity and profitability goals of the company. Southwest Airlines promotes both intrinsic goods and extrinsic goods, but gives more importance to the former than the latter, as MacIntyre would suggest.

Compare this with managing one's job or career in accordance with what is found in most LinkedIn postings. This social network tends to give more value to an instrumental dimension of people's careers, when it prioritizes our ambition of getting a better job opportunity through pay, personal prestige and professional status. Such activity does not consider the internal good of work, and it ignores the possibility that a present job can be satisfactory and fulfilling. LinkedIn's valuation of work is almost exclusively based on pay and professional status, which are external goods from MacIntyre's perspective. This is corruptive and hardly contributes to our personal thriving.

MacIntyre's categories of practices and institutions were never meant to be exclusive of each other, however. Clearly, practices and the goods internal to them can only be sustained insofar as institutions and the external goods they pursue are available. Firms need to be productive and earn profits. However, productivity and profits in an ethically constituted and managed firm are understood as necessary means and conditions. Internal goods remain as the ultimate ends or goals of the enterprise. Work in organizations, therefore, should not be conceived as pure practices or pure institutions. Rather, both dimensions ought to be recognized in all forms of work, while always safeguarding the priority of practices over institutions.

Moreover, the distinction between practices and institutions in MacIntyre mirrors, to a large extent, that found between intrinsic and extrinsic motivations (MacIntyre 1981). Work performed with an intrinsic motivation imitates a practice, inasmuch as it seeks goods internal to the activity above all. Work done with an extrinsic motivation comes closer to an institution, since it puts money, honor, prestige, status and the like before excellence in the activity itself.

When work is performed with an intrinsic motivation, it gains in "meaning." "Meaningful work" is work done with a purpose and awareness of personal objectives, in line with one's principles and values such as self-mastery, growth, development and committed service to the common good (Fairlie 2011). "Meaning" becomes a major source of worker satisfaction. Insofar as meaningful work facilitates autonomy and participation, it likewise becomes "engaging work." "Engaging work" consists of productive activities in which workers are encouraged to exercise autonomy in decision-making, as opposed to simply executing other people's orders (Schwartz 1982; Bainbridge 1998; and Sayer 2009). Meaningful and engaging work results in a greater sense of authorship in workers. Additional responsibilities in workers are more than offset by less frustration, apathy, stress and anxiety.

- For MacIntyre, therefore, virtuous work—one that contributes to the common good—comes closer to a practice than an institution. It seeks excellence and internal goods above effectiveness and external goods. It prioritizes intrinsic motivations over extrinsic motivations. Virtuous work enhances meaning and engagement.

3. Catholic Social Teaching: an organizational culture or corporate *ethos* supportive of virtuous work

Organizations such as firms are shaped not only by the actual behavior of individuals who work in them, but also by what that behavior leaves behind, in terms of institutional knowledge, principles, values and so forth. This milieu corresponds to their unique organizational culture. In the same way that a country's culture is often defined as its shared attitudes, beliefs, customs and written and unwritten rules developed over time, the same may be said of a company. Corporate culture provides an organization its social and psychological identity or *ethos*.

Perhaps the most important overarching goal for HR managers is to create an atmosphere supportive of virtuous, meaningful and engaging work in companies. Catholic Social Teaching (CST) provides a set of guidelines to help them in this task, permitting workers to discern the good in practice and search for excellence in the exercise of their profession and the conduct of their life as a whole.

The most relevant fundamental CST principles in shaping organizational culture are: human dignity (Pontifical Council for Justice and Peace, Compendium of the Social Doctrine of the Church, henceforth CSDC: 105, 132), the common good (CSDC: 164, 165), subsidiarity (CSDC: 186) and participation (CSDC: 189).

In consonance with human dignity, HR managers ought to consider employees always as "the firm's most valuable asset" and "decisive factor of production" (CSDC 344), giving priority to them and their personal development over capital, profits or any other economic objective (Congregation for the Doctrine of the Faith 1986). In line with the principle of the common good, HR managers should bear in mind that the ultimate purpose of business and firms is to "contribute to the development of people and the human community" (CSDC 369). The reason for being of firms is the extent to which they can further the goal of human flourishing.

The principles of subsidiarity and participation go hand in hand, as both refer to the proper respect afforded to employee capacity for autonomous decision-making. Subsidiarity in the firm means providing employees assistance, training and the resources to decide for themselves (Alford and Naughton, 2001). People usually want to decide for themselves, although they may not have the know-how, habits, skills and experience to make good decisions. HR managers are responsible for preparing employees to make the right decisions. Contrary to these principles is a paternalistic management style, in which superiors always make decisions, denying workers any possibility of engagement and meaning.

The principle of participation, on the other hand, imposes on individuals the right and duty to contribute to the cultural, economic, political and social life (Vatican II, *Gaudium et Spes*, in Flannery 1996) to the best of their abilities.

Participation means acting in a responsible manner aimed to foster the common good of the organization. Responsible participation means the need to take action in favor of others.

In accordance with the aforementioned CST principles, HR managers ought to fashion an organizational culture that allows workers to thrive. That means creating an atmosphere in which workers can freely and rationally decide the right way to do the right things, aiming at the common good of the organization. When employees make decisions this way, they contribute to shaping a virtuous *ethos* for the organization.

We can see an example of how a virtuous corporate *ethos* was developed in the Manchester United soccer team under its coach, Sir Alex Ferguson. This soccer team has been one of the most successful sports firms in the past 30 years. Under Ferguson, Manchester United's culture focused on excellence. For Ferguson, his job as a manager was like that of a teacher, encouraging and inspiring people to become better. He understood the Club's role as providing players not only technical skills, but also helping them become better people, offering a chance for integral personal development. Ferguson understood his work as helping the team grow together, producing a bond and creating a spirit among members. Part of his job was to instil values in players, pushing them to always do better and never give up. Ferguson's work ethic spread throughout the Club. It became unacceptable for a player not to give his all, not to give his best. This was something that everyone in the team thought about, not in an individualistic manner, but as members of a group. Trusting one another, not letting mates down, helps build character and enhances team pride (Elberse 2012).

This corporate *ethos* turns every job position into a space for personal development. This is what putting people first in the organization means. Pfeffer and Veiga (1999) have devised a list of seven HR principles to develop a virtuous corporate *ethos*:

i   Job security: many benefits follow from this, as workers freely contribute knowledge and increase efforts to enhance productivity
ii   Selective hiring: positions are assessed on the basis of initiative, judgment, adaptability and the ability to learn
iii   Self-managed teams and decentralization: they foster accountability and responsibility for organizational success in every member of the firm
iv   High compensation contingent on organizational performance: it attracts more experienced and better prepared employees to the firm
v   Extensive training: knowledge and skills are a basic component of high performance work
vi   Reduction of status differences: high performance is based on the ability of the organization to tap the ideas, skills and efforts of all people, making them feel valued as a result
vii   Information sharing: successful firms are high-trust organizations.
   • HR managers are responsible for promoting meaningful, engaging and virtuous work through their impact on corporate culture. As we have

seen, CST provides them with resources to do this through the principles of human dignity, the common good, subsidiarity and participation.

4. Innobe aims for the big league

Entry barriers in the business consultancy sector tend to be lower than in other industries. This is particularly the case in developing countries, due to the difficulty of enforcing non-compete agreements. In such economies, the number of firms in consulting can be huge. Any professional can start his or her own company, set up a website and work from home or the nearest Starbucks Café.

Consultancies can be divided into three categories: one-person operations, co-working professionals and consolidated firms with consultants and analysts. Owners of consolidated firms have management responsibilities, doubling as HR managers.

Such firms face an important risk: the consultants they hire are potential competitors. This poses a dilemma between the need to develop the firm's human capital and the risk of developing a potential competitor.

The firm's owner and HR manager decides who gets hired, how they get paid and the professional training they receive. This is the case of *Innobe Consulting*,[1] a Chilean firm that provides innovative solutions for human resource management to the private and public sectors in Chile, Peru, Colombia and Mexico.

Innobe was founded in 2000 in Chile. Although one of Latin America's most competitive economies, Chile performs poorly on innovation and R&D, ranking 85th and 92nd, respectively, in the World Economic Forum's Global Competitiveness Report 2015–2016. This is an important disadvantage for a country that needs to diversify the drivers of economic growth, but also potentially a great opportunity for Innobe.

Innobe was founded by its current owner and manager, John, and has developed 45 original innovation programs. Over the course of 15 years, it has worked with several dozen clients in the private and public sectors of different Latin American countries, designed more than 150 innovation processes, organized workshops for more than 31,000 employees and promoted more than 15,600 innovation ideas in firms with a budget of more than US$90 million. According to John, these figures could double over the next two to three years. For John, 2016 was an important year in turning Innobe into a large consulting firm.

Although Innobe programs offer standardized services, they have a real impact on companies when the leading consultant is capable of understanding the client's circumstances (organizational structures, culture or industry, among others). Its business model is based not only on successful programs but also, and more importantly, on the consultant's skill in adapting each program to the client.

All Innobe's programs are built using Innovation Management Office (IMO), an original methodology designed by John, which is based on strategic pillars through which to achieve high standard results.

Innobe work style

From the beginning, John wanted to develop a team with a multidisciplinary approach. This meant that, in terms of formal education, consultants were only required to have a university degree. In addition, John always tried to develop teams with consultants from different backgrounds. As a result, a professional qualification in innovation was not a requirement of the selection process; formal education in innovation was an advantage but never a condition.

Training programs in innovation for the consultants, tailored to each professional, were always very important for John, not only as a means of increasing sales but also as a means of human development through work.

With this in mind, he has developed his firm in accordance with a clear philosophy of work that can be summarized as follows:

Work is an opportunity for personal development and satisfaction. This means that Innobe views work as an opportunity for personal growth. It tends to hire professionals with less experience, but high development potential, usually under 30 years of age. Moreover, the type of university degree they hold does not matter much and its consulting teams are formed by engineers, lawyers, psychologists and graphic designers, among others, but, regardless of their original profession, they must share an interest in and passion for innovation.

Personal growth means not only professional development but also personal quality of life. With this in mind, Innobe seeks to hire professionals who value a long-term project of personal development that implies hard work, but never at the expense of personal and family life. It offers flexible work schedules, part-time work for mothers with newborn children, and sick-child benefits for female consultants.

The company's work process is based on the same innovation policies it offers clients. It is therefore crucial to set aside time for research in order to incorporate new ideas for management innovation programs at Innobe itself. This process includes team work and weekly meetings, known as "Innobe Mondays," at which new ideas are evaluated.

From John's perspective, consulting professionals need to understand that their work is not only about providing a sound methodology for the formulation of new ideas, but rather about believing that everyone has the potential to come up with new ideas for improving a business. Consultants should always bear in mind that innovation is not only possible but also crucial for every company. The consulting process is not only about selling technical tools to develop new ideas, but also about promoting the importance of every member of the client's firm in providing new ideas cooperatively with colleagues. An important part of the consultant's job is to promote the creation of solutions by the whole community of workers, not just the top of the hierarchy, in which every employee, no matter his or her position, has the *right* and the *potential* to innovate.

With this motto in mind, John has developed two important tools for the consulting process. The first is the "ideas workshops" in which every member of the client's firm participates in a bid to develop new ideas and solutions. The second is a technological platform, known as "Innovation Facebook," through which every employee can propose ideas and solutions, which can be seen and commented on by every member of the firm.

Finally, for John, it is essential that consultants focus on achieving results. The value of their work lies not only in the process or in changing cultures, but also in the tangible results for the client in terms of productivity and economic performance. This is in line with the idea that any firm needs to change in order to survive in a competitive market. To just keep doing the same is a death sentence for any company. Innovation is not only important but also an imperative for every organization.

Innobe today

At present, Innobe has 14 full-time consultants, five associate consultants, an accounting and finance manager, and an IT manager, besides the founder who leads the company. Full-time consultants have three areas of work: project management, innovation consulting or design and communications management. Each consultant forms a team for a particular project and roles change according to the project. In one project, a consultant may act as the innovation consultant and, in another, as the design and communications manager. According to the founder, the firm encourages employees to form work teams in a voluntary manner, allowing consultants to choose the role they want to play in each project. There is, however, a permanent marketing team, formed by four consultants, responsible for drawing up business proposals for potential clients and closing deals.

Consultants receive a fixed salary, plus a variable income depending on the projects in which they participate. This is in line with general practices in the industry where consultants' pay usually has a fixed and a variable component. Innobe consultants can also give classes in its academic program for clients, for which they receive an additional US$80 per hour, while marketing employees receive an annual bonus if they meet their sales target.

Except for the leading position of the founder, the company has a flat organizational structure, and this has a key impact on the organization since all human relations are based on trust. It also means that there are no career or promotion policies or opportunities for increased responsibility, so consultants' aspirations take the form of increased salaries or access to training.

In the case of additional training, five consultants have been able to undertake graduate studies in innovation, financed partially by the firm. Furthermore, four consultants have been encouraged to teach classes on innovation management at different universities, with no salary discount for the time they are out of the office.

Even though the industry has low entry barriers and this firm has no policy for career mobility, turnover is very low. In 2016, 21% of employees in Chile indicated that they had changed job during the previous six months, a figure that reached 23% among 25–34-year-olds,[2] but only two people left Innobe that year. Moreover, they did so not to start their own company but, in one case, to work for a competitor and, in the other, for a university.

A difficult year

2016 was a very difficult year for Innobe in terms of personal relations and work quality. John discovered that the service provided to clients by a couple of consultants fell short of expectations. Moreover, the autonomy given to employees had opened the way to the creation of cliques that were manipulating the role of the consultants in every project. This problem, reported by one of the firm's old consultants, led John to survey client satisfaction. The results were not alarming, but neither were they encouraging. Clients perceived a deterioration in the service but, given their very good opinion of the founder's technical capacity, viewed it as something temporary. John's conclusion was that consultants had too much autonomy and were treating clients as if they were their own. This was a major concern for John because he realized that, if the situation persisted, it would eventually damage the company's growth prospects.

John did not abandon his plans for growth and decided to reformulate and formalize the consultants' performance, objectives and results. It was time to act and solve two problems: that of growing the company and of giving Innobe consultants a new role. The goal was to turn Innobe into a bigger and more professional organization. This would, in John's view, only be possible if the consultant's job were redefined and divided into two different roles: senior and junior consultants. The new Innobe would need a large team of analysts, so those consultants with more experience would take on senior positions, managing a team of analysts. Senior consultants could be evaluated not only in terms of sales and project management, but also as team managers responsible for keeping human resource costs in line with the income from each project. For John, this was the way to increase the professionalization of the company's consulting activities.

Under this strategy, Innobe would in the future hire only junior consultants whose job would be more heavily weighted towards analytical tasks. Senior consultants would lead relations with clients and serve as a bridge between their needs and junior consultants. Each senior consultant would eventually have a regular team of analysts and, depending on demand, hire temporary consultants for specific projects.

This structure implies a new vertical relation between senior consultants and the firm's other employees, and incorporates new metrics for assessing results. Moreover, in a context in which new generations of professionals are less inclined to stay in the same job for long, it has the advantage of making the loss of a junior consultant less serious. For John, turnover will cease to be a challenge in the new Innobe.

However, although this looked like a good plan, John still had some doubts. The big question was how culture would be preserved in Innobe, whilst professionalizing the consulting position and increasing profits.

With these questions in mind, John began to look for new junior consultants. One of the candidates, Mary, was very interesting. She had just graduated from the University of Chile with a joint degree in business and psychology, having taken the latter because of her interest in HR innovation processes. On graduating, she received several offers from large consulting firms to work as a junior analyst in an HR position. But, in a best-case scenario, she would only have an opportunity to innovate in HR five years into her career. A small consulting firm would, she believed, give her the opportunity to do something more than analytical work. In fact, her expectations were very high and, as she told the manager during her first interview at Innobe, she wanted to be given the task of redesigning performance evaluation for Innobe clients and take a leading role in managing relations with clients. To put it briefly, she wanted to do "exciting things" and have a real impact on other people's problems.

As John realized, she was a perfect candidate for Innobe's past structure. However, in its new form, it would have to forego candidates with a spirit of innovation, choosing instead those with demonstrated analytical skills. Was John doing the right thing? He was not sure.

Case discussion guidelines

This case highlights the importance of approaching work as a meaningful activity and the role of HR managers in developing a virtuous organizational culture. It illustrates the understanding of the different dimensions of work and how this can affect productivity and action. The case could also be used to show how HR policies and practices can contribute to thriving institutions.

Guide questions

1   Should John hire Mary?
    Mary's interview indicated that the new structure of Innobe poses some challenges.
        The instructor can ask students to identify the advantages and disadvantages of hiring Mary.
        It is important to highlight the consequences of the hiring decision. The aims include attracting talented people and growing the business.
        Specify how HR's guiding moral principle is related to HR strategy and practices.
        Differentiate between extrinsic and intrinsic motivation.
2   What are the advantages and disadvantages of the new and the old structure?
    The instructor can ask students to vote for the structure they prefer.
        Innobe works in a competitive industry where company employees are key to its success. This is also an industry with very low entry barriers and differentiation is very important. Developing intrinsic motivation is a big advantage, because extrinsic motivations are very easy to replicate.
        The company founder has played a huge role in developing its culture. He created a business model with a strong sense of meaning. His philosophy is that work should be an opportunity for personal development and satisfaction.

The concrete actions taken to develop this virtuous culture include Innobe's strategy of hiring young professionals. This company does not focus on their undergraduate degree, but rather on their interest in and passion for innovation (intrinsic motivation). It also has a training program that seeks to foster human development as well as the growth of the business.

The result of this strong sense of meaning is that Innobe can develop a service with a real impact on clients, because the leading consultant understands their circumstances and really gets involved in the process.

Innobe tries to give meaning to what its employees do and enable them to identify with their work. The instructor can go through the decision-making process.

3   How does the corporate culture impact Innobe's structure?

Innobe has a clear focus on the person and its HR policies are consistent with the owner's philosophy. However, its growth has posed a challenge. One of the problems is that the strong sense of meaning may not be reaching everyone. For some Innobe employees, their work may not be something with which they identify and they may undertake it in a merely transactional manner (extrinsic motivation).

People need to feel important and valued. The instructor can discuss how to turn work into a virtuous activity, explaining the difference between production (*poiesis*) and action (*praxis*) and how the development of intrinsic motivation affects the final outcome.

Other challenges for Innobe are respecting employee autonomy in decision-making while fostering cooperation among organization members.

4   How can the new structure maintain meaningful work for junior consultants?

This question helps students develop action plans. They should be able to identify different challenges in organizations. It is different to talk about meaningful work when people have been with a company for several years and when they are new to it.

This new structure should continue to develop both the production and the action aspects of work. Communications and the evaluation system should also take both aspects into account.

Check the recruitment process and the training program. The instructor should explain how HR systems (like recruitment, training, evaluation, compensation and so forth) are related to a virtuous corporate culture.

5   Is innovation a good of excellence?

Notes

1 Not the firm's real name as per the founder's request.
2 www.randstad.cl/sobre-nosotros/noticias/randstad-news/chile-rotacion-laboral-baja-6-puntos-en-tres-anos-influenciada-por-la-caida-en-las-proyecciones-de-crecimiento-del-pais/ (accessed September 27, 2017).

References

Alford, H.J. and Naughton, M.J. 2001, *Managing as if faith mattered*, Notre Dame, IN: University of Notre Dame.

Aristotle. 1995, 'Nicomachean ethics', in J. Barnes (ed.), *The complete works of Aristotle*, Princeton, NJ: Princeton University Press.

Aristotle. 1995, 'Physics', in J. Barnes (ed.), *The complete works of Aristotle*, Princeton, NJ: Princeton University Press.

Aristotle. 1995, 'Politics', in J. Barnes (ed.), *The complete works of Aristotle*, Princeton, NJ: Princeton University Press.

Bainbridge, S.M. 1998, 'Corporate decision making and the moral rights of employees: Participatory management and natural law', *Villanova Law Review*, 43(4), 43–741.

Becker, B.E., Huselid, M.A. and Ulrich, D. 2001, *The HR scorecard: Linking people, strategy, and performance*, Boston, MA: Harvard Business Press.

Benson, T. 2016, 'Motivating millennials takes more than flexible work policies', *Harvard Business Review*, 11 February.

Congregation for the Doctrine of the Faith. 1986, *Instruction on Christian freedom and liberation, "Libertatis conscientia"*.

Elberse, A. and Dye, T. 2012, 'Sir Alex Ferguson: Managing Manchester United', *Harvard Business School—Business Case*, 9-513-051; 20 September, 1–25.

Fairlie, P. 2011, 'Meaningful work, employee engagement, and other key employee outcomes: Implications for human resource development', *Advances in Developing Human Resources*, 13(4): 508–525.

Flannery, A. (Ed.) 1996, *Vatican Council II: Constitutions, decrees, declarations: The basic sixteen documents*, Northport, NY: Costello.

Macintyre, A. 1981, *After virtue*, Notre Dame, IN: University of Notre Dame Press.

McCarthy, N. 2016, 'Millennials place work/life balance before career progression', *Forbes*, 11 May.

O'Reilly, C.A. and Pfeffer, J. 1995, *Southwest Airlines: Using human resources for competitive advantage*, Stanford University, CA: Graduate School of Business.

Pfeffer, J. and Veiga, J.F. 1999, 'Putting people first for organizational success', *The Academy of Management Executive*, 13(2): 37–48.

Pontifical Council for Justice and Peace. 2004, *Compendium of the social doctrine of the church*, Vatican City: Libreria Editrice Vaticana.

Sayer, A. 2009, 'Contributive justice and meaningful work', *Res Publica*, 15(1): 1–16.

Schwartz, A. 1982, 'Meaningful work', *Ethics*, 92(4): 634–646.

Ulrich, D. 2013, *Human resource champions: The next agenda for adding value and delivering results*, Boston, MA: Harvard Business Press.

7

VIRTUES AND COMMON GOOD IN CORPORATE LEGAL PRACTICE

Kemi Ogunyemi and J. Brooke Hamilton, III

Learning objectives

In this chapter, we shall:

- Describe the societal purposes of the legal function and how it relates to the purposes for which businesses operate and individuals live their lives.
- Describe where legal compliance and ethics are located in the organizational structure of the firm and what activities are needed to carry them out.
- Discuss how legal compliance and ethics activities fit within the Aristotelian epistemic architecture.
- Explore how corporate legal practitioners fulfill MacIntyre's requirements for the virtues in three steps:
  1 showing how practices affirm and promote virtue
  2 demonstrating how practices fit within the context of individual lives and roles
  3 arguing that virtuous lives enable the development of the legal profession and community

- Discuss how legal compliance and ethics practices could be exercised in accordance with the principles of Catholic Social Teaching (CST).
- Illustrate the concrete virtues demanded in the legal compliance and ethics functions through three mini-case studies.

1. The common good and the purpose of law and ethics

The common good includes "all those social conditions which favor the attainment of the full human potential" (John XXIII, *Mater et Magistra* (MeM) 1961: 65). One of the tools to maintain the common goods of security and peace is human law. Governments use laws to protect peace and order, distribute duties and regulate their enforcement, and defend human rights. Despite errors caused by unjust and bad laws, laws generally achieve the aim of maintaining order and equity. The foundation for all law is the recognition of and respect for the dignity of the human person (Vatican II, *Gaudium et Spes* (GeS): 17).

Ethics is a less formalized system than the law. In relation to the law, ethics can be described as a set of values, rules, principles, obligations and concerns that guide behavior. These guides are adopted by societies and individuals because they allow people to live and work together in complex social settings and pursue common and individual interests (Haidt 2007; Tenbrunsel and Smith-Crowe 2008). Ethics connects us with others and guides and constrains our actions so that we can live happy lives. Laws aim to preserve a minimum of ethical behavior to facilitate and enrich human community. Ethics reaches where the law does not.

Rather than being created, interpreted and enforced by governments, as is the case with the law, ethical guides can involve religious, societal, group and individual sources and sanctions. Though ethical guidelines are generally accepted as essential to orderly functioning, the consensus in understanding what they are could, at times, be erroneous. This could prompt individuals to dissent from the consensus on what is right or wrong. Heroes such as Mahatma Gandhi and Martin Luther King Jr. dissented in favor of the common good to bring about change in the consensus, while villains such as Adolph Hitler dissented against the common good and are rejected as ethical exemplars.

Persons and organizations who benefit from legal and ethical protections for their dignity and well-being should recognize their obligation to follow and promote the law and ethics for the good of others as well. The law and ethics are not ends in themselves but means to achieve a virtuous life—one that promotes the best in human beings.

An economic organization can aim to insure compliance with the law and ethics because that makes business sense. Following the law and being ethical promote stakeholder loyalty, insure a good reputation and minimize exposure to litigation. The organization can also aim to enable creative ethical behavior to promote stakeholder flourishing (Mackey and Sisodia 2013).

"Compliance" protects the organization from employees' illegal and unethical behavior, while "ethics" promotes excellence in their behavior. Being conscious of this distinction enables the organization to work more effectively towards both (Sharp Paine 1994).

In some organizations, the legal function is responsible for both ethics and compliance. In others, ethics is located in a separate ethics office or in the audit office, reporting directly to the Board of Directors. Working towards training in and fostering ethical behavior is one way to prevent unethical behavior. Establishing compliance measures also helps prevention, but it goes beyond deterrence to detect and punish unethical behavior.

a. The law and virtue ethics

On the surface, the ethical theory that appears to resonate most with the concept of law is deontology. Yet, the other two main theories, virtue ethics and utilitarianism, also have a relationship to the use of laws. Virtues might be identified from the point of view of social duties (Homer), from the point of view of man striving to flourish by achieving his deepest purpose (Aristotle, Aquinas and CST) or from the point of view of man seeing the utility of certain ways of acting (Franklin) (MacIntyre 1982). In all three cases, law is a tool to be bent towards an end. When the end is the flourishing of man, the law is better oriented towards serving humanity.

As will be discussed as follows, especially in the section on CST, the law is meant to serve the common good. Individuals and corporations create and use the law for this purpose, by their votes, lobbying and campaign contributions. Non-virtuous persons are unlikely, as individuals or as officers of the corporation, to create laws that serve the common good.

Because they aim to promote the common good, laws should ensure fairness reigns and due consideration is given to what can be demanded or legislated universally. The law is not simply for one individual's happiness or one company or industry's profits but for human flourishing in general.

Pointing to the consequences of obeying the law or not emphasizes its utilitarian aspect and offers reasons for ethical behavior based on the best outcomes for all affected. Laws cannot cover every eventuality, however, and there can be errors in their creation or application. A law might be erroneous in its very substance because it enjoins some intrinsically evil action. In such a case, no one is bound to follow. On the other hand, a law might still be erroneous, even if what it enjoins is not intrinsically evil. In either case, it could be called a bad law. In the case of the second type of bad law, a person is not expected to follow, while using legitimate channels to address its shortcomings. The benefits of obeying the law do not always outweigh the costs to the individual or to the community constituted by the corporation. It may be difficult to assess how paying the correct tax when the regulator can be bribed so that one gets away with paying less is better than limiting the corporation's tax duties. The preservation of the common good in such a situation may depend to a large extent on the character (virtue) of the individual or individuals in corporations.

Virtue ethics enjoins the virtuous man to obey the law in the interest of the common good and to strive to make good laws. The person would be guided by law to cooperate with others to create external goods and distribute them fairly. This means giving equals an equal share and unequals (because they work harder, achieve more or need more for example) unequal shares. The discipline that comes from obeying the law promotes a number of internal goods as well— justice, fortitude, temperance, equanimity and so forth.

b. The law and the virtuous person

The law is a guide and a support for the virtuous person. If it has been created by virtuous persons, it is likely to be a good tool to facilitate the path to virtue for individuals. The law shows where to tread and imposes limits; it may also establish the consequences of trespassing boundaries. The law protects everyone's freedom by curtailing each one's freedom. This limitation of freedom is interpreted by virtue ethics within the Catholic tradition (Grisez and Shaw 1988; Grisez 2001) as a perfection of freedom when persons act virtuously. Freedom is seen as a hierarchy, with physical freedom at the base, psychological freedom (choice) at the middle and moral freedom or virtue at the top. Freedom is not really curtailed, but perfected in the higher level because the person constrains him or herself by choosing to do what is legally required and ethical.

The law does many things that, given time, the person would arrive at doing individually. The law saves citizens time and effort. If organizations are places where human beings are degraded or dehumanized, those organizations are thereby illegitimated. Corporations are only legitimate if they encourage the flourishing of the persons working in them and work for the common good (MeM: 65 and 91).

When a corporation engages lawyers in the compliance function, these professionals enter into a fiduciary relationship with the corporation. Like some other officers of the company, they are specially trusted to always act in the best interests of the organization. Due to that trust, they are given legal power over the resources of the company. They act on behalf of the company in interactions with other employees and with external entities with which the organization relates. Fiduciary obligations are expected to be carried out with the highest standard of care, and a lawyer who places personal interest over that of the corporation would have breached this duty. Thus, the lawyer who enters into the compliance function of a corporation is freely committing him or herself to work with that corporation's efforts towards the common good and human flourishing.

Within a corporation striving for an ethical culture in pursuit of the common good, both the legal perspectives (laws, policies, processes, procedures, sanctions) and moral perspectives (ethics, virtue, character-building, policies and processes rewarding good behavior, and good example) are essential. Both approaches work hand in hand (Sharp Paine 1994). To understand how organizations can encourage virtue, it is important to revisit the distinction between a compliance orientation and an integrity or values orientation (Sharp Paine 1994). Compliance aims to guarantee conformity with externally imposed standards, primarily the law and company policies. Efforts to prevent criminal misconduct include education regarding what is required or proscribed, limiting choices by employees based on rule-specified actions, vigorous auditing, controls and penalties. The behavioral assumption is that employees are autonomous and look out for their own self-interest. The goal of compliance programs is to prevent, detect and punish legal violations. Many organizations, hoping to take advantage of the 1991 US Federal Sentencing Guidelines for companies, instituted compliance-based programs with the seven elements described in the law (Sharp Paine 1994; Driscoll et al. 1998). The reduced fines for violations and the benefits demonstrated to follow from a strong ethics and compliance culture also occasioned the creation of a whole industry of compliance services providers as well as compliance and ethics officer associations such as the Ethics & Compliance Initiative (www.ethics.org).[1]

While essential, a compliance program is not enough to engage employees in the creative use of moral imagination (Sharp Paine 1994; Werhane 1999) or to sustain a culture that promotes excellence in employees rather than the self-interested management of one's own career (Jackall 1988). It is also important to independently promote ethics in businesses. Even when the legal compliance function is responsible for promoting ethics, it is more effective to use the two-pronged approach, rather than expect to achieve ethics by pushing compliance or compliance by pushing ethics. Organizations should distinguish the compliance activities that target the prevention of criminal misconduct and the ethics or integrity activities that foster responsible conduct. The ECI's Principles and Practices of High-Quality Ethics & Compliance Programs is a good place to begin (www.ethics.org/research/hqp-standards/blue-ribbon).

- Law and ethics provide guidance for how individuals should live a virtuous life that promotes the best in humans. Economic organizations follow this guidance to provide benefits for themselves and for the good of those they affect, thereby promoting their individual good and the common good. They do this both by compliance functions and policies that ensure that employees follow the law and ethics programs promoting ethical choices and virtuous behavior.

2. Aristotelian perspectives into the legal function

Law is as old as the oldest human societies. For the Greeks, law was a guide for humans to live in harmony with self and others. For the Romans, law was promulgated based on what was considered equitable, fair and just. Various civilizations have created laws to achieve some good for the community, especially when that might conflict with the good of individuals.

Aristotle taught that to understand something, we should look to the end or purpose it serves. For him, and Plato as well, the law is the voice of reason in agreement with nature to achieve an end, a good. The best way to understand the legal function in a corporation—as the counterpart to societal law—would be to look at its end—the counterpart good. This good is what gives the legal function its raison d'être in the corporation. If the good is its genuine end, then the law in the corporation must be crafted in such a way as to work towards that end; it determines the content and structure of the legal function (Lear 2009).

In a firm, human beings are helped to achieve *eudaimonia* (Lear 2009). The different functions of the organization, including the legal function, would contribute to this. Usually translated as flourishing, *eudaimonia* or holistic success as a human being includes internal and external goods, with an emphasis on the internal goods. It is in great part through acquiring the internal goods, for example, meaningfulness and virtue (Sison and Fontrodona 2012), in the course of carrying out their work, that individuals in the firm attain fulfillment as human beings. External goods such as higher salaries or better cafeteria food tend to be more instrumental and mediate than the internal. While they contribute to happiness, they are further away from *eudaimonia* in terms of what is really important for human beings to fulfill their purpose. The priority of internal goods over external goods is also rooted in their orientation towards the common good. Internal goods tend to work towards the good of the whole community, while external goods tend to engender friction and competition since, by nature, they need to be distributed among individuals (MacIntyre 1982).

While internal goods are worth choosing as constituents of happiness, external goods derive their worth from being instrumental to happiness and aiding virtuous action (Lear 2009). Virtuous action is essential, since the *eudaimonia* ultimately entails living in a way proper of *eudaimon* (Gavin 2006, 2009). For Aristotle, the good in question is not the good of one or several individuals, but the good of the human being (Kraut 2006). Virtue, according to Aristotle, is part of what constitutes *eudaimonia*, so human beings should attain virtue not only because virtue can be instrumental for other goods, but because virtue is part of what fulfills individuals and makes them flourish. Law, on the other hand, is attractive only because it supports virtue and serves other goods.

Thus, law, for Aristotle, is a tool to achieve universal justice, the *eudaimonia* of the community for which it is promulgated. It is meant to be obeyed. Aristotle acknowledges that laws may have deficiencies, although he is not too clear about the issues raised by laws that are mistaken in their ordination to *eudaimonia*, either because the lawmakers are mistaken in regard to *eudaimonia* or in the way to achieve it (Young 2009).

According to Aristotle, the core mission of economy is the moderation of scarcity (Pfeffer 2016). When humanity converts that mission into one of acquisitiveness or chrematistics, then the money-making drive is alienated from the pursuit of *eudaimonia*. A concern for the common good provides grounds upon which to build solutions (Sison and Fontrodona 2012).

• Societies and firms create laws to balance the common good with the good of individuals in order to achieve *eudaimonia*, human flourishing or fulfillment. Within the firm, this flourishing depends on individuals acquiring internal goods such as meaningfulness and virtue in carrying out their work, as well as the more instrumental and mediate external goods such as higher salaries and better cafeteria food. Law is attractive because it supports virtue and is a tool to achieve justice. The end or purpose of economic activity is the moderation of scarcity that promotes flourishing, not the money-making drive that alienates individuals from pursuing fulfillment.

3. MacIntyre and the law in the corporation

For MacIntyre, the community's laws should promote human flourishing. Individuals can only truly flourish within their communities. The good of the individual should be respected while working for the good of the community; both are connected, inseparable (Garcia 2003; MacIntyre 2015). One of the marks of responsible agents, according to MacIntyre, is that they see their true good as achievable only by respecting and contributing to the common good (MacIntyre 2015).

The responsible corporation would thus be bound to respect and contribute to the common good of society, as it acts to advance the good of all stakeholders. Adherence to the law is one of the tools that help to achieve this balance between the common good and stakeholder satisfaction. The law specifies what is required—externally to the company, as government laws, policies, regulations and so forth, and internally to the company, as policies, procedures, codes and so forth, to protect the common good. The practice of law comprises a set of practices, each of which is a complex human activity, has goods internal to it and has standards of excellence by which it is measurable (MacIntyre 1982). For example, one of the measures of a lawyer's integrity is the good faith with which he or she handles whatever the company has entrusted to him or her as a fiduciary.

The legal function in the corporation focuses on ethics as well as compliance to nurture a corporate culture that facilitates ethical behavior of morally responsible agents (MacIntyre 2015). The measures established to promote an ethical culture aid the internal development of virtuous habits in agents. Measures put in place for compliance set external boundaries for the same purpose. The law helps, in some degree, to keep shareholders from a heedless drive to acquire profit for its own sake, without regard for the proper hierarchy of goods suggested by MacIntyre (2015) and Pfeffer (2016), among others.

Hence, the principles suggested by MacIntyre to solve the problems generated by the divorce of economic activity from ethical concerns (MacIntyre 2015) are achievable by using the law as a defining and restraining tool. Professionals who are part of this practice are responsible for making sure that the common good and stakeholders' good are achieved. They reach this balance by finding the good insofar as their engagement in the practice evolves. Their life as professionals practicing law can be broken down into smaller bits or practices and is influenced by the daily tasks they have to carry out and by how they live out the virtues.

Some core legal practices of lawyers within the corporation include, in no particular order:

a   the drawing up of legally binding documents within the corporation (codes, employee contracts, supplier and customer contracts and so forth.);
b   the monitoring of compliance by the corporation with the country's laws and societal and industry regulations;
c   the protection of the company and the individuals within it from litigation;
d   and providing legal advice with regard to activities that the corporation is considering undertaking.

It is the responsibility of legal practitioners to develop and keep current the requisite knowledge and skills to carry out these tasks.

Legal practitioners also need to develop attitudes proper to the attainment of their personal good and a meaningful life. In the first place, there are the virtues—the excellent ways of acting—that legal practitioners have in common with people in other practices at the generic level. Besides these, the virtues of legal practitioners in particular take on more perspective and color, specified by the achievement of the goal or good of the practice (Higgins 2003).

To get a sense of particular virtues, consider the advisory aspect of the legal function as a practice. Imagine Team A, which views their practice through a capitalist focus on the good of the firm as expressed in profitability, and Team B, whose practice is characterized by a sensitivity to the common good and to the flourishing of employees and the whole community. Team A has a shareholder and Team B a stakeholder perspective. Both teams might be asked to provide legal advice for business decision alternatives regarding where to locate a new branch in an emerging market. Team A's focus is to achieve the least cost and risk to the firm, while staying within the law and avoiding civil litigation to maximize profit. Team B, while concerned with maximizing profit, might, in addition, look at laws in more developed countries to recommend actions not strictly required by law in the country where they operate. Team B might suggest paying fair wages in that country rather than the legal minimum wage. They could suggest product quality measures unenforceable by law in a country that probably also lacks organized consumer voices and credible human rights and civil society organizations. Looking at the dearth of environmental regulation in the targeted country, Team A might see an opportunity to get away with unrestricted emission levels, while Team B might strive to match best practices in places where such emissions are regulated. Team B would take into account not only the good of the corporation but also the personal flourishing of people connected with it and the common good of all affected by its operations. The current operations of some corporate members of the UN Global Compact provide further examples of Team B behavior (www.unglobalcompact.org).

Team B would better reflect a corporation that is an Aristotelian community of practice. The persons of Team B would become better persons because of their efforts to practice responsibility in their work and contribute to the good of the community as well as of individuals. Team A might work efficiently to make more money for the company, at least in the short term. However, Team A's concept of the corporation would be lacking in some good by chasing profitability and achieving external goods for some, while destroying both internal and external goods for others (employees, customers, people living in the community and so forth.). Team B would have demonstrated greater consciousness of the common good and higher regard for human flourishing. Team A would have a "compliance only" perspective on the function of the law, while Team B would be interested in "compliance plus integrity."

TABLE 7.1 Description of the two teams

	Team A	Team B
Ethos	Conform with externally imposed standards	Conform with externally imposed standards **plus** self-govern according to chosen standards
Objective(s)	Avoid criminal misconduct and minimize the risk of prosecution	Avoid criminal misconduct and minimize the risk of prosecution **plus** enable responsible conduct
Standards	Abide by criminal and regulatory law	Abide by criminal and regulatory law **plus** integrate company values, social responsibilities, global best practices
Concerns	Protect the good of shareholders	Protect the good of shareholders while respecting the individual good of stakeholders as well as the common good of society
Goods	Safeguard profits (focus is on external goods)	Use skills and knowledge to identify, analyze and resolve risks to profits while maintaining virtue, finding meaning and achieving excellence (focus includes internal goods)
Alignment	Could have protected profits by any other means, including illegal activities	Needs to be in this practice to achieve the objectives embedded in it

Transposing some of Sharp Paine's (1994) distinctions into a description of the two teams, we could expect to have (Table 7.1):

The virtues most relevant to the work of Team B would include

- discernment—to identify all the issues in the problem under study;
- prudence—to foresee all sides to the issue and the implications of the possible actions that could be taken, as well as the recourse to advice as may be needed;
- fairness—the ability to balance the interests of the corporation with the interests of other stakeholders;
- a long-term view of the impacts of the corporation's activities on others, and so forth.

As a member of the team develops these habits, he or she becomes a more balanced and thoughtful person. This part of the good, internal to the practice, devolves on the individual himself or herself.

The cardinal virtues are developed according to their peculiar manifestations for the role:

- moderation—to call a halt when an activity of the company could be very profitable but could cause unnecessary harm to other stakeholders;

- courage—to defend the rights of individuals and of the organization, as well as defend society from the organization when necessary;
- justice—a well-developed understanding of fairness;
- and practical wisdom—to discern issues and to balance interests within and without the corporation.

By ignoring internal goods, Team A might end up not being able to flourish (MacIntyre 1982); it might become excellent at cutting costs, but that is not the actual goal. It would have missed developing the skills needed for the excellence of the practice—in this case, the provision of the best legal advice for business decisions.

The team comparison illustrates why MacIntyre sees virtues as superior to rules and duties in determining what makes for a moral life (Garcia 2003). He expects that through habits of living according to the virtues, each person is able to serve the common good of the whole community (MacIntyre 1981), and through the return to Aristotle, corporations might become places of practice in which ethics is applied. MacIntyre (1981) describes the kind of practice that supports the attainment of individual goods and the common good reflected in Team B.

Within this context, MacIntyre identifies the danger of compartmentalization. A lawyer could compartmentalize his life so that he can work "well," while being a man of bad character in other spheres. This would not fit the Aristotelian notion of good character and would not signify a virtuous person (MacIntyre 2008). It is important, therefore, to look at persons in the legal function not only with regard to one aspect of their lives, but also with regard to how they are at home or at social gatherings. The habits they develop in work should, in principle, spill over to enrich the other activities and relationships outside the workplace, since their lives are single narratives (MacIntyre 1982). This transference of virtue is true, even though the practices in each domain are different and virtues would need to be specified differently. This way, the internal goods of knowledge, meaning and virtue lead to the legal practitioner's *eudaimonia* (Higgins 2003), to the good of the community (the corporation) and to the common good (the society) according to the nature of these three domains as interdependent entities (MacIntyre 1994).

- According to MacIntyre, responsible firms achieve their true good by balancing respect for and contribution to the common good with their concern to create profits. The law specifies practices and standards for how this balance can be secured, while ethics promotes the habits individuals need to make choices to achieve it. Thus, a responsible firm might move beyond a "compliance only" approach by using the laws and environmental regulations of more developed jurisdictions to guide its operations in less developed areas. In adopting this "compliance plus integrity" practice, the firm would also foster the development of virtues necessary for the *eudaimonia* of internal and external stakeholders.

4. The legal function through the lens of Catholic Social Teaching

Catholic Social Teaching (CST), contained in scripture and church documents including papal encyclicals[2] (Klein and Laczniak 2009; Sison et al. 2016), supports the normative role of the common good as the end of the corporation, and implicitly, the legal function within it (GeS: 35 and 63; John Paul II, *Centesimus Annus* (CA) 1991: 35[3]; Abela 2001; Stabile 2005; Klein and Laczniak 2009). This common good is "the sum total of social conditions which allow people, either as groups or as individuals, to reach their fulfilment more fully and more easily" (CSDC: 164). Thus, there is a relationship between the common good of the corporation and the personal good of each individual employed by it (Sison and Fontrodona 2012). CST has been developed to identify social challenges and propose solutions that work for common good and human flourishing; this is also applicable to business (Klein and Laczniak 2009; Fremeaux and Michelson 2015). Even when the corporation may have been set up to pursue profit (financial or social), there are constraints on how it is set up and how it operates to ensure the common good and human flourishing (Pius XI, *Quadragesimo Anno* (QA) 1931: 28 and 135; John Paul II, *Laborem Exercens* (LE) 1981: 9, 12 and 17). These constraints make up the content of the law—the law in society and the law by which the corporation governs itself. Thus, the law works towards ensuring that one person's progress does not come at the cost of others (Fremeaux and Michelson 2015; Pfeffer 2016).

According to Thomas Aquinas, the law is an ordinance of reason for the common good made and promulgated by one charged with the care of the community. Thus, it presupposes reason; it has to be reasonable in the sense that it should be morally just and for the common good. Second, it should be made by a competent authority. Third, it must be officially published so that it's known to those who should obey it. Having the law moderate possible excesses of the corporation could appear contrary to another principle of CST, the principle of subsidiarity (QA: 79), which enjoins government not to intervene in spheres in which private organizations could govern themselves. However, since private organizations are, at times, conglomerations of self-interested individuals, it is necessary that there be some protection for the rest of society (MeM: 20–21, 81 and 151; GeS: 31 and 55; LE: 6 and 9). This is the reason behind the principle of subsidiarity. This protection takes the form of a legal framework within which corporations operate, and CST expects government to fulfill this purpose for the common good (LE: 17; CA: 15, 8 and 11). Government lays down the minimal laws necessary, and the corporation responds with a legal function that ensures compliance and regulates the internal matters of the organization.

CST also goes into more detail in applying Aristotelian concepts, coming up with concrete principles to guide human interaction. Yet, since the virtues (or excellences) provide the criteria for determining humanly successful action leading to *eudaimonia* (Gavin 2009), Aristotle's position is firmly in consonance with

CST. If a firm does not advance both the external goods and internal goods for a person, it is not in line with the true meaning of work and does not respect the rights of workers (Leo XIII, *Rerum Novarum* (RN) 1891: 40–42; LE: 10, 16fw). In terms of external goods that enable employees to flourish, a corporation must provide fair pay, decent working conditions including work-family conciliation policies and so forth. While as part of the internal goods, it must allow workers to act as free beings (opportunities to use their initiative and a right to unionize may be included here) and to grow in knowledge, skill, meaning and virtue through the practices in their job. It is in this later aspect of *doing* (CST following Aristotle) that the subject acquires internal goods as distinct from the external goods of the subject's *making* (Sison and Fontrodona 2013).

CST says that the corporation must enable human flourishing, and it should be judged by how it protects or undermines the life and dignity of the human person (Stabile 2005; Fremeaux and Michelson 2015) made in the image of God (Sison et al. 2016). Thus, the legal function helps to check on the corporation's activities so that it is considerate of possible effects even on those only remotely connected to it (Stabile 2005). With the legal function serving its purpose, the firm's activities tend to respect the dignity of the staff and refrain from infringing their human rights. Such a firm allows workers to participate and have a voice and to associate in smaller groups to their mutual benefit (e.g., staff cooperatives, unions and so forth), constantly orienting them through codes, policies, procedures and reward systems.

A good picture of what CST views as the role of the corporation is expressed in the word "stewardship" (RN: 22[4]; Stabile 2005), which reflects an understanding of the universal destination of goods, very much part of CST (CSDC: 171fw). "Stewardship" incorporates the ideas of an attitude (often translated into laws) that protects the physical environment, for the common good of humanity including generations to come (CSDC: 166; Benedict XVI, *Caritas in Veritate* (CiV) 2009: 50[5]; Klein and Laczniak 2009; Francis Laudato Si' (LS) 2015: 116[6]). Going beyond the law as a source of regulation for the common good to stewardship helps cover the gaps inherent in the law. The law is not perfect and may fail. It is an instrument or tool and therefore prone to error. In any case, virtue cannot actually be legislated—acts that are not free cannot be virtuous.[7] Hence, while recognizing the importance of the law and the legal function, one must also recognize the limits that can only be overcome by the striving for excellence. Recognition of the respect and consideration owed to human dignity and understanding that all goods are universally destined to human flourishing are of great import here. This is why, in promoting the compliance approach, proponents have usually emphasized that the integrity approach is even more important and that the two should be used together (Sharp Paine 1994). This is in line with the focus of virtue ethics on the agent, in contrast to looking primarily at the law or at consequences.

Particular attention needs to be given to helping workers to find ways to integrate the demands of work and family. CST emphasizes the responsibility of employers—those who work in corporations need to earn what they need to support their families and also need to have working hours that allow them the time required to build and sustain a rich family life (CA: 10^8; Guitián 2009). Responsibility for watching out for this aspect might be located in the legal and ethical compliance function, in the human resource function or in both. Responsibilities would entail fulfilling the legal minimum with regard to wages and work-family related policies (maternity and paternity leave periods, annual leave periods, working hours and so forth), as well as going beyond the minimum to find and to implement what is fair, humanly speaking, especially in countries where the regulatory infrastructure is very minimal.

Another tenet of CST is the precedence of the subjective dimension of work over the objective dimension (CSDC: 271). The legal function primarily works towards achieving this by the support given to the human resource function. Indeed, in small firms, the legal function and the human resource function often reside in the same person or team.

- CST, in scripture and church documents, supports the balance of the common good and stakeholder satisfaction as the purpose of the corporation. CST specifies social conditions needed for people to reach their fulfillment and suggests ways in which the firm can achieve this balance, respecting the constraints of law and promoting virtues.

5. Experiences from the Nigerian Bar Association

Through 24 interviews with legal and compliance professionals across a variety of industries, we seek to examine how the aforementioned ideas work in practice. A total of 85 years of corporate legal experience was under scrutiny, with interviewees coming from a variety of sectors including oil and gas, banking and other financial services, logistics, telecommunications, advertising, construction, real estate, manufacturing, energy and power, consulting, entertainment and media, and mining and exploration. The findings are presented as follows under the main themes into which they have been clustered, based on the importance and recurrence of certain concepts.

> The Corporate Legal Compliance Function: Practices for the Common Good (Interviews with Legal Counsel – members of the Nigerian Bar Association – on their Professional Practices in the Compliance Function within their Companies)

The legal function advises and guides the organization and its people such that they do not run afoul of the law.

> We have to make sure that every transaction and everything that we do are in compliance with the Laws of the Federal Republic of Nigeria, the

rules, directives, regulation, notes, announcements of the Securities and Exchange Commission of Nigeria and the Nigerian Stock Exchange. So, there is also a compliance unit that the firm has, and the legal unit and the compliance unit usually work hand-in-hand to make sure that the firm is compliant.

The job scope of the legal function would typically cover: participating in the articulation of group or corporate office's strategic goals and objectives and taking ownership for communicating the same to employees and ensuring a common understanding of roles, responsibilities and accountabilities; managing board and shareholder relationships and performing secretarial and administrative duties to the organization; providing advisory services on issues that relate to the legal and regulatory framework within which the organization operates and liaising with relevant regulatory bodies as required; managing relationships with external solicitors and ensuring compliance with agreed service levels; drafting, negotiating, administering, interpreting and advising on agreements, letters, forms and other legal documents as required by the group for both internal and external stakeholders; providing some guidance, leadership support and strategic direction to other functions in the execution of the organization's activities; and keeping informed of changes in regulation and proactively advising the organization.

In the process of doing their job, they review everything that passes through the other functions with this perspective of protecting the organization from external and internal harm. In the words of one of the interview subjects, the questions asked by the legal department in every situation are: "are we breaking any laws?", "are we binding ourselves to something that we would not like?," "are there irregularities?," "are there things that should be included that are not included?"

In addition, the legal department develops guides to help others practice virtue—codes of ethics, codes of conduct, conflict of interest policies and so forth, all "put in place so that everyone is basically aware of what is expected of them in terms of honesty and ethical behavior by the firm." Lawyers in the firm tend to see conflict ahead of others and are able to advise them, for example, with regard to precision in wording or documentation, and so forth.

A field for the practice of virtue: internal goods

According to one of the respondents

> compliance is the key to corporate governance in an organization, which the legal department – acting in its advisory capacity – must ensure is carried out to the best of its abilities. To achieve this, it is necessary that the legal department can be trusted and is sincere because, most times, whatever advice emanates from the legal department is believed to be right and beneficial to the company; thus, integrity comes to play.

It is particularly important for an organization that intends to be virtuous to be guided by legal advice as an aid to practical reasoning, as "even minor violations of law or compromise on integrity level may tend to lessen management's, shareholders' or customers' confidence ... and create reputational issues."

A variety of virtues were self-acknowledged to be instrumental in enabling the performance of the function and therefore enabling excellence of the practice. These included integrity, hard work, discipline, honesty, diligence, faith, fear of God, perseverance, fortitude/toughness, patience, fairness (justice), compassion, selflessness, attention to detail, faithfulness, punctuality, obedience, respect for dignity, people skills (amiability), openness to learning, maturity, respect for confidentiality, truthfulness and discretion. The list of virtues finds resonance with MacIntyre's list, though more with the Aristotelian and the Catholic traditions (justice, courage/fortitude, *phronesis*) than with the Homeric (physical strength, bravery), Franklin (cleanliness, silence, industry) or Austenian (constancy, amiability) virtues (MacIntyre 1982). They are more related to the attainment of internal goods (core virtue ethics) than to social duties or to successful outcomes (MacIntyre 1982). When questioned about the sources of training in virtue, interviewees almost unanimously attributed it to family, religion, school and professional training, and on-the-job experience. One person also made reference to the influence of reading material on a person's character.

Flourishing of the employees: external goods

Compliance with local laws is good for the country and is the responsibility of the legal function. This department ensures that the company complies with incorporation and registration laws, tax laws, employment and labor laws, safety standards and so forth. A number of companies apply international laws where the country is silent or laws are weak. In these ways, companies live up to the principles of participation and of solidarity,[9] whereby they collaborate with government and other organizations to make society a humane environment for all (John Paul II, *Sollicitudo Rei Socialis* (SRS) 1987: 39–40; GeS: 30–32). Within the company, they also help to lay down the policies and procedures that improve probity and transparency for everyone—approvals, company seals and so forth.

Within the organization itself, legal department work also translates into efforts to pursue the individual and common good of the firm's employees. This happens in several ways, for example:

- "employees can rely and be confident in performing their daily job functions with confidence, of the legal unit as a backup on clarifying legal issues that may occur when interacting with clients";
- "risk is better managed and unnecessary litigation could be avoided which eventually protects the employee... When risk is minimized, losses are reduced which leads to profitability, progress and ultimately employees keeping their jobs";

- oversight of the Human Resource function to ensure compliance with labor laws, insurance laws, pension laws and so forth, e.g., due process in disengagement and prompt payment of entitlements;
- "policies and procedures that encourage accountability, promote a good working environment and also protect the rights of staff within the firm";
- the provision of mediation and arbitration services when there are conflicts among employees or between employees and the company, e.g., a case where the employee was aggrieved with regard to health entitlements;
- protection, e.g., complaints on their behalf, e.g., a protest against sexual harassment of an employee by an industry regulator;
- support to be law-abiding citizens through counsel for their own needs:

> people are now aware of the fact that they should try as much as possible to comply with laws… People have been sensitized to the importance of this and are more sensitive to the impact of their actions. … teaching our people to be law abiding citizens. … instances, where people seek our counsel on personal matters and we provide our opinion.

Flourishing of the employees as members of the community

The internal goods that accrue to legal practitioners and confer excellence on them in a way that leads to flourishing derive from virtues embedded in practices. There are also manifold benefits to other persons deriving from the legal department's taking their responsibility seriously to ensure that the law is followed. Primarily, it fosters growth in virtue. For example, the legal function pushes other persons in the firm to excellence by asking questions—nothing is taken for granted. The legal department constantly asks: "What is the purpose of this document, transaction, meeting and so forth?" Through their interaction with the legal department, people develop sharper analytical thinking skills and deepen their ability to understand issues. Also, "it forces everybody to think through completely and honestly, because we cannot agree to or sanction anything that is not valid." Other employees also learn to consider every activity extensively in advance—including its potential downsides, so as to draw up plans to avoid or mitigate foreseeable negative side effects. Overall, the burden of responsibility and accountability placed on each person helps and encourages that the individual be thorough and pay attention to detail.

- Besides, employees also grow from imbibing the culture of the organization— if it is an ethical organization, the ethos around them helps them be better people. They learn "to work by a well-spelt-out set of objective(s), to place integrity above profiteering and benefits (and to) … integrate more into society by easily adapting to a "rules-regulated" larger society." In the process of

> ensuring that the staff are aware of the policies concerning what actions might have legal consequences, they are groomed on what is acceptable in the workplace as well as in the general society. Such boosts virtue. A state of improved virtue is a step towards personal development.

Staff whose ethical character has improved can apply it to whatever professional or social context they might later find themselves. This is ultimately a way of contributing towards the common good, since it entails developing people to be more virtuous (MeM).

- It was therefore clear, also from the empirical evidence, that the legal and compliance function has a very important role in the achievement of the common good. Corporate lawyers bear special responsibility to look at every activity of the firm in its entirety and consider all possible eventualities. Those in the legal function are required to pay huge attention to detail, be extremely careful with the choice of words and information disclosure, and demanding from their colleagues. They protect the firm and keep it running smoothly and profitably; they wield a lot of power, given the information at their disposal. For the firm to thrive, those in the legal function must be very disciplined, ethical, honest and law-abiding. Interviewees warned about the destructive potential of a corrupt legal function—the crafting of tax avoidance mechanisms, obstruction of stamp duties provisions and so forth. As commented by one of the interview subjects, "knowledge in the hands of someone without these virtues can be very destructive to the profession and the society at large."

Meet the company lawyer

Company or Corporate lawyers provide legal guidance for their employers. They typically work for large companies, perhaps as part of legal teams, but they may also be self-employed and contract themselves out to many different firms.

Corporate lawyers spend their careers focusing on the legal issues businesses face. Usually, they spend little time in courtrooms and, instead, turn their energies towards the transactions of the firm with internal and external stakeholders. In this regard, they assist in the negotiation of contracts with employees, customers, suppliers, unions and so forth; partnerships, investments and acquisitions; corporate governance matters; compliance with legal requirements and those of industry and societal regulatory bodies, and so forth. Because of the fiduciary nature of the relationship, the client's business and legal interests are always at the forefront of the corporate lawyer's mind.

A day in the life of a corporate lawyer prioritizes the role's primary responsibility to ensure that the employer's business transactions are in compliance with the law. The corporate lawyer must research the law implicated by every transaction and advise clients of any negative effects it might create. In addition to regular duties, corporate lawyers ensure that clients' legal decisions translate to a strong bottom line—i.e., enhance profitability. For example, a corporate lawyer may consult with a company's marketing department to understand whether and how settling a dispute could affect the company's marketing prospects or hurt sales that quarter.

Other activities that fill the day of the corporate lawyer include:

- Consulting and handling all corporate legal processes—registration, permissions, filing and so forth.
- Developing company policy and position on legal issues.

- Support the human resources function in the drafting and vetting of internal policies, compliance with the country's labor law requirements, the establishment of disciplinary processes, engagement and disengagement processes and so forth.
- Researching, anticipating and guarding company against legal risks.
- Consult and handle all corporate legal processes (e.g., intellectual property, mergers & acquisitions, financial/securities offerings, compliance issues, transactions, agreements, lawsuits, patents).
- Guide managers and ensure compliance with rules and regulations.
- Structure, draft and review reports and other legal documents.
- Appear as the company in legal proceedings (administrative boards, court trials and so forth).
- Draft and administer contracts.
- Negotiate deals and attend company meetings.
- Arranging for the delivery of legal paperwork.
- Typing correspondence and legal paperwork.
- Transcribing court proceedings and other recorded meetings.
- Scheduling, coordinating and confirming court dates, appointments and meetings.

The role of a corporate lawyer also includes ensuring the legality of commercial transactions and advising corporations of legal rights and duties, including the duties and responsibilities of corporate officers. They must have knowledge of aspects of contract law, tax law, accounting, securities law, bankruptcy, intellectual property rights, licensing, zoning laws and the laws specific to the business of the corporations for which they work, for example, banking, maritime or telecommunications laws, and so forth.

Challenges facing a Company Lawyer include:

1   A Unique and Demanding Skill Set
    Corporate lawyers must have a varied skill set, including business and financial acumen. It is crucial for corporate lawyers to understand the business effect of any legal decisions. They must be proficient in legal research to ensure that their clients are in compliance with the most recent rules and regulations. They must also be excellent writers so as to communicate with clients and, if a client becomes embroiled in litigation, the court or other arbitration forum. Finally, corporate lawyers must be skilled negotiators because they need to bargain on behalf of clients. Other skills needed by a corporate lawyer are:
    - Attention to detail
    - Keen observation skills
    - Excellent time management skills
    - Strong organizational skills
    - Impressive communication skills
    - Excellence of judgment for making important decisions within the scope of their duties on a daily basis

2   The Requirement for Confidentiality
     If a corporate lawyer's internal company clients are not assured of confiden-
     tiality, they will be less likely to seek legal advice, but keeping confidences
     can shelter society's access to vital information.
3   Representation for the Company in Legal Dealings
     The practice of corporate law is generally less adversarial than that of trial
     law. Lawyers for both sides of a commercial transaction are less opponents
     than facilitators. They have been characterized in this role as "the hand-
     maidens of the deal." Transactions take place amongst peers. There are
     rarely wronged parties, underdogs or inequities in the financial means of
     participants. Corporate lawyers structure transactions, draft documents, re-
     view agreements, negotiate deals and attend meetings. However, it could
     happen that the company is involved in a trial. In such cases, the usual prac-
     tice is that the corporate lawyer appears as the company, but an independent
     lawyer is retained to plead the case. It is considered contrary to the ethics
     of the profession for a corporate lawyer to actually represent the company
     as a trial lawyer.

Ethniki Corporation's Mike

Mike Eze was a man who learnt and embraced a very strong value system quite
early in his life at the knees of his grandmother. For him, there could only be
right or wrong, black or white and no greys or shortcuts in between when it
came to integrity. Even as a child, he had a reputation for owning up to his
wrong actions and bearing the consequences. His core value was integrity, and
integrity, to him, meant doing the right thing even when no one was watching.

Over the years, he came across some isolated ethical and unlawful challenges,
like the intervention of his mother in changing his national youth service corps
posting; colleagues paying court officials to get papers filed in court; demands
by customs officers for payment of duty on goods exempted from duty; and so
forth. He always tried not to bow to intimidation, but to keep to the right thing.

However, thus far, he had experienced the toughest challenges to maintaining
his value system in his role with Ethniki Oil Services Limited as "Company Secretary and Legal Adviser." The oil and gas sector, closely regulated in Nigeria,
was very exposed to demands for questionable payments that had come to characterize the Nigerian public service sector. Saddled with the responsibility of
ensuring the company's compliance with corporate governance policies and code
of ethics, Mike discovered very early on that it was difficult to practice integrity
in the tough environment, and he began to develop strategies to avoid compromising his ideals. He had to be very clever to get internal buy in for his "quaint"
ideas from some of his bosses and colleagues, who were interested in profits at all
costs. Gradually, this led him to develop a personal integrity statement. Mike also
soon realized the need to inculcate integrity and ethics into the culture of the
company as a whole, and so he devised and implemented strategies that served

to train, guide and advise staff, promote ethical behavior, monitor the ethical climate, and report and punish unethical practices.

As the Legal Adviser and Company Secretary, as well as the unofficial Compliance and Ethics Officer, Mike occupied a very important and precarious position within the Company. He was tasked with ensuring that the company, as well as every employee, management, business associate and other affiliates, was legally and ethically compliant. He had to consider the legal implications of any act, omission, conduct or policy of the company that could result in legal suits, sanctions or punishments. Incidents of demands and offers to facilitate and expedite official duties—which amounted to bribery, fraud, sub-standardization of products and services—and embezzlement of company funds—which amounted to forgery, cheating, stealing, obtaining by false pretenses, fraudulent false accounting, and other offences and malpractices—were rife in the industry. These vices were unethical, illegal and unlawful, and were, in fact, criminal offences that ordinarily should be prosecuted. In the face of all these, Mike took on the burden of setting up a system to ensure ethical and legal compliance within the Company.

Over time, Mike had demonstrated to a number of his colleagues that a good attitude to work, information dissemination, communication, values, respect, accountability, honesty, good working relationship, monitoring and compliance with the law are keys to building integrity. He did a great job, with transparency and honesty, and he, to a large extent, succeeded in curbing corruption and restoring ethics and values in the Company. He led by example, he never compromised, and that made the transformation in his workplace possible.

Unfortunately, despite all his efforts, there were often instances of being caught off guard. Such a one was the new problem facing Mike—he was under pressure to be involved in a bribe. The company had inadvertently flouted a building regulation, and the city council officials were asking for a hefty bribe to overlook it. The alternative was to demolish the construction so far (of a prospective new branch) and cost the company multiples of the amount being asked for by the regulators. Mike's bosses were putting pressure on him to assign someone to discreetly pay on behalf of the company. Everyone knew that other companies had done it in the past and succeeded. Mike had begun to wonder if he had been overdoing things and whether to make an exception this time, for the common good of Ethniki Oil Services Ltd.'s internal stakeholders, given the huge financial cost a demolition would entail.

All in a day's work

My name is Jane. I am 27 years old. After I was called to the Bar six years ago, I completed the expected year in the National Youth Service Corps and got a good job almost immediately afterwards. I am one of the lucky ones that have never had to look for a new job. Having started as a legal assistant, I am now a legal officer for one of the biggest multinational companies in Nigeria, at the head office located on the Lekki peninsula, in Lagos State. I am well paid—it is a good company—and I have hopes of one day becoming the Chief Legal Officer, but sometimes I feel like I have no real life. I keep wondering when I will have time to develop any interests or relationships outside my office, when I will settle down to raise a family of my own. Having moved out of my parents' home once I started Law School, I now live alone in Anthony Village, which is in Lagos mainland. It takes me two to three hours to get to work. This morning, I listened to a radio program while in the traffic. The presenter was talking about a man called MacIntyre and his ideas about flourishing at work and growing in virtue while doing good to one's community. It sounded attractive but utopian—this man does not know what my work is like. Let me give you an idea and you will see how impossible it is to match the lofty language of MacIntyre to the reality of life:

5:00 am: Alarm goes off, wake up, check Blackberry. See that 10 e-mails directed to me on the meetings and court appearance I have today have come in since I put down my phone at 12:00 am. Respond to two of the 10 e-mails. Try to prepare breakfast, but realize I can't make it because, while I was writing those two e-mails, I've had clients send me meeting planners for 8:30 am and 10:00 am calls. *(For the uninitiated, clients rarely ask if I can take a call; sometimes I'm told to get on the line in five or ten minutes; sometimes I get sent random meeting planners.)*

5:15 am: Review the meeting plan and what I need to do before the court hearing today. Look over all the documents.

6:00 am: Shower. Brush teeth. Hope I have clean shirts and a pressed suit in the wardrobe. No time for breakfast. Don't want to be late for the meeting.

6:45 am: Get into my official car and hit the road to the office. Read more e-mails while on train and respond to another two or three while in traffic on 3rd mainland bridge.

8:15 am: Arrive at office. Start printing documents for 8:30 am meeting

8:30 am: Meeting gets moved to 9:00. Thank God! I do not expect it to last more than an hour, or I'd already have a conflict. Use extra time to look over documents I expect I'll be discussing in 9:00 meeting to make sure I am prepared.

9:00 am: Jump on call. Fortunately, Client wants to reschedule the meeting at 10:00 am because he is going to the child's school for a PTA meeting. I inform client I have another meeting at 10:00 and client asks me to push that meeting for him. I try to dodge by proposing 10:30 and promising to keep the other meeting to 30 minutes. Meanwhile, four new e-mails come in while I am on the call. I get two more meetings, Skype call with another three clients and to regularize the company's annual returns at the Corporate Affairs Commission.

10:00 am: Get on second meeting. Have no idea what it will be about, but assume I can handle it because it is with an unsophisticated client that we love. I field another six e-mails while at the meeting and mark a document at my desk, occasionally paying attention to the client, but I never look at her because I'm just trying to get done what I need to get done to not fall further behind.

10:30 am: I recap call with my boss (the Managing Director). I then get on the 10:30 am meeting with the 9:00 am client and try to pay attention because the client is a business-side managing director. I check the news anyway.

11:00 am: Drive to Court for the 12:00 court hearing. But arrive in Court at 11:45 am.

12:00 pm: Have a short pretrial briefing with the lawyer handling our case.

1:05 pm: Judge finally calls our case. She says: "I didn't get a chance to look at your papers. Can we adjourn this for a month?" I smile through my teeth and nod: *"as the Court pleases."* Funny how, every time *we* ask for extension of time to address something, it's a big deal.

2:30 pm: Take a few minutes to skim the news; get coffee. Return to desk and begin researching and going through documents drafted for a proposed contact for one of our deals. Attempt to do this without interruption, but answer the phone every 10 or 15 minutes and lose train of thought.

3:15 pm: My boss calls to ask me if I've seen e-mails that just came in and if I've reviewed the documents attached—252 pages, came in five minutes ago. I tell him, no, I have not yet reviewed the documents, but I will as soon as I can and generally try to determine whether the matter is urgent.

4:00 pm: Begin catching up on e-mails; see that I missed two calls while reviewing documents and hope clients/boss are not mad at me for missing them. Try to determine the importance of what I have missed.

4:30 pm: Things are quiet, so catch up on a document that has sat on my desk for more than a week.

5:00 pm: Close of work. But the *"fire drills"* begin. My boss says one of our clients wants to sign a set of documents today, none of which we have seen. I stay back to review them and to get tax review. I skim as fast as I can, isolating key points.

6:30 pm: Three clients have already sent me e-mails on other documents that I need to prepare, and I have two more meeting planners, both via Skype calls at 8:30 pm. I ignore all to perfect the documents that are for signing today.

7:00 pm: I jump on one of the calls and find out this client also wants documents signed tonight. Meanwhile, my boss's personal assistant drives by and drops a 200-page markup on my desk. He spends 30 minutes in my office trying to discuss it despite my telling him that other matters are in process and need to be closed out.

7:30 pm: I've been hit with two more clients who want to sign documents today. I now have five projects that are trying to get done by today. I push things forward to the extent I can, do the least possible amount of work I am okay with on each project and push things out. I am on and off calls with each client for next three hours while turning the documents.

8:30 pm: I'm now waiting for comments on three of the five matters. The other two have died: false alarms. I catch up on e-mails.

9:00 pm: I hit the road, hoping to get home in an hour.

10:30 pm: At home now, try to prepare dinner, catch up on e-mails not related to hot projects.

11:15 pm: Have dinner. Return to hot deals. Continue going back and forth (I'm still receiving 12–15 e-mails an hour on these projects) for next two hours.

1:15 am: Try to catch some sleep and get ready for tomorrow's hot deals. Corporate Affairs Commission is first on my list tomorrow morning, since it is on the mainland.

You see what I mean? And, even if I had listened to that radio program before the day I'm describing, my thoughts would still be the same: *"Now, how does one make MacIntyrean sense out of this?"*

Case discussion guidelines

- Mini-Case 1: Looking at the typical corporate lawyer, (a) identify the practice(s); (b) discuss what goods are internal to the practitioner engaged in the practice(s); and (c) explain the benefits to the wider community.
- Mini-Case 2: Remind Mike why he should not focus solely on cutting costs for the company—give reasons that pertain to (a) him as a professional; (b) him as a person; (c) the company; and (d) the community.
- Mini-Case 3: Help Jane find the rhythm in the routine and the random. Advise her about (a) the practice(s) she is engaged in; (b) the relationship of her routine to internal and external goods; (c) the relevance of her work to the common good of her firm and of society.

For all three, the students can work in groups and make presentations to the plenary.

Final reflections

To show how the legal function relates to the purposes for which businesses operate and individuals live their lives, the chapter has discussed legal compliance and ethics within the firm in the light of three traditions—Aristotle, CST and MacIntyre. Since the purpose of the legal function, like that of the whole firm, is the common good and flourishing of the individuals working in the organization, its practices must affirm and promote human virtue and so develop the profession and the community.

A common good orientation helps to avoid seeking wealth for its own sake, but rather, for the service of one's real needs and with consideration for the interests of others—of both present and future human communities. Both MacIntyre and CST use Aristotelian concepts and insights to resolve potential conflicts. The legal compliance and ethics function in a corporation can be a tool for achieving the good of the corporation, while respecting and ensuring human flourishing.

The law and ethics are not ends in themselves; they are means for human persons to achieve a virtuous life and so fulfill their greatest purpose. When an organization ensures that it complies with the law, it contributes towards the achievement of the common good and protects the rights of persons both within and without the corporation. It also helps the corporation to reduce the potential costs of not being law-abiding. When the corporation mandates the legal function to promote ethical sensitivity and behavior within the organization, this will further help each employee to grow in virtue and become a better person, which would in turn help the whole community—inside and outside the corporation—to be better.

Using a discussion of two hypothetical legal teams A and B, with lesser or greater common good orientations, the chapter simultaneously albeit imperfectly illustrates an Aristotelian community of practice, a MacIntyrean approach to the pursuit of virtue and the CST tenets in operation. As depicted in the illustration, apart from the cardinal virtues, Team B would end up practicing discernment, prudence, fairness, foresight and concern for others, and would thus become better persons due to these internal goods. These goods help them to become better at achieving the goal of the practice, which goes beyond the economic shrewdness that may be the specialty of Team A. The common good would also be better served by Team B, especially if the Team B person achieves consistency in the different spheres of his or her life. A Team B style corporation would therefore foster human flourishing and promote the common good as a good "steward" for the human ecosystem.

The insights from the interviews illustrated specific ways in which the individual's striving for virtue and excellence interweaves the fabric of professional practice and produces both internal and external goods for the person and the community. The three mini-cases present scenarios of the practical challenges faced by these professionals and provide a basis for greater student engagement and deeper discussions.

Guide questions

1 How much responsibility does a company lawyer have for ensuring that his employer keeps the common good in sight in decisions made on behalf of shareholders?

2 How much responsibility does a company lawyer have for ensuring that her employer keeps human flourishing as an objective, side by side with its profit objective, in its activities?

3 What is the relevance of the legal department in the efforts of the corporation to attain its goal?

4 What aspects of human flourishing can be furthered by a good legal department?

5 How can a staff of the legal department help his colleagues to achieve (a) external goods and (b) internal goods?

6 How can a corporation ensure that its legal function functions well?

7 How important is it for corporations to be (a) governed by law and (b) law-abiding?

8 Which virtue is most important for a legal practitioner working in a firm as part of its legal team?

Notes

1 Laws that encourage compliance and ethics best practices include the UK Bribery Act (UKBA); the US Foreign Corrupt Practices Act (FCPA); and the King Code of Governance for South Africa. The same goals are espoused by organizations such as the Institute of Corporate Governance, Nigeria (ICGN); the Organization for Economic Cooperation and Development (OECD); and the UN Global Compact (UNGC). It could be an interesting exercise for the course participants to research and develop a table listing resource providers in this regard from all over the world, with web addresses, so that the whole class can see how many organizations are involved.

2 A complete compilation is given in the Compendium of the Social Doctrine of the Church (CSDC).

3 "the purpose of a business firm is not simply to make a profit, but is to be found in its very existence as a community of persons who in various ways are endeavoring to satisfy their basic needs, and who form a particular group at the service of the whole of society."

4 "that he may employ them, as the steward of God's providence, for the benefit of others."

5 "This responsibility is a global one, for it is concerned not just with energy but with the whole of creation, which must not be bequeathed to future generations depleted of its resources. Human beings legitimately exercise a responsible stewardship over nature, in order to protect it, to enjoy its fruits and to cultivate it in new ways, with the assistance of advanced technologies, so that it can worthily accommodate and feed the world's population. On this earth there is room for everyone: here the entire human family must find the resources to live with dignity, through the help of nature itself—God's gift to his children—and through hard work and creativity. At the same time we must recognize our grave duty to hand the earth on to future generations in such a condition that they too can worthily inhabit it and continue to cultivate it."

6 "Our "dominion" over the universe should be understood more properly in the sense of responsible stewardship."

7 This, however, does not mean that every free act is virtuous or that all obedience to the law is virtuous. People constantly freely choose to obey or disobey the law. Besides, as explained earlier, in the case of a law that enjoins intrinsic evil, it would be virtuous to freely disobey the law.

8 "… we must go on to the second sphere of values which is necessarily linked to work. Work constitutes a foundation for the formation of family life, which is a natural right and something that man is called to. These two spheres of values-one linked to work and the other consequent on the family nature of human life-must be properly united and must properly permeate each other. …Obviously, two aspects of work in a sense come into play here: the one making family life and its upkeep possible, and the other making possible the achievement of the purposes of the family, especially education. … It must be remembered and affirmed that the family constitutes one of the most important terms of reference for shaping the social and ethical order of human work."

9 Embedded in Catholic Social Teaching (CSDC: 189 and 192fw).

References

Abela, A. 2001, 'Profit and more: Catholic Social Teaching and the purpose of the firm', *Journal of Business Ethics*, 31: 107–116.

Benedict XVI. 2009, *Encyclical letter 'Caritas in veritate'*, Vatican City: Libreria Editrice Vaticana. (http://w2.vatican.va/content/benedict-xvi/en/encyclicals/documents/hf_ben-+xvi_enc_20090629_caritas-in-veritate.html, Accessed September 27, 2017).

Driscoll, D., Hoffman, W. and Murphy, J. 1998, 'Business ethics and compliance: What management is doing and why', *Business and Society Review*, 99: 35–51.

Francis. 2015, *Encyclical Letter 'Laudato Si'*, Vatican City: Libreria Editrice Vaticana. (http://w2.vatican.va/content/francesco/en/encyclicals/documents/papa-francesco_20150524_enciclica-laudato-si.html, Accessed September 27, 2017).

Fremeaux, S. and Michelson, G. 2016, 'The common good of the firm and humanistic management: Conscious capitalism and economy of communion', *Journal of Business Ethics*, 1–9. DOI: 10.1007/s10551-016-3118-6.

Garcia, J.L.A. 2003, 'Modern(ist) moral philosophy and MacIntyrean critique', in C. Murphy Mark (ed.), *Alasdair MacIntyre*, New York: Cambridge University Press, 94–113.

Gavin, L. 2006, 'Human good and human function', in R. Kraut (ed.), *The Blackwell guide to Aristotle's Nicomachean Ethics*, Oxford: Blackwell Publishing Ltd., 1–11.

Gavin, L. 2009, 'Human excellence in character and intellect', in G. Anagnostopoulos (ed.), *A companion to Aristotle,* Oxford: Blackwell Publishing Ltd., 419–441.

Grisez, G. 2001, 'Natural law, God, religion, and human fulfillment', *American Journal of Jurisprudence,* 46: 3–36.

Grisez, G. and Shaw, R. 1988, *Beyond the new morality: The responsibilities of freedom*, Notre Dame, IN: University of Notre Dame Press.

Guitián, G. 2009, 'Conciliating work and family: A Catholic Social Teaching perspective', *Journal of Business Ethics,* 88: 513–524.

Haidt, J. 2007, 'The new synthesis in moral psychology', *Science*, 316(5827): 998–1002. DOI: 10.1126/science.1137651.

Higgins, C. 2003, 'MacIntyre's moral theory and the possibility of an *Aretaic* ethics of teaching', *Journal of Philosophy of Education*, 37(2): 279–292.

Jackall, R. 1988, *Moral mazes: The world of corporate managers*, New York: Oxford University Press.

John XXIII. 1961, *Encyclical Letter 'Mater et magistra'*, Vatican City: Tipografia Poliglotta Vaticana. (http://w2.vatican.va/content/john-xxiii/en/encyclicals/documents/hf_j-xxiii_enc_15051961_mater.html, Accessed September 27, 2017).

John Paul II. 1981, *Encyclical Letter 'Laborem exercens'*, Vatican City: Vatican Polyglot Press. (http://w2.vatican.va/content/john-paul-ii/en/encyclicals/documents/hf_jp-ii_enc_14091981_laborem-exercens.html, Accessed September 27, 2017).

John Paul II. 1987, *Encyclical Letter 'Sollicitudo rei socialis'*, Vatican City: Vatican Polyglot Press. (http://w2.vatican.va/content/john-paul-ii/en/encyclicals/documents/hf_jpii_enc_30121987_sollicitudo-rei-socialis.html, Accessed September 27, 2017).

John Paul II. 1991, *Encyclical Letter 'Centesimus annus'*, Washington, DC: United States Catholic Conference. (http://w2.vatican.va/content/john-paul-ii/en/encyclicals/documents/hf_jp-ii_enc_01051991_centesimus-annus.html, Accessed September 27, 2017).

Klein, T. and Laczniak, G. 2009, 'Applying Catholic Social Teachings to ethical issues in marketing', *Journal of Macromarketing*, 29(3): 1–22.

Kraut, R. 2006, 'Introduction', in R. Kraut (ed.), *The Blackwell guide to Aristotle's Nicomachean ethics*, Oxford: Blackwell Publishing Ltd., 1–11.

Lear, G. 2009, 'Happiness and the structure of ends', in G. Anagnostopoulos (ed.), *A companion to Aristotle*, Oxford: Blackwell Publishing Ltd., 385–403.

Leo XIII. 1891, *Encyclical Letter 'Rerum novarum'*. (http://w2.vatican.va/content/leo-xiii/en/encyclicals/documents/hf_l-xiii_enc_15051891_rerum-novarum.html, Accessed September 27, 2017).

MacIntyre, A. 1981, *After virtue*, Notre Dame, IN: University of Notre Dame Press.

MacIntyre, A. 1982, 'The nature of virtues', *The Hastings Center Reports*, 11(2): 27–34.

MacIntyre, A. 2008, 'How Aristotelianism can become revolutionary: Ethics, resistance, and utopia', *Philosophy of Management*, 7(1): 3–7.

MacIntyre, A. 2015, 'The irrelevance of ethics', in A. Bielskis and K. Knight (eds.), *Virtue and economy: Essays on morality and markets*, New York: Routledge, 7–21.

Mackey, J. and Sisodia, R. 2013, *Conscious capitalism: Liberating the heroics spirit of business*, Boston, MA: Harvard Business School Press.

Pfeffer, J. 2016, 'Why the assholes are winning: Money trumps all', *Journal of Management Studies*, 53(4): 663–669.

Pius XI. 1931, *Encyclical Letter 'Quadragesimo anno'*, Boston, MA: St. Paul Editions. (http://w2.vatican.va/content/pius-xi/en/encyclicals/documents/hf_p-xi_enc_19310515_quadragesimo-anno.html, Accessed September 27, 2017).

Pontifical Council for Justice and Peace. 2004, *Compendium of the social doctrine of the church*, Vatican City: Libreria Editrice Vaticana.

Sharp Paine, L. 1994, 'Managing for organizational integrity', *Harvard Business Review*, 72(2): 107–117.

Sison, A.J.G. and Fontrodona, J. 2012, 'The common good of the firm in the Aristotelian-Thomistic tradition', *Business Ethics Quarterly*, 22(2): 211–246.

Sison, A.J.G. and Fontrodona, J. 2013, 'Participating in the common good of the firm', *Journal of Business Ethics*, 113: 611–625.

Sison, A.J.G., Ferrero, I. and Guitián, G. 2016, 'Human dignity and the dignity of work: Insights from Catholic Social Teaching', *Business Ethics Quarterly*, 26(4): 503–528.

Stabile, S. 2005, 'A Catholic vision of the corporation', *Seattle Journal for Social Justice*, 4(1): 181–224.

Tenbrunsel, A.E. and Smith-Crowe, K. 2008, 'Ethical decision making: Where we've been and where we're going', *The Academy of Management Annals*, 2(1): 545–607. DOI: 10.1080/19416520802211677.

Vatican Council II. 1965, Pastoral constitution on the church in the modern world *'Gaudium et spes'*, Vatican City: Vatican Polyglot Press. (www.vatican.va/archive/hist_councils/ii_vatican_council/documents/vat-ii_const_19651207_gaudium-et-spes_en.html, Accessed September 27, 2017).

Werhane, P. 1999, *Moral imagination and management decision making*, Ruffin series in business ethics. New York: Oxford University Press.

Young, C. 2009, 'Justice', in G. Anagnostopoulos (ed.), *A companion to Aristotle*, Chichester and Malden, MA: Blackwell Publishing, 457–470.

8

PRACTICAL WISDOM IN CORPORATE GOVERNANCE

Alejo José G. Sison and Matthias P. Hühn

Learning objectives

This final chapter seeks to:

- Explain the virtue of practical wisdom (*phronesis*) in contrast to the vice of cunning (*panourgia*), its counterfeit.
- Show how corporate governance consists essentially in the sustenance of institutions and contributes to their flourishing.
- Illustrate how practical wisdom (*phronesis*) acts as an attitude, outlook or subjective frame that allows us to correctly evaluate the merits of each particular case and act on them.

Practical wisdom (*phronesis*) has all but been lost in corporate governance. By "practical wisdom," we mean something like "prudence," "practical reason" or "practical rationality" applied widely to ethics, economics, business, politics and social relations. Yet, none of these purported equivalents really hits the mark. Each carries its share of unwanted baggage. "Prudence," for instance, speaks of a careful regard for future interests, synonymous with "calculation" or the disposition to earn a huge return from an investment, even at the expense of others. One would not expect that from a virtue.

Similarly, by "corporate governance" we mean something akin to (general) management or what used to be called "business administration." It is not limited to decisions taken by the board, "the ex-post bargaining over the quasi-rents generated by the firm" (Williams 1985; Zingales 1997) or even how suppliers of finance assure themselves returns (Shleifer and Vishny 1997). Rather, in the best of cases, it refers to how stakeholders—especially the board and management—collaborate in a principled fashion to seek the common good of the company. Corporate governance is a particular instance of the art of governing or (Aristotelian) politics applied to firms. In the end, it determines "who gets what, when, where, how and at what price."

This chapter deals with practical wisdom in corporate governance making use of insights from Aristotle, Catholic Social Teaching (CST) and MacIntyre. The first part explains Aristotelian practical wisdom (*phronesis*) in contrast to the vice of craftiness (*panourgia*). Next comes a description of the link between practical wisdom and the common good of the firm in CST. In third place is an account of corporate governance according to the MacIntyrean categories of "practices" and "institutions." And lastly we present a case that illustrates how practical wisdom in corporate governance can be embedded in individual biographies and the traditions of communities of enquiry.

1. Aristotle on practical wisdom (*phronesis*) and its counterfeit (*panourgia*)

Aristotle defines "practical wisdom" (*phronesis*) in the Nicomachean Ethics (henceforth NE: 1144a) as the virtue of choosing the suitable means to the right end. In truth, "practical wisdom" may not be the best translation for *phronesis*, given that *sophia*, the intellectual virtue of knowing things in their first principles and final ends, is also rendered as "wisdom" (NE: 1141a). This translation, therefore, may lead to a confusion between a "theoretical wisdom" (*sophia*) and a "practical wisdom" (*phronesis*). Further, there is another practical virtue concerned with making things, the "productive skill" or *techne* (NE 1140a). By contrast, "practical wisdom" refers to right action in the moral sphere, to doing things. The difference between these two practical virtues, *techne* and *phronesis*, is the same one between excellence in making and doing.

What are the distinctive features of practical wisdom (*phronesis*), for want of a better term? First, it's practical orientation as a moral virtue (NE: 1103a). Here it diverges from *sophia*, which is wisdom, but theoretical, not practical; and *techne*, which is practical, but concerned with making, not doing. Practical wisdom (*phronesis*) is the virtue of doing the right thing the right way. It deals with particular or concrete realities, not universal or abstract ideas; these are contingent events that may or may not occur, and if they do, they may happen one way or another (NE: 1139a). That is why practical wisdom involves deliberation and choice or decision-making (NE: 1140a–b). One does not deliberate over what is already given (for example, death and taxes). Neither does one choose when there is just a single option; decisions require freedom to choose among multiple options. Practical wisdom also entails following through with the right action. Without this final step, there is no practical wisdom because there is no practice. Practical wisdom, therefore, establishes harmony among rational deliberation, choice and behavior.

A second feature of practical wisdom is normativity, a command or prohibition, but in a way beyond mere rule-following. That's because outside of "moral absolutes" or exceptionless prohibitions (such as not taking the life of the innocent) (NE: 1110a), ethical rules are always formulated in general terms. They cannot take into account all the relevant particulars involved in implementation. Hence, proper rule-following invariably needs "prudential judgment" or practical wisdom. For instance, when a traffic-enforcer metes out punishment to a speed-limit violator, he has to consider whether there was a medical emergency, by how much was the limit exceeded, the road and weather conditions, if there was any sign or warning and so forth. There may be procedures to determine the punishment, but rules will still have to be interpreted and decisions could be just or unfair. There is no such thing as a self-implementing rule. Because human beings are not all-knowing, they cannot establish perfect rules or foresee all circumstances. There will always be room for practical wisdom in the interpretation and implementation of rules.

Third, practical wisdom is like a charioteer that guides and a mother that begets all the other virtues (NE: 1145a); without it, no genuine virtue exists. Because every bit of virtue-knowledge is connected, to judge or evaluate any action morally is to compare its worth relative to others. For instance, each alternative in the daily morning dilemma "should I rise or remain in bed?" brings mutually exclusive and freighted consequences. Practical wisdom makes this connection possible by providing a common fount or source among the different virtues. For this reason, many ethicists maintain the "unity of the virtues" thesis, meaning no single virtue can be truly present without the others (Telfer 1990). Practical wisdom plays a crucial coordinating role among the different moral virtues.

In fourth place, practical wisdom implies a "qualified agent account" (Hursthouse 1999: 28), according to which an action will be right and virtuous if and only if it is what a virtuous agent would characteristically do in comparable circumstances. Aristotelian practical wisdom therefore rejects the "neutral, third-party observer" standard utilized in the natural sciences. Practical wisdom involves the right perceptions, desires, feelings, motivations, judgments and actions according to a moral, not a physical, standard. The "objective standard" in decision-making and action is the "subjective judgment" of the practically wise agent. The subjective moral disposition of the agent—not any mechanical skill or theoretical knowledge—is the determining factor in practical wisdom. Understandably, this creates some form of circular reasoning, since only the practically wise person can identify and carry out practically wise behavior. But, this difficulty can be explained by the different stages in the psychological development of virtues and skills. To the degree that an apprentice or novice is initiated and advances in a virtue such as practical wisdom or a skill such as piano-playing, the novice's perception, judgment and performance changes until it approximates that of a virtuoso or expert. These internal changes have repercussions on external behavior critical to the virtue or skill (NE: 1144b, 1147a). Observable conduct by itself, without knowledge of the underlying feelings and motivations, is not a valid criterion for practical wisdom.

Aristotle actually has a name for the mere appearance or "fake" practical wisdom: *panourgia* ("craftiness," "cunning" or "astuteness") (NE: 1144a). This is the quality possessed by someone who goes through the motions or external displays of practical wisdom, because he is effective in getting things done and efficient in making use of resources, but is morally indifferent to the goal or end.

His perception, feeling, judgment and action are not informed by virtue but by mere compliance with rules. There is no internal commitment. This describes the behavior of the perfect bureaucrat or manager who always obeys orders, whatever they may be, due to a lack of ethical scruples. Think, for instance, of the compliant Nazi concentration camp officer.

The main difference between a person of practical wisdom and one of cunning, therefore, does not lie in external behaviors, since both may be engaged in the same activities. Rather, it's in the internal dispositions and commitment to a certain goal or lifestyle as final end. In this vein, Aristotle states that Socrates was, for the majority, indistinguishable from the Sophists, because they were equally surrounded by young people eager to learn (despite Socrates' insistence that he knew nothing). Besides charging fees for instruction, the Sophists differed profoundly from Socrates in their lifestyle choice: the Sophists were after wealth and power, while Socrates sought virtue (Metaphysics 1004b). This choice of a final end meant all the difference for their internal dispositions and whether they had practical wisdom or its counterfeit, craftiness.

In summary, practical wisdom is similar to craftiness since both refer to rational choice and deliberation regarding the means to an end. But whereas craftiness is indifferent to the moral nature of the end, exclusively "maximizing" results or output, practical wisdom requires that the end be "right," in accordance with virtue and the ultimate end of human life that is flourishing (*eudaimonia*). Practical wisdom consists of doing the right thing the right way.

Aristotle lists practical wisdom among the character traits (*ethos*) that a speaker must have to convince or persuade an audience ("Rhetoric," henceforth Rh: 1356a, perhaps the first manual not only in public speaking, but also in leadership). Together with virtue (*arête*) and goodwill (*eunoia*), practical wisdom allows speakers and leaders to form correct opinions over concrete, contingent issues, enabling them to express views justly and fairly, and ensuring sound advice to listeners. They form the basis of a person's credibility and trustworthiness. Aristotle distinguishes three ways these personal traits prove useful (Rh: 1358b): in a deliberative mode, to exhort or dissuade from future action, by showing potential benefit or harm; in a judicial mode, to approve or condemn past action in accordance with innocence or guilt; and in a demonstrative mode, to indicate what is honorable or, on the contrary, shameful. Morally excellent and skillful public speakers and leaders influence audiences in a manner respectful of their freedom and reason.

Thus, the parallelisms between rhetoric and leadership, on the one hand, and management and governance, on the other, begin to emerge. And for all these related activities, practical wisdom proves crucial.

- For Aristotle, practical wisdom (*phronesis*) consists of doing the right thing the right way. Cunning (*panourgia*) means acting efficiently, regardless of the end.

2. Practical wisdom and the common good of the firm from the Catholic Social Teaching perspective

We shall now apply practical wisdom to the governance of a corporation. The first step consists of establishing the proper end or goal of the firm.

Grounded on Aristotelian-Thomistic traditions as well as Catholic Social Teaching (CST), the "common good theory" (Sison and Fontrodona 2012) states that the purpose of the firm lies in "participatory work" or "collaborative production." John XXIII admonishes "that all parties cooperate actively and loyally in the common enterprise, not so much for what they can get out of it themselves, but as discharging a duty and rendering a service to their fellowmen" (John XXIII, *Mater et Magistra* (MeM) 1961: 92). This end or objective is "common" not only because of the non-rivalrous and non-excludable features of production (similar to "public goods"), but also because it can only be attained if all the individual members of the group jointly attained it. It implies that "workers have their say in, and make their contribution to, the efficient running and development of the enterprise" (MeM: 92), notwithstanding the unity of direction set by management. The common good account of the firm, therefore, is contrary to the profit-maximizing neoclassical economic version, since profits strictly cannot belong to several people or be shared. On the other hand, the common good could only be achieved by the group to the extent that each member achieves it, much like victory in a team sport. Although the members of a side play different roles, it is the whole team that wins.

Firms exist to produce goods and services necessary for flourishing (*eudaimonia*) beyond the capacity of individuals and families (Sison and Fontrdona 2012). This is known in Aristotelian parlance as "artificial chrematistics," the acquisition or production of material means needed for flourishing. Firms are voluntary associations human beings form, often as extensions of families, to satisfy particular economic requirements. For instance, if a European wanted to build a vessel to travel and trade with people in Asia, he would most likely have to source manpower, expertise and capital beyond his family and enlist the cooperation of like-minded people. He would constitute something very similar to a firm.

"Collaborative production" accomplishes the common good of firms in two, hierarchically ordered ways (Sison and Fontrodona 2012). First, through the production of a variety of goods and services and the generation of profits, all of which, together, comprise the "objective dimension" of work. These constituents of the objective dimension can be distributed more or less equitably, but not shared, strictly speaking. More importantly, collaborative production also actualizes the common good of firms by developing knowledge, skills, meanings and moral excellences in the workers who take part. This "subjective dimension" of work is so-called because it inheres directly in the workers and is inseparable from them, forming part of their immaterial worth or value. It demands that employees not be treated as "mere cogs in the machinery, denying them any opportunity of expressing their wishes or bringing their experience to bear on the work in hand, and keeping them entirely passive in regard to decisions that regulate their activity" (MeM: 92). More than the objective dimension, the subjective dimension comes closer to the core of human dignity. Also, its elements are such that they can truly be shared, they entail no rivalry or excludability, and the whole of humankind would be better off if we had more of them.

In the dominant neoclassical economic framework, corporate governance is largely a matter of rule-making ("codes of conduct"), plus the creation of incentives and sanctions aligned with shareholder interests (Sison 2000b). The common good theory takes a more complete approach, setting rules, identifying goods and specifying the virtues (Sison 2008). Rules are, of course, necessary, as they provide immediate guidance, especially regarding prohibited behaviors: "Do not pay bribes to government officials." However, for permissible behaviors, rules are too general to help: "It is not, of course, possible to lay down hard and fast rules regarding the manner of such participation, for this must depend upon prevailing conditions, which vary from firm to firm and are frequently subject to rapid and substantial alteration" (MeM: 91). Joint deliberation about the "goods," the hierarchy of goals, objectives, values and so forth to be collectively pursued is also needed. For example, the commitment to people's health urged Johnson & Johnson to recall the possibly tainted Tylenol bottles immediately, instead of following other more "economic" lines of action. But still, the third element comprising the virtues, particularly practical wisdom (*phronesis*), is vital. Virtues link objective rules and goods through subjective action, developing integral human excellence. The virtues allow one to properly interpret rules and judge which among competing goods are to be realized and how. Moreover, virtues accrue in the subject or agent, creating "moral capital" (Sison 2003), the right disposition for ethical actions.

By establishing collaborative production in its double, hierarchically ordered subjective (knowledge, skills, virtues and meanings) and objective (goods, services and profits) dimensions as the common good of the firm, we lay down an ethical conception of the corporation. Following the principle of the priority of labor over capital, we ensure that

> when a man works, using all the means of production, he also wishes the fruit of this work to be used by himself and other, and he wishes to be able to take part in the very work process as a sharer in responsibility and creativity at the workbench to which he applies himself.
>
> *(John Paul II,* Laborem Exercens *(LE) 1981: 15)*

Instead of getting lost in excessive, bureaucratic centralization as a production instrument, he realizes that he is "a true subject of work with an initiative of his own" and "working for himself" (LE: 15).

While in the neoclassical economic view, there was only room for craftiness (*panourgia*) in maximizing profit at whatever cost, now it is possible to cultivate practical wisdom (*phronesis*), aided by the existence of rules and shared goals, objectives and values.

• CST principles, in putting people before profits and the subjective dimension of work above the objective dimension, uphold practical wisdom and reject cunning or craftiness.

3. A MacIntyrean account of corporate governance

In this section, we shall frame corporate governance in terms of two closely related MacIntyrean categories, "practices" and "institutions."

Practices are

> any coherent and complex form of socially established cooperative human activity through which goods internal to that form of activity are realized in the course of trying to achieve those standards of excellence which are appropriate to, and partially definitive of, that form of activity, with the result that human powers to achieve excellence, and human conceptions of the ends and goods involved, are systematically extended.
>
> *(MacIntyre 2007: 175)*

Examples of practices are chess, football, farming, architecture and the creation of Aristotelian political communities. They are considered a "universal feature of human cultures" (MacIntyre 1994: 287). Practices involve two things: goods that cannot be obtained or achieved outside of the cooperative activity ("internal goods") and "standards of excellence" by which performance is partially judged. Practices also yield two results: the development of distinct capacities for excellence and improvement in the understanding of the specific ends and goods.

The definition of practices shows how closely they resemble instances of practical wisdom. Both pursue goods or ends internal to the activities themselves, such as the "morally right action" for practical wisdom and the proper performance of the practice, be it chess, football, farming and so forth. Objectives are "path-dependent" and cannot be obtained through other means. Furthermore, the standards of excellence only make sense to those who have been initiated and are involved in these activities. Practical wisdom is desirable exclusively to humans, not to robots. Similarly, excellence in practices is appreciated only by those who know the rules and objectives and have participated in them. Otherwise, chess, for example, would simply appear as moving tokens across a checkered board. Third, practical wisdom and practices result from cooperation, not competition. One learns practical wisdom by imitating the virtuous example of another, and one agent's practical wisdom does not detract but contributes to another's. Likewise, one learns to play chess well by following the strategies of a master, and there is no limit to the people who are good in chess. An increase does not harm chess-playing; instead, it spurs further development and excellence.

For their part, "[I]nstitutions are characteristically and necessarily concerned with [...] external goods. They are involved in acquiring money and other material goods; they are structured in terms of power and status, and they distribute money, power and status as rewards" (MacIntyre 2007: 194). Institutions refer to the procurement and distribution of external goods, some material (money) and others related to the material (power and status). Institutions are necessary because they "sustain not only themselves, but also the practices of which they are the bearers. For no practices can survive for any length of time unsustained by institutions" (MacIntyre 2007: 194). Thanks to the external, material goods that institutions provide, practices, with their internal goods, survive.

Institutions, then, are similar to the realms in which craftiness is exercised. First, both seek external goods. Craftiness is the skill of effectiveness and efficiency regardless of the goal or objective. Craftiness "works" indifferently of the end. Second, anyone can observe excellence in institutions and craftiness, without need of previous understanding, involvement or experience. All one sees are the external results, that there are more and that this was achieved through the efficient use of resources. Any neutral, third-party observer—even machines—could attest the efficacy of craftiness and institutions; no moral commitment is needed. And third, the goals of institutions and craftiness are matters of competition, not cooperation. Their ends are objects of a zero-sum game; one's gain is necessarily another's loss. This is clear in the case of money.

Both institutions and practices, on the one hand, and external and internal goods, on the other, are intimately related such that they form "a single causal order" (MacIntyre 2007: 194). Because of this, "the ideals and the creativity of the practice are always vulnerable to the acquisitiveness of the institution, [...] the cooperative care for the common good of the practice is always vulnerable to the competitiveness of the institution" (MacIntyre 2007: 194). Due to the dependence of practices on institutions, agents could seek external goods (money, status and power) in themselves, forgetting about internal goods altogether or subordinating them to external goods. This situation describes corruption or the loss of integrity of practices and institutions (MacIntyre 2007: 195); practices are distorted and institutions invade, rather than support them (MacIntyre 1994: 289).

At this point, the parallelism between practices and practical wisdom, on one hand, and institutions and craftiness, on the other, stops. Although practices and practical wisdom rely on external goods supplied by institutions to achieve internal goods, we should not say that practical wisdom depends on craftiness or that one could only exercise practical wisdom thanks to another's craftiness. Virtue owes nothing to vice. Rather, we should find a way to acquire the necessary external goods without falling to craftiness. We should look for institutions ruled by practical wisdom, not craftiness. How is this possible?

First, we have to recognize that external goods sought by institutions are not "goods in themselves," but "goods in respect of another" or "instrumental goods." It is foolish to seek them for their own sakes. We should strive for them only to the extent that they lead to superior "internal goods" or "goods in themselves" as those provided by practices. The second step lies in setting boundaries or limits in which institutional goods could be "internalized" and put at the service of practices. For instance, when a hospital asks how much profit it should make, the answer should not be "as much as possible." It would be a corrupt hospital and institution, beholden to craftiness and dedicated mainly to accumulating external goods. Rather, the response should be "as much money as needed to fulfill the overriding practice of improving people's health." Such hospital or institution would then be governed by practical wisdom and supportive of practices.

Institutions are not to be censured outrightly. External goods are goods necessary for cultivating practices. More importantly, "the making and sustaining of forms of human community—and therefore of institutions—itself has the characteristics of a practice, and moreover of a practice which stands in a peculiarly close relationship to the exercise of the virtues" (MacIntyre 2007: 194). The making and sustaining of institutions can be transformed into a practice with its internal goods and standards of excellence. Moore identifies this practice as "governance" (Moore 2012). Governance—corporate governance—becomes a "second-order practice" in which institutions supply the right amount of external, material resources to be sustainable and supportive of "first-order," core practices (in the hospital example, caring for the sick). Proper deliberations, decisions and actions surrounding the sustenance of institutions is a matter of practical wisdom, not craftiness.

Before explaining how this "second-order" practice of maintaining institutions or governance relates to practical wisdom, let us draw its connections with the corporate common good (Sison and Fontrodona 2012). Collaborative production as the corporate common good dovetails seamlessly with the MacIntyrean categories of practices and institutions. The "subjective dimension" of collaborative production that gives rise to knowledge, skills, meanings and virtues refers to practices, while the "objective dimension" that goes after economic goods, services and profit refers to institutions. Just as practices and institutions form a single causal order, so too do the subjective and objective dimensions of the corporate common good. Although the subjective dimension, like practices, pursues superior internal goods, this would not be possible without the objective dimension, equivalent to institutions, which provides external goods. Likewise, a properly governed institution seeks just the right amount of external goods to be self-sustaining and enabling of core practices. Thus, practical wisdom represents the excellence of the second-order practice of maintaining institutions or governance. By contrast, a corrupt institution seeks external goods over any core practice. There, craftiness reigns, as the turf of Weberian bureaucrats and managers.

Corporate governance is a second-order practice of acquiring the right amount of external, material resources to maintain an institution and promote first-order or core practices with internal goods. Practical wisdom is the excellence or virtue corresponding to this second-order practice of governance.

However, defining the practice and good internal to governance is just the first of three conditions MacIntyre requires for genuine virtues (MacIntyre 1994: 284). Besides identifying practical wisdom as the virtue of governance, we have to examine how it can be "institutionalized." This is the "governance of virtue," the ways in which virtues can be cultivated among the members of the firm (Moore 2012). How does corporate governance "crowd in" virtue instead of vice? How do we recover practical wisdom in corporate governance?

- MacIntyrean practices resemble instances of practical wisdom, while institutions, instances of cunning. Proper corporate governance is a second-order practice dependent on the virtue of practical wisdom.

4. The recovery of practical wisdom in corporate governance and the "institutionalization" of virtue

MacIntyre states that genuine virtues enable the achievement of three kinds of goods (MacIntyre 1994: 284): (1) those internal to practices; (2) those of an individual life; and (3) those of the community. Three steps must be taken, therefore, to fully develop practical wisdom in corporate governance, such that institutions are sustained, core practices supported and virtues promoted or "institutionalized" among firm members and the community.

We have already complied with the first step, framing corporate governance as a second-order practice, the sustaining of institutions supportive of core practices, with the corresponding virtue of practical wisdom. We now turn to the other two conditions.

Governance does not take place in the abstract, but is always carried out by particular people, with their life stories or biographies. The good represented by the practice of governance needs to be located within the narrative unity or story of individual lives. A person is necessarily someone's son or daughter, probably a brother or sister, perhaps a spouse, maybe a father or a mother. Besides being a corporate executive, that person plays a variety of roles in different life spheres or domains. Invariably conflicts will arise from these roles. For instance, should people favor close relatives when hiring? Should duties towards relatives take precedence over the good of the company, in need of competent professionals? Although there may be policies concerning hiring, there is also "managerial discretion." There will always be opportunities to put practical wisdom in governance to the test. A practically wise corporate governor should make the right decisions in such situations, fulfilling family duties without sacrificing professional integrity and firm loyalty.

The next and final step concerns contextualizing practical wisdom through engagement with different traditions or "communal modes of inquiry" (equivalent to the "best practices") in governance. For instance, due to the breadth of company operations and investor backgrounds, executives may have to choose between a German-style dual (supervisory and management) board with worker representation and an Anglo-Saxon style unitary board with an "imperial" Chair and CEO (Sison 2000a). Each would have its pros and cons in monitoring, performance targets, compensation, efficiency and so forth. Practical wisdom enters into play in such a decision. Which alternative best reflects the company's value systems and supports its core practices? Which is more conducive to the flourishing of firm members and the organization? It behooves a governor trained in practical wisdom to choose in the interest of the common good of the firm. Practical wisdom in governance is sufficiently established only when this final stage is reached.

Essential to the recovery of practical wisdom is the proper understanding of the virtues. These are distinctively human excellences found in multiple operational tracks, producing positive feedback among them. They are "goods" not only because they satisfy the right desires, but also—and above all—because they lead to flourishing, the final end of human beings. Certain features of practical wisdom—such as its practical orientation towards right action, normativity beyond rules, and ability to engender and coordinate—differentiate it from all the other moral virtues. In MacIntyrean terms, practical wisdom corresponds to a "practice" that seeks a path-dependent internal good and a non-rivalrous, non-excludable object of cooperation; its standard of excellence is known only to qualified agents initiated in the specific practice. ("Institutions," by contrast, pursue external goods that, as objects of competition, are zero-sum; their standard of excellence is available to neutral, third-party observers.)

We should distinguish practical wisdom from its counterfeit, craftiness. In corporations, this can only be possible if we posit a "proper end" different from the "maximization of shareholder value" proposed by neoclassical economic theory. This is the "common good of the firm," consisting of participatory work or production insofar as it yields subjective (knowledge, skills, meanings, virtues) and objective (products and profits) results. Corporate governance, then, is the management of the firm in accordance with its specific rules, goods (especially its "common good") and virtues. In MacIntyrean parlance, corporate governance consists of the (second-order) practice of sustaining and maintaining institutions.

Besides the definition of a specific practice, virtues require embeddedness in individual lives and continuity with community traditions. Practical wisdom helps governors navigate role conflicts and advance "best practices" among traditions. Fulfilling these biographical and sociological requirements is fundamental to the institutionalization of practical wisdom in governance. Virtuous corporate governance qualifies as a "good of an individual life" in which agents successfully play multiple roles in different spheres or domains. Corporate governance with practical wisdom represents a "good of a community" when agents meaningfully engage with traditions to discover "the best way to lead" at any given moment.

• The institutionalization of practical wisdom in governance requires embeddedness in individual biographies and community narratives or traditions.

5. Producing scoops of pure goodness at Ben & Jerry's Unilever

"This is too good to be true!" David thought to himself while he stood with six friends—he couldn't make himself think of them as colleagues—and "tested" different mega-cool ice cream flavors at Ben & Jerry's test lab. He'd only been with Ben & Jerry's for half a year and had felt like he'd arrived where he always wanted to be from day one. This was his 6th test session—courtesy of Chris, one of the Flavor Gurus, who had messaged him and the others that the Flavor Creating crew was working on marrying Brazilian vanilla, Scottish malt whisky and *umeboshi* (pickled Japanese plums). Tina, one of his closest colleagues in Marketing, was also munching away and rolling her eyes at either Don's unlikely but true stories about even more outrageous flavors that didn't make it or because her brain was overloaded with the aromas attacking it from all points of the gustatory compass at the same time.

David and Tina had hit it off right from the start because, like him, she had really wanted to work for Ben & Jerry's and had also taken a massive pay cut in exchange for an even bigger happiness raise. Both were serious overachievers by nature: while Tina had worked for L'Oreal for three years, David had worked for the Boston Consulting Group for five years. Both had really liked the people they worked with, the prestige their jobs gave them and the sensational salary they got. But, they had both sensed that something had been missing: the connection between the employees, the work and the world in general was only skin-deep, they had felt. Not at Ben & Jerry's, where everybody worked to spread the love 24/7! What they were doing right now was called "coning together" and was one of the ways in which Ben & Jerry's wanted to make people come together. After his first day at work, Tina had taken David to the freezers where employees picked up their three daily free pints, sat with him on the grass on Thatcher Brook and told him that after three years at Ben & Jerry's she still couldn't believe how good work could be! David suspected that almost everybody shared this feeling: at Ben & Jerry's, totally different people met and created Value and not profits. It was just like one of the founders, Ben Cohen, had said in 1988: "It's really interesting what you can do with business when you don't care about making a lot of money." David and Tina had come across the statement in a case they had done in their Business Ethics class. It had stuck with both of them.

Ben Cohen and Jerry Greenberg didn't want their friendship to end after school and were looking for something they wanted to do and could do together. Their first effort (selling bagels) failed, but their second attempt was super successful right from the get-go. Somehow, what they produced and how they produced it created value for employees, customers, suppliers and even the wider community as a whole. Instead of doing what many see as the important prerequisite for the success of a business, i.e., to systematically extract more value from society than they produce, Ben and Jerry had always thought their success would actually be based on the very opposite: to help the community to achieve its goals better. Successful business, to both founders, must be a variable sum game, and one that should be a lot of fun to play for all involved.

David had actually gotten infatuated with the company before he discovered that he also liked their products. He had attended the top-ranked University of Pennsylvania's bachelor in business program on a full lacrosse scholarship and despite being fiercely competitive, he found himself in his Business Ethics class fascinated by the idea that business isn't about competing and raking in profits, but about cooperation. His professor argued that a successful business is very often based on the belief that business creates something that customers find valuable, and that connects the values of the company with the values of a group of people. Many companies lose sight of that mission, but some don't and are rewarded by stunning and sustained success. Ben & Jerry's was the example the professor used.

The company was founded by two high school friends whom David would have described as utter losers: totally unsporting (they became friends because of that!) with no competitive bone in their body. Their main goal in life was to hang out together and make enough money selling ice cream to finance a simple life. A superficial look at their business's story could make one believe that they essentially stumbled into success by sheer luck: Dumb and Dumber on steroids. They first bummed around doing odd jobs, Jerry was rejected by med school three times, they unsuccessfully tried to sell bagels (United Bagel Service), then took a $5 correspondence course in ice cream making from Penn State of all places, scratched together $8,000 and borrowed $4,000 more, and in May 1978 opened an ice-cream parlor in a disused gas station in Burlington, Vermont. And customers queued from day one to get a scoop. To satisfy demand, reach more customers and get over the winter, they started filling their concoctions into pint cartons in an old spool and bobbin mill in Burlington. Since the ice cream hit the spot with more and more people (a lot actually: between 1984 and 1987, they grew from $4 to 32 million and today their turnover is over $1 billion!), they used a little-known clause about stocks and brokering to raise money for a new manufacturing plant and created a Vermonters-only public company. In 1988, the two hippies with a plant on Thatcher Brook were named US Small Business Persons of the Year by the original neo-Con himself: President Reagan. Ben famously had to borrow a suit from a waiter to not look completely out of place in the White House.

This sounds phenomenally phishy (available in pints since 1997): two Social Justice Warriors, who know a legal loophole that allows them to sell shares to finance the explosive growth of their business, who then get a gong from an arch-capitalist president (Reagan, also an ice cream fan, created the National Ice Cream Month in 1984). To top it all off: in 2000, they join the dark side officially by selling out to Unilever. The end of a fake fairy tale, just like Body Shop and L'Oreal. But just like their super premium ice cream, which is so good only because there are chunks of goodies hidden beneath the creamy surface, there are a lot of rich details that make Ben & Jerry's a very special company, even after they became part of a multinational company (Figure 8.1).

Our three-part Mission guides our decision making

Our Product Mission drives us to make fantastic ice cream — for its own sake.
To make, distribute, and sell the finest quality all natural ice cream and euphoric concoctions with a continued commitment to incorporating wholesome, natural ingredients and promoting business practices that respect the Earth and the Environment.

Our Economic Mission asks us to manage our Company for sustainable financial growth.
To operate the Company on a sustainable financial basis of profitable growth, increasing value for our stakeholders, and expanding opportunities for development and career growth for our employees.

Our Social Mission compels us to use our Company in innovative ways to make the world a better place.
To operate the company in a way that actively recognizes the central role that business plays in society by initiating innovative ways to improve the quality of life locally, nationally, and internationally.

FIGURE 8.1   Ben & Jerry's mission.

What fascinated David most was how Ben and Jerry had managed not only to stay true to their personal ideals, but how they had embedded these values, and thereby their characters, in the DNA of the company. They personally had always wanted to lead a good and simple life, and when the company grew in leaps and bounds, they initially wanted to sell because, as Ben Cohen said: "We were afraid that business exploits its workers and the community" (Kahn 1990). In the end, they decided to trust themselves more than received wisdom and worked on created a caring company. They believed that a happy life is based on doing well because one did good (unsurprisingly, one of their flavors is called Brownie Chew Gooder). In their own words: they wanted to "create linked prosperity for everyone that's connected to our business: suppliers, employees, farmers, franchisees, customers, and neighbors alike." That touched a chord in the lacrosse player in David. A big part of the joy of playing lacrosse, or any sport for that matter, was being your best in a team and making others better through your own excellence. Ben Cohen and Jerry Greenfield simply included more people in their team: everybody! How did they build spreading the love into the structure of the company? On the highest level by explaining that Ben & Jerry's has three connected and equally important missions in life: a social mission, a product mission and an economic mission.

In David's Business Ethics class, they had talked a lot about the missions and how this was different from conventional ways of thinking about strategy. The shareholder approach turned a company into tool to turn out a profit. Apart from the shareholders, the "company" had no humans connected to it, not even employees and customers. That made little sense to anyone in class. The stakeholder approach had humans in the picture, but split into groups whose interests where often clashing. Ben Cohen and Jerry Greenfield's approach took it one level higher and asked fundamental questions that many businesses never ask, but are naturally important questions to all humans: What should I do with my life/ with this company? Why should I do this? The Ben and Jerry never differentiated between themselves as business people and private individuals. They wanted to "make fantastic ice cream," create "sustainable [and] profitable growth" and "make the world a better place." Like in any life, the answers to all the questions are not easy and always require compromises, but can be achieved without compromising fundamental values. David had never looked at business like this and recognized the similarities to questions he asked himself. For instance, in lacrosse: he never cheated, didn't hurt an opponent when the referee wasn't looking and wasn't angry when a teammate scored and he didn't. It wasn't about winning every game at any cost and being the star. Happiness came from being excellent in a community. If he'd won through cheating, that would have devalued success. You cared first about your own team, just like Ben & Jerry's had issued stocks to Vermonters only at first. But when there was a chance to help the opposing team out, you did that too, because it strengthened the wider community of lacrosse players. David, in a tournament, had once joined the other side, because due to a flu epidemic they didn't have enough people on the bench to replace two players who got injured during the match. When the other guys won the tournament, his whole team was invited in the celebrations, and it had almost been as if both teams had won because they appreciated the excellence of each other. Celebrating with more people is just more fun.

When someone in class asked whether selling ultra-high calorie ice cream could be an ethical business, when the cause number one for unhappiness and health issues in the US was obesity, David had an answer that convinced his classmate. First, there is goodness in achieving excellence in what we choose and almost nothing is perfect, but we can strive to make it perfect. Lacrosse was a contact sport and David had hurt people unintentionally while trying to win. Was lacrosse therefore unethical? Is producing cars unethical, because many people die in car wrecks? Second, the possible negative impact on people's lives was mitigated by the other two missions. And third, if one accepts the premise that nothing in life is perfect, individual responsibility cuts both ways: people who abuse ice cream make the choice to do so. Ben Cohen and Jerry Greenfield were never ideological (they call it partisan) about anything; they always sought out the virtuous middle ground. This pattern could be easily deduced from everything they did. They always had had an anti-capitalist sentiment (maybe Jerry rebelled against his stockbroker father), but one of the three missions was economic success. Their ice cream was and still is made from all-natural ingredients that have been fairly traded, but the chunky flavorings could contain artificial stuff when it supported the social mission. The brownies in Chocolate Fudge Brownies contain additives but are produced by Greyston Bakery. The bakery offers job opportunities to the homeless as well as those who served numerous years in prison or are recovering from alcohol or drug addictions, which therefore supports Ben & Jerry's social mission (Grace 2015).

When David was in his last semester of his bachelor's degree, he received multiple offers from top consultancies and very consciously decided to go to BCG because the five people who interviewed him were not only incredibly nice and super smart, but they also appreciated him as a person. Like all consultancies, BCG is a partnership, and that meant that the atmosphere was collegial and rank didn't matter so much. BCG also offered its employees opportunities to do good and had even founded its own charity, the Center for Social Impact. Work at BCG was exhilarating: he was one of the very few new-hires who didn't have a master's or even a doctorate, and working with smarter people and being staffed on projects in different industries meant that he learned something every day. The 60-hour weeks were not an issue for someone who all his life wanted to test and expand his physical and mental abilities, and on top of it, his colleagues were cool people. And then there was the material side of being a strategy consultant: staying at the finest hotels, flying business class, filling his bank account (he had no student debt) and not having the time or energy to spend it on anything, apart from the mandatory tailor-made blue suits he wore. He went from being a student, living in a nice but pretty basic dorm, to renting an apartment in Manhattan, relaxing in VIP lounges in airports and staying on the Club floors of five-star hotels. After four years, David realized that something was missing. At first, he didn't understand what it was: he had been promoted and would be promoted again soon to run his own projects, he had developed his expertise and was now assigned to the financial services industry, his colleagues were great, he was full of energy. He hadn't changed, the work hadn't changed, but he felt different. He sat in team meetings and wasn't excited about the projects anymore. He felt disconnected from his colleagues whose lives and conversations seem to revolve around their mileage and hotel loyalty program accounts.

One evening, his team worked late and they ordered pizzas and ice cream, which they ate in their project office at the client's headquarters building. Suzy, their project leader, had just found a trick to get to highest status level with two airline programs, which got everybody very excited, but he found himself zoning out. He was suddenly back in his Business Ethics classroom talking about Ben & Jerry's and from there drifted to wondering what it would be like to work for them. Taking another spoonful of Americone Dream, he felt more than he thought that it must be very different from working for BCG. They worked on producing something that made people happy (that feeling was probably induced by the fudge-covered waffle he was chewing on) and produced it in a way that was morally excellent, and they did not only work for their clients but for everybody. Suddenly, he realized that his three colleagues were laughing at him, and he heard Suzy say, "I have to try Ben & Jerry's! Davey, you look like you are in love!" A smile spread across his face as he replied, "I think you are right: I am in love with Ben & Jerry's, Suzy!"

The decision was essentially made there and then, but being a trained consultant, he didn't trust his gut feeling and analyzed Ben & Jerry's as best as he could from the outside. He looked at their website, watched all the interviews with Ben Cohen and Jerry Greenfield and scoured the media for articles on Ben & Jerry's. What he found was encouraging. Even the super-critical liberal New York Times was full of praise for Ben & Jerry's: How the social mission of Ben & Jerry's survived being gobbled up (Gelles 2015) gave a glowing account of how Unilever, unlike Starbucks with La Boulange, didn't turn it into a "soulless subsidiary." Paula Caligiuri (2012) thinks that it has a lot to do with the actions of another individual, Yves Couette, Ben & Jerry's first post-takeover CEO. Many observers even opined that Unilever's soul was positively affected by the takeover and that this was part of the attraction that Ben & Jerry's had for Unilever (Reuben 2012). Ben & Jerry's supported Occupy Wall Street, which was aggressively against any multinational company, and Unilever didn't try to shut it down.

This was another thing that David liked about Ben & Jerry's: they were progressive (David thought of himself as a conservative), but they were so incredibly positive about the world and they really believed in personal freedom. On that evening when he made the decision to apply to Ben & Jerry's, he read on the package of Americone Dream: "Nation! This pint contains 1776% of your recommended daily allowance of freedom! It may be illegal to lick the Lincoln Memorial*, but with this ice cream you can do the next best thing and lick liberty! *seriously, it is" (Ben & Jerry's Website). He experienced this lighthearted commitment to spreading the love every day at work. In his opinion, this was the personal wisdom of the two founders embedded in the culture and structure of the company. It allowed Ben & Jerry's to support Occupy Wall Street and both sides of the conflict, Big Business (Unilever) and aggressive anti–capitalists, to like them and maybe understand the other side a bit better.

Unilever, when they executed what was essentially a hostile takeover bid, understood that they would be buying just a product range if they were unable to keep the two characters that gave the company its unique character. And in typical fashion, Ben Cohen and Jerry Greenfield created an independent board of directors and staffed it with very unlike characters who are "heroes for ice cream and hungry for justice" (Ben & Jerry's Website). Ben and Jerry are not even members of the board! As is typical for wise people, one doesn't know what they will do, but when they have acted, one can see the wisdom in their action. The company grew without an organization chart because an org chart creates a hierarchy, and the two kibbutzniks wanted equality, not distance. For the first 15 or so years, this value was expressed by limiting the difference between the highest and the lowest paid employee to a 5:1 ratio. The strategy consultant David (he had been on two M&A projects) was amazed at this. Unilever wanted the two founders to stay and gave them a board of directors and total freedom to define how they would stick around. Ben and Jerry had apparently managed to create trust at Unilever, despite the fact that they didn't want to sell. Staying true to themselves, the two founders revived an old idea. After Jerry, who had left Ben & Jerry's in 1982 to be with his girlfriend while she was doing her PhD in Arizona, returned in 1985, he created and ran Ben & Jerry's Joy Gang. Having failed three times to gain admission to medical school, he had always found managing boring and thought his best contribution to Ben & Jerry's would be to take the boredom out of work for others as well. The activities of the gang included 15-minute massages for the shift workers, Barry Manilow Day, Manufacturing Appreciation Day (managers dressing up as their favorite workers), Name The Face Contest and about a thousand other seriously weird happenings (Carmicheal).

Now Ben, the more serious manager, joined him in running in a new version of Ben & Jerry's Joy Gang. In an interview (Wieder 2003), the gastronomic gangbangers described their role:

JERRY: Well, we're still employed at the company, but we're not involved in operations or management. So we have no responsibility, no authority, and very little influence.

Q: How does that feel?

JERRY: Funny. Very funny. It's very different. We're somewhat goodwill ambassadors for the company, which I like, because—and I think this is true for Ben—we both want to help promote the values of the company, not simply to sell more ice cream, but the other things that the company stands for and works for.

David had met them while they stopped by, but most of the time they spend on the road being not brand ambassadors, but value ambassadors, which, when David thought about it, was the same thing at Ben & Jerry's: they sold goodness. Jerry's humility and sense of humor was something that David noticed immediately when meeting them: of course they had tons of authority, responsibility and influence, just not the formal type. And they never wanted that type of authority because it came at the expense of other people's freedom, joy and creativity. When people in the company listened to them when they were still the owners, they could never be sure that it wasn't their formal authority that was followed. That probably worried two people who grew up in the anti-authoritarian movement of the 1960s a great deal. People's perceptions of how companies are should be governed, i.e., by the managers and owners, are something they struggled against all their lives. Now that they were freed of the burden of being dictators-against-their-will, they could be even more active and outspoken. David remembered with a grin how the pair had been arrested at a Democracy Awakening rally in Washington DC and how he expected a new ice cream flavor to mark the event. Ben Cohen and Jerry Greenfield seemed to have achieved the unthinkable, namely, that a big leviathan of a company like Unilever gave freedom to its employees. The maybe most important precedent was set a few years earlier: Unilever lobbied heavily to not have to tell consumers on the packaging whether the products contained genetically modified organisms, and Ben & Jerry actually lobbied the governor of Vermont to legally require GMO labeling (Boyle 2014). David, who had no opinion on this topic, and actually disagreed with Ben and Jerry on other issues, looked at how the two sides engaged each other. He thought he saw a pattern in how the two ice cream activists acted in this and other instances, and what he saw made him like the company even more. Instead of making the argument on an emotional and political level, i.e., that GMO food is harmful, they appealed to higher order values: freedom and honesty. Consumers should be informed so that they can make their own individual choices. Not only was that smart, because how can anyone argue against honesty without losing trust, but it was also a wise way of reminding all other businesses that they are losing sight of what really matters (trust, honesty, respect, freedom) in favor of short-term profits. The actors in business and life, at the end of the day, were humans, and all humans have to be able to look into the mirror without flinching. Putting values with a small v (profit, growth) before Real Values was a sure way of not being happy with oneself. If David recognized this, he thought it highly likely that some top managers at Unilever also saw the wisdom in this. Just like Ben & Jerry's, Unilever had a founder, who based the success of his business on creating value for society: he had a social mission. Lord William Lever thought that hygiene is a prerequisite to a happy and healthy life and wanted to alleviate the terrible conditions for England's poorest. He sold soap, not in bulk to shops, which at the time sold it by weight to consumers, but wrapped in small pieces of paper, selling them directly to consumers. In one fell swoop, he established the idea of branding individual products, cut out middlemen and made soap popular among the masses. That, however, wasn't enough for him. Just like Ben & Jerry's wanted not only to improve the lives of customers, Lever also cared about the happiness and well-being of his employees. In 1887, he built a model village for his employees, Port Sunlight, and just like Ben Cohen and Jerry Greenfield, he supported progressive social causes and democratic ideals.

In some matters, Lever was keen to allow the residents of Port Sunlight a degree of democratic control, and this seems to have led to a common conviction that he was in favor of women's suffrage: a belief that possibly stems from a situation arising in connection with the Bridge Inn, a Port Sunlight temperance "pub" that was opened in 1900. Lever was a lifelong teetotaler, and he naturally assumed that the Bridge would be "dry." Within two years of its opening, however, representations were made to change its status to a licensed house. Lever promptly announced that he would not impose his own views and that the issue would be decided by a referendum, insisting somewhat unconventionally for that time that women would take part. With the added proviso that the Bridge would only become a true British "pub" if a supermajority of 75% was in favor, Lever probably felt confident that the outcome would support his abstemious sentiments. But in the event more than 80% voted for a liquor license and even though some people petitioned Lever urging him to use his absolute authority in Port Sunlight and ignore the referendum, he refused to do so.

Maybe some Unilever executives really wanted to breathe a soul into the governance structures of their company, David thought to himself. There was a lot of wisdom in that, because rules are applied or disregarded by individuals. But if all individuals shared a belief that certain higher-order rules based on higher-order values are simply good in any possible circumstance, then everybody would govern their own behavior. There would be no need to police employees' observance of company policy because they all shared the same values.

And just like Lord Lever was wise enough to give his employees the freedom to disagree with him on not drinking alcohol because he recognized that respect and freedom are higher-order values, Unilever managers agreed to disagree with their Port Sunlight, Ben & Jerry's, on GMO labeling. When David thought about it, he remembered his Business Ethics professor talking about one major difference between modern approaches to ethics and virtue ethics: virtues lie in the middle between two vices and that enabled people to have different assessments. In effect, there were many ethical solutions for one problem: two wise people could stand on two different sides of an issue, and both could be ethical at the same time! Morality was not always about right and wrong, black and white. Unilever respected Ben & Jerry's decision, just as Ben & Jerry's allowed David to have different opinions on any issue. It was about respect and freedom creating the basis for being a happy but disagreeing member of a company.

Comparing Unilever and Ben & Jerry made another thing clear to David: values, individuals and communities must never be separated and they must be cared for. Otherwise, over time, rules replace values and good practices. When rules are simply applied without reflection and because employees fear negative consequences, values disappear, individuals become selfish and communities are replaced by machine-like organizations. On top of that, there was probably also a tendency for companies to control more and ratchet up the punishments and thereby destroy the very base for a community to flourish: trust. No joy in working in such an environment.

As he was chewing on a piece of tangy *umeboshi*, David looked at his friends chatting and joking and was very happy with the decision to forego a life in business class to help spread the love while coning together.

Case discussion guidelines

1   Why did David not stay with BCG and work in their Center for Social Impact?
     The idea is to break the separation between work and life, which is very strong in students without work experience. Character cannot be split into work and private life. Many traditional companies today give their employees opportunities to do good and many companies are engaged in philanthropy. David wanted his daily work filled with meaning, instead of trying to put a social band-aid on his real job, which was creating profit for the company.
2   How does the structure of Ben & Jerry's reflect the character of the two founders?
     Students should understand the respective roles of character and rules. All individuals are governed by their character, and if they have to change their character to conform to corporate rules, they might not like that. The triple mission should be discussed. Long-term profitability is flanked by what and how the company produces its goods and what the social impact (in- and

outside the company) is. All three missions depend on each other; the relationship is not antagonistic: the more social value is produced, the more profits are generated.

3   What is the role of rules when it comes to ethical behavior?

Rules are not self-enforcing: either individual members of a corporation follow the rules or they don't. Students should understand that the logical sequence is not rules then behavior, but values, rules, behavior. Thus, in a company where the rules are based on shared values, they are more likely to be followed. In a virtue ethical framework, rules give guidance to employees—they help them to make better decisions. Governance is an environment that can allow individuals to develop excellence. If, however, it is set up to force compliance, it destroys.

4   How can there be objective and flexible rules in virtue ethics?

Students have been raised to view every value as equally important, and in order to understand virtue ethics, they need to understand why virtue ethics thinks there are objective/absolute rules. Objective rules refer to highest-order values that are agreed upon within a community. Respect and freedom are examples of such values. Students should be asked if they have some values that are really important for them. The goal is to enable students to see that how these values are expressed in action is flexible, because in virtue ethics, the mean covers a wide range of possible actions.

References

Aristotle. 1971, *Metaphysics* (trans. and notes C. Kirwan) Oxford: Clarendon Press.

Aristotle. 1985, *Nicomachean ethics* (Irwin, T., trans.), Indianapolis, IN: Hackett Publishing.

Aristotle. 1991, *Aristotle on rhetoric: A theory of civic discourse* (Kennedy, G.A., trans.) Oxford: Oxford University Press.

Ben & Jerry's. 2016, 'Why Ben and Jerry just got arrested', (www.benjerry.com/whats-new/2016/ben-and-jerry-arrested, Accessed September 27, 2017).

Boyle, M. 2014, 'Ben & Jerry's GMO food fight. The ice cream maker's support for GMO labeling clashes with parent Unilever's opposition', (www.bloomberg.com/news/articles/2014-07-31/gmo-labeling-ben-and-jerrys-parent-company-unilever-at-odds, Accessed September 27, 2017).

Caligiuri, P. 2012, 'When Unilever bought Ben & Jerry's: A story of CEO adaptability', (www.fastcompany.com/3000398/when-unilever-bought-ben-jerrys-story-ceo-adaptability, Accessed September 27, 2017).

Gelles, D. 2015, 'How the social mission of Ben & Jerry's survived being gobbled up', (www.nytimes.com/2015/08/23/business/how-ben-jerrys-social-mission-survived-being-gobbled-up.html?_r=0, Accessed September 27, 2017).

Grace. 2015, 'You won't believe who bakes the brownie bits in Ben & Jerry's ice cream', (https://spoonuniversity.com/lifestyle/ben-and-jerrys-brownie-bits-baked-by-former-inmates-drug-addicts, Accessed September 27, 2017).

Hursthouse, R. 1999, *On virtue ethics*, Oxford: Oxford University Press.

John XXIII. 1961, *Encyclical Letter 'Mater et magistra'*, Vatican City: Vatican Polyglot Press. (http://w2.vatican.va/content/john-xxiii/en/encyclicals/documents/hf_j-xxiii_enc_15051961_mater.html, Accessed September 27, 2017).

John Paul II. 1981, *Encyclical Letter 'Laborem exercens'*, Vatican City: Vatican Polyglot Press. (http://w2.vatican.va/content/john-paul-ii/en/encyclicals/documents/hf_jp-ii_enc_14091981_laborem-exercens.html, Accessed September 27, 2017).

Kahn, T. 1990, 'For new age ice-cream moguls Ben and Jerry. Making 'Cherry Garcia' and 'Chunky Monkey' is a labor of love', *People Magazine*. (http://people.com/archive/for-new-age-ice-cream-moguls-ben-and-jerry-making-cherry-garcia-and-chunky-monkey-is-a-labor-of-love-vol-34-no-10/, Accessed September 27, 2017).

MacIntyre, A. 1994, 'A partial response to my critics', in J. Horton and S. Mendus (eds.), *After MacIntyre: Critical perspectives on the work of Alasdair MacIntyre*, Notre Dame, IN: University of Notre Dame Press, 283–404.

MacIntyre, A.C. 2007 [1981], *After virtue* (3rd ed.), London: Duckworth.

Moore, G. 2012, 'The virtue of governance, the governance of virtue', *Business Ethics Quarterly*, 22(2): 293–318.

Reuben, A. 2012, 'Did Ben & Jerry's change Unilever?', (www.bbc.com/news/business-18167345, Accessed September 24, 2017).

Shleifer, A. and Vishny, R. 1997, 'A survey of corporate governance', *Journal of Finance*, 52: 737–783.

Sison, A.J.G. 2000a, 'The cultural dimension of codes of corporate governance: A focus on the Olivencia Report', *Journal of Business Ethics*, 27(1/2): 181–192.

Sison, A.J.G. 2000b, 'Integrated risk management and global business ethics', *Business Ethics: A European Review*, 9(4): 288–295.

Sison, A.J.G. 2003, *The moral capital of leaders. Why virtue matters*, Cheltenham, UK; Northampton, MA: Edward Elgar.

Sison, A.J.G. 2008, *Corporate governance and ethics. An Aristotelian perspective*, Cheltenham, UK; Northampton, MA: Edward Elgar.

Sison, A.J.G. and Fontrodona, J. 2012, 'The common good of the firm in the Aristotelian-Thomistic tradition', *Business Ethics Quarterly*, 22(2): 211–246.

Telfer, E. 1990, 'The unity of the moral virtues in Aristotle's "Nicomachean ethics"', *Proceedings of the Aristotelian Society*, 90(1989–1990): 35–48.

Wieder, T. 2003, 'Coneheads – Ice-cream icons Ben and Jerry may have sold their famed company, but the pair still has the scoop on Boston's favorite dessert', *Boston Phoenix*. (www.bostonphoenix.com/boston/news_features/qa/documents/03073228.asp, Accessed September 27, 2017).

Wikipedia. 2017, 'William Lever, 1st Viscount Leverhulme', (https://en.wikipedia.org/wiki/William_Lever,_1st_Viscount_Leverhulme, Accessed September 27, 2017).

Williams, O. 1985, *The economic institutions of capitalism*, New York: The Free Press.

Zingales, L. 1997, "Corporate governance," *NBER Working Paper Series*, n. 6309. (www.nber.org/papers/w6309, December, Accessed September 27, 2017).

9

CONFUCIAN TRADITIONS IN VIRTUE ETHICS

Richard Kim, Reuben Mondejar, Richard Roque and Javier Calero Cuervo

Learning objectives

In this chapter, we will:

- Explain the basic framework of Confucian virtue ethics, demonstrating how it supports a conception of business inseparable from moral ends and the common good.
- Identify how a core Confucian virtue, ritual propriety, is relevant to business practices.
- Show how some behaviors such as gambling commonly observed in Confucian communities are compatible with virtue ethics and business.

On one interpretation, Confucian ethics is a form of virtue ethics, a normative theory that takes the cultivation of certain robust character traits as foundational for both acting and living well (Yearley 1990; Ivanhoe 2000; Sim 2007; VanNorden 2007; Yu 2007; Angle 2009). In this chapter, we explore how the Confucian moral framework supports the view that the proper end of a business is the promotion of the common good. We will focus on the way Confucians—more specifically, the early Confucians represented in the *Analects, Mencius* and *Xunzi*—prioritize moral virtue over material welfare and understand proper governance as requiring the ruler to truly care about the flourishing of the people. Additionally, we will identify and explain how a key virtue in Confucian ethics, *li* (ritual propriety), is relevant to business practice.

1. Confucians on the hierarchy of goods

The Confucian vision of a well-ordered, flourishing society achieved through a turn to social civility and personal cultivation is exemplified in the teachings of Confucius (Kongzi 551–479 BC), contained in the *Analects*. One of the primary aims of Confucius was to move rulers to cultivate virtues and govern with benevolence:

> If you try to guide the common people with coercive regulations and keep them in line with punishments, the common people will become evasive and will have no sense of shame. If, however, you guide them with Virtue, and keep them in line by means of ritual, the people will have a sense of shame and will rectify themselves.
>
> *(Analects: 2.3)*

Instead of focusing on law and punishment as the primary tools of governance, the ruler should seek above all to establish a culture that forms the ethical character of people. Once people have well-ordered attitudes and beliefs, they will be internally motivated to live according to the law. The most important step is for the ruler himself to develop the moral qualities of deep compassion and wisdom necessary for truly caring about the welfare of the state. For the state to flourish, the ruler must prioritize the common good above any other goal, including military power or territorial dominance. Only when the ruler truly cares about the good of people and keeps their good as the primary end of governance will the state flourish. Confucius himself exemplifies this focus on human welfare: "One day the stables burned. When the Master returned from court, he asked, 'Was anyone hurt?' He did not ask about the horses" (*Analects:* 10.17). Given that horses were expensive and stable workers possessed a low social status, Confucius' question clearly expresses prioritization of human lives over material goods. Underlying Confucius' ethical thinking is a system of values distinguishing between the noble and base, the broad-minded and petty: "The gentleman cherishes virtue, whereas the petty person cherishes physical possessions. The gentleman thinks about punishments, whereas the petty person thinks about exemptions" (*Analects:* 4.11).

These remarks identify one important insight virtue ethics can bring to our understanding of business. Contrary to what many economists claim, it is incorrect to characterize human beings as solely motivated by narrow self-interest, as *homo economicus*. How we conceive our interests or well-being is deeply shaped by our ethical outlook and the values we endorse. For Confucians, having a properly formed character is a necessary condition for a correct understanding of well-being. On the Confucian view, the gentleman or sage not only has the right kind of character, but also a true understanding of what really matters in life and what constitutes human flourishing.

Mencius (Mengzi 391–308 BC), in the beginning of an eponymous work (perhaps the most influential Confucian text in East Asian intellectual history after the *Analects*), is found in conversation with King Hui of Liang. The king, notorious for his greed and power, initiates the dialogue saying, "Sir, you have come, not regarding one thousand *li* as too far. Surely you will have something to profit my state?" Mengzi responds with a poignant rebuke:

> Why must Your Majesty say, 'profit'? Let there be benevolence and right-eousness and that is all. Your Majesty says, 'How can my state be profited?' The Counselors say, 'How can my family be profited?' The scholars and commoners say, 'How can I be profited?' Those above and those below mutually compete for profit and the state is endangered.[1]
>
> *(Mencius: 1A1)*

Like Confucius, Mencius also gives priority to virtue or moral goodness over profit. This passage exemplifies two key points for our topic: (1) focusing on one's narrow self-interest, whether from the perspective of personal welfare or business interests, is counterproductive, and (2) virtue or moral goodness offers the most stable way of realizing material goods. The basic line of reasoning behind (1) and (2) might be briefly reconstructed in the following way. When people become solely preoccupied with profit or self-interest, the result is a more competitive mindset that decreases social cohesion and increases vices such as callousness and greed. Ultimately, this results in diminished trade and productivity. While Mencius recognizes that profit and material goods are legitimate ends of both the state and people, the most effective way to realize these ends is by helping every-one develop morally good attitudes and dispositions (i.e., the virtues), since they are necessary for the proper social conditions that promote trust, reciprocity and justice—conditions that are crucial to the production and flow of material goods.

It would be a misunderstanding, however, to take Confucianism as seeing the value of virtues in wholly utilitarian terms. Like many virtue ethicists, Confucians hold a non-consequentialist view of what makes actions right. There are certain kinds of acts—those that go against certain Confucian virtues—that are never permissible. The early Confucian Xunzi (310–219 BC) says of the "true king":

> "Even if they could obtain the whole world by performing a single act that goes against *yi* ("righteousness") or by killing a single innocent person, they would not do it" (*Xunzi*: 54–55). And in Mencius we also find certain absolute prohibitions, as revealed in his comments about the actions of sages: "if any could obtain the world by performing one unrighteous deed, or killing one innocent person, he would not do it".
>
> *(Mengzi: 2A2.24)*

Applied to business, these two elements of Confucian ethics—the non-consequentialist perspective and the priority of moral excellence over material goods—yield two important claims: good business practices cannot be detached from moral considerations, and when business practices are properly situated within a moral framework, they are more likely to succeed.

Based on the foregoing discussion, Confucian virtue ethics provides several important thoughts relevant to the ethics of business. The first is that the leader has to consider the common good rather than just self-interest. The virtue of "ren" (benevolence or humaneness) prompts him towards a mission orientation that gives weight to moral reasons.

It is useful to recall that the Ming and Qing dynasties saw a growth of the Confucian merchants ("Ru shang"), which originally began during the Qin Dynasty. Many well-known merchants gave food, medicine, shelters and other goods and established schools for the poor and those afflicted by disaster.

Today, there is an emerging revival of Confucianism and the promotion of the Modern Confucian Merchant, whose basic qualities are as follows:

a   Upright moral character;
b   Ability to balance profit with righteousness;
c   Courageousness and a competitive spirit;
d   Spirit of innovation and entrepreneurship;
e   Management centering on the good of the people.

The promotion of the common good as articulated earlier also relates to the mission of the enterprise. In this context, the enterprise mission could take a "stakeholder approach", since it advocates "solidarity," which aims at achieving the common good of all stakeholders: customers, suppliers, community, government, investors, employees and competitors. Another important issue is recognizing the need to optimize benefits—in other words, create value for each stakeholder.

• Confucianism endorses a hierarchical ordering of human goods that prioritizes moral goodness and virtue over material goods and profit. It is only through a proper formation of character that one can fully appreciate the differences between the higher and lower goods and have an accurate understanding of what matters in life. Moreover, it is only by first gaining the virtues that material goods can be effectively achieved, at the level of both the individual and state.

2. Applying Confucian concepts to a Chinese NGO

A company that would typify this stakeholder approach is Carpenter Tan, a wooden accessories manufacturing, franchising and retail enterprise based in Southwest China that went public in the Hong Kong Stock Exchange in late 2009. The company's mission includes assisting people with disabilities enter the labor market by providing them with appropriate training so they move from welfare reliance to self-reliance. Their goal is: "Strive to provide more employment opportunities for people and improve their quality of life and enrich the content of life for them." More than 50% of the company's employees (over 300) at the manufacturing facilities are handicapped and have some form of disability. These persons include the deaf, speech-impaired, disabled and those who suffer from learning disabilities.

The core values are in honesty, hard work and achievement of happiness, whilst at the same time, they aim to make a significant contribution to society.

To the end-customers: the company employs rigorous quality control and informs them of any weak points of their product. To the franchisees: the company adopts a measured pace of limiting the number of new franchisees, so as to ensure that the existing franchisees are able to generate a profit. To the employees: the company provides education and training programs, and encourages the pursuit of job excellence through sharing and on-site training. The company also has established a share option scheme for employees for up to 10% of the issued capital of the company. To its shareholders: the company generates a return on equity of approximately 30% during the past three years, with an average dividend payout ratio of 50%. To the government: the company employs disabled persons, generates jobs and pays lower preferential rate taxes. To society at large: The company encourages its employees to take time to be involved in social programs in remote villages, to provide training to the children and to engage in various community services such as donating books, stationery and money to poor students or going to nursing homes, chatting with the elders and helping them overcome any physical or emotional challenges. In addition, the company established an internal foundation for poor employees or those who urgently need money as a result of serious illness. The company has also made a significant donation of RMB 2 million for earthquake disaster. To the environment: Although the company consumes wood for its products, it plants more trees around the country to protect the environment.

From the aforementioned, it appears that the stakeholder approach has created a virtuous circle between the company and its stakeholders. Its operations deliver benefits to all its stakeholders that, in turn, lead to an enduring support by the stakeholders for the company. It is worth noting that while the share option scheme is primarily for employees, it is also available to other stakeholders of the company such as suppliers, customers and service providers.

Carpenter Tan is one of few social enterprises that have recently arisen in Greater China that has managed to achieve significant profitability and growth. Social entrepreneurship is still in an embryonic stage in China, and as awareness grows and Impact Investment makes inroads, we expect many more social entrepreneurs with innovative business models to emerge, creating significant financial and social value.

- Carpenter Tan is an excellent example of a social enterprise that has achieved both significant profit and growth by focusing on a business model that is genuinely concerned with a moral end—improving the lives of those with disabilities. By aiming at the good of both employees and customers, and focusing on virtues such as honesty and hard work, Carpenter Tan highlights the Confucian idea that profit is a natural corollary of virtue and that morality and economic success can be integrated for the good of all.

3. Confucianism on the virtues of ritual

The Confucians prioritized virtues over other goods such as wealth and power. But what are the Confucian virtues? In the *Analects,* we find Confucius advocating certain traits of character: "goodness" (*ren*), "courage" (*yong*), "trustworthiness" (*xin*), "understanding" (*shu*) and "filial piety" (*xiao*). Mencius and Xunzi discuss, albeit in different ways, virtues such as "righteousness" (*yi*) and "ritual propriety" (*li*). Because different early Confucian texts give different, though not necessarily incompatible, accounts of the virtues, and since there are numerous ongoing debates about the nature and scope of Confucian virtues, we will turn our attention to just one virtue that lies at the heart of Confucian ethics: the virtue of ritual propriety (*li*).

The Confucians did not neatly separate the virtue of ritual from the practice of rituals, perhaps because the good of rituals is closely connected to the value of ritual practice. With this point in mind, we will focus mostly on the value of ritual practices. Reflecting on the value of rituals can bring to light a number of points that, as we will later see, are relevant to business.

The Confucian conception of ritual is broad, covering not only large-scale ceremonies such as weddings and funerals, but also small gestures such as handshakes or bows and appropriate manners of speech. The Confucians take rituals as lying at the heart of any well-ordered society, helping to establish a proper moral framework for social interactions and for participating with others in significant social events. Rituals underscore the Confucian conception of human beings as social creatures that cannot be understood outside of familial and communal contexts. The complete realization of human potential, on the Confucian view, requires the fulfillment of the key roles that partially constitute one's identity: being a daughter, son, mother, father, worker or leader. But how exactly do rituals help one fulfill these roles? Rituals provide the proper rules and boundaries of social interactions, thereby regulating how one should comport oneself in both everyday activities and major events. By attaching a socially recognizable meaning to rituals, e.g., a bow expresses a gesture of respect towards another, proper emotions and intentions are communicated that strengthen social bonds and decrease the risk of negative feelings such as hostility or resentment that can lead to social erosion.

Rituals are at the heart of Confucian virtue ethics because they provide reliable and consistent guidance for behavior and emotion regulation:

> "The Master said, 'If you are respectful but lack ritual you will become exasperating; if you are careful but lack ritual you will become timid; if you are courageous but lack ritual you will become unruly; and if you are upright but lack ritual you will become inflexible.'"
>
> *(Analects: 8.2)*

Here, Confucius seems to anticipate certain findings in contemporary social psychology, noting how easily our character can become fragmented and breed vice.

Rituals, Confucius seems to suggest, help unify the virtues by harmonizing the different inclinations and emotions and rectifying wayward dispositions.

From a modern perspective, Confucian rituals may appear too inflexibly tied up with socially acceptable norms. But while it is fair to say that Confucians value the importance of tradition and upholding ritual practices passed down through generations, they do not advocate blind conformity. Confucius himself was open to revising the rituals, depending on the role and function that a specific ritual serves: "The Master said, 'A ceremonial cap made of linen is prescribed by the rites, but these days people use silk. This is frugal, and I follow the majority. To bow before ascending the stairs is what is prescribed by the rites, but these days people bow after ascending. This is arrogant, and—thought it goes against the majority—I continue to bow before ascending'" (*Analects*: 9.3). Here we see Confucius both willing and unwilling (on different occasions) to follow the majority with regard to ritual practices, based on considerations about the nature of their ends and particular context.

Consider another intriguing passage in the *Analects*: "Zigong wanted to do away with the practice of sacrificing a lamb to announce the beginning of the month. The Master said, 'Zigong! You regret the loss of the lamb, whereas I regret the loss of the rite'" (*Analects*: 3.17). What Confucius seems to identify here is the loss of certain goods internal to the ritual, which would be lost without the sacrificial lamb. Borrowing from Alasdair MacIntyre's influential definition, we might characterize goods internal to rituals as those goods that can only be achieved by participating in the particular ritual and can only be understood by those who participate in the ritual practice (MacIntyre 2007[1981]). Far too often, those outside a particular tradition can easily fail to grasp the significance of a particular practice, because they are unable to appreciate how a particular element of a practice or ritual constitutes an essential aspect of a tradition. Confucius clearly affirms that the sacrificial lamb played a critical, irreplaceable role in the ritual practice and believes the loss of the lamb would have entailed the loss of the rite, and therefore, the loss of whatever goods were internal to it.

Another important aspect of rituals is that they require wholehearted participation: "Sacrifice as if [they were] present" means that, when sacrificing to the spirits, you should comport yourself as if the spirits were present. The Master said, "If I am not fully present at the sacrifice, it is as if I did not sacrifice at all" (*Analects*: 3.12). Proper engagement in ritual requires commitment and mindfulness. Simply going through the motions is insufficient.

Let us now identify three goods tied to the practice of ritual:

1   Social Cohesion. Rituals help signify the recognition of dignity and value towards others. By conferring interpersonal actions with socially shared meaning—hugs indicating affection, for example—rituals strengthen social bonds.

2   Role-Fulfillment. One of the central aspects of living well, on the Confucian view, is the fulfillment of one's fundamental roles. Because rituals help

define the boundaries of proper speech and behaviors, they help individuals understand how to act properly in different circumstances.

3   Emotional Fulfillment. Rituals not only help mark out significant events in one's life—e.g., graduation, marriage, death—but they also help human beings give shape to emotions that are often difficult to express. The best example here is the ritual of funeral. We find a way of expressing grief, which allows us to cope with loss.

- Ritual provides a social script that helps regulate interpersonal conduct in ways that increase respectful attitudes and behaviors. Rituals also help to define social roles, which helps to establish boundaries of conduct and social expectations, mitigating potential areas of social conflict. Finally, rituals help give shape to deep feelings such as grief at the death of loved ones or joy at the celebration of new life. Because rituals take place within a public setting, they help give meaning to certain social events, which can help bind the members of communities.

4. Manuel and the *Ouro* casino-hotel in Macau

"Who were the losers in the game of gambling?" The question echoed repeatedly as Manuel boarded his flight in Zurich, to get back home to Macau and take over his father's business.

Manuel's father, Mr. Vong, ill and in his late 70s, is the owner of a historic hotel whose early-nineteenth-century, Portuguese-inspired façade was listed as part of Macau's tangible heritage. The *Ouro* morphed into an exclusive 88-suite premium hotel that recently attracted high rollers to its quiet Coloane village location in the southernmost part of Macau. All other casino hotels were located in the Macau peninsula, Taipa and the Cotai region.

Mr. Vong was a frugal, quiet, self-made man. He was a likeable, trusted and a respected businessman. Mr. Vong attributes his success to holding on to the virtues taught and lived by his parents, who were staunch followers of Confucian values. In 2002, just two years after Macau's handover to China, Mr. Vong agreed to the offer made by Mr. Hou's company to operate the gaming tables at the *Ouro* for the 20-year concession granted by the Macau Special Administrative Region (S.A.R.).

In 2002, the central government of the People's Republic of China designated Macau as the only place in China where it is legal for citizens to gamble. This designation catapulted Macau to become the world's top Gross Gaming Revenues (GGR), earning $27.98 billion in 2016 (Gaming Inspection and Coordination Bureau 2017). While the Chinese, in general, have a liking for gambling, it was the Portuguese government, administering the small enclave of Macau in Southern China since the sixteenth century, that decided to legalize the activity in 1847, overseeing the Chinese operators of games of luck and fortune.

Casino operators in Macau were happy with their earnings, which they reinvested to expand their properties. Meanwhile, the government of the Macau S.A.R. was also cashing in from tax revenues with an effective tax rate of 39% of Gross Gaming Revenues.

Just as Manuel was relishing delicious dim sum, Katrina, his best friend who operates a successful traditional Chinese medicine business in Macau, quipped: "So how are you going to reconcile your Confucian values with running a hotel with a large stake in gambling?" It was a valid concern for Manuel, given what he had read concerning the risks faced by the gambling industry in Macau due to "money laundering issues" and the need for better oversight on gamblers and junket promoters.

Legalized in 2010, junket operators coordinate high roller gamblers to play at VIP tables, contributing 70% of casino revenues. Junket operators serve as lenders to high stakes gamblers who play at VIP rooms; they receive 40% of the casino's take in return. The junket operators also help guests to coordinate accommodation, transportation and entertainment when they come to Macau. The *Ouro* Hotel's 88 rooms have been totally taken over by junket operators.

Manuel understood that the well-being of *all* stakeholders and profits were necessary to keep the *Ouro* Hotel business competitive. He knew that games of chance were deeply embedded in Chinese culture and also believed it to be a legitimate form of rest and leisure. Moreover, gambling is legal in Macau and is a major driver of the economy, providing employment and revenues to the government as well as sustaining the livelihood of thousands of citizens. But, "Where's the limit?" Manuel pondered and asked: "How does the gambling industry promote human flourishing and the common good in Macau?"

In November 2015, China cracked the nation's biggest "underground bank," which handled 410 billion yuan ($64 billion) of illegal foreign-exchange transactions, as the authorities tried to rein in capital outflows (Macau Daily Times 2015). The effects of the anticorruption drive have been compounded by the broader economic slowdown nationwide. "From a peak of around $30 billion in gambling revenue in 2013, revenue from high rollers at Macau's casinos has fallen more than 50 percent. Players have been defaulting on loans from junket operators or taking longer to repay. Fraud has also been an issue" (Gough 2015).

In April 2016, it was noted that the Macau authorities had established stricter accounting standards for junket operators, leading to the non-renewal of license for 35 operators for failure to submit financial accounts (Macau Daily Times 2016). The *Ouro* Hotel took the hit too, as its occupancy rate fell to 60%—the hotel's worse performance in history.

Reflecting on how Macau has changed in the past 17 years—the economic benefits and social costs—Manuel had given serious thought to a number of issues: "Should *Ouro* Hotel consider foregoing the renewal of the gaming concession when its term ends in 2022?" "Is the gambling business consistent with Confucian values?" Through his reading about the history of gambling in China, Manuel had come to believe that Confucius had a saying that "a gentleman does not gamble." This belief (whether or not Confucius really had said this) yielded a significant influence on the rules and regulations laid down by many Chinese imperial rulers throughout history to restrict gambling. It should be pointed out that in Macau it is illegal for government employees and civil servants to gamble at casinos in Macau, except for a few days during the Chinese New Year celebrations.

Manuel was also saddened by the situation of his good friend Joe, whose gambling addiction fostered other vices that made a mess of his health, marriage and family. Joe's history somewhat mirrored the five stages identified in a publication on Counsellors' reflection on gambling (Tang 2008): from being a *Social* gambler (for socialization, like small bets in *mahjong*) to a *Regular* gambler (for leisure activity to kill time), to a *Transitional* gamblers (i.e., a person who experienced a sad turn of event in life and turned to gambling to escape stress), to a *Problem* gambler (i.e., a person's daily family, social and professional life are jeopardized by gambling) and finally to being a *Pathological* gambler.

A study commissioned by the Social Welfare Bureau of the Macau S.A.R. found that 2.5% of a sample of 2,000 residents in Macau aged 18 and above were probably suffering from gambling disorder (IAS 2017). The same report also observed that "the results showed that only 43% of the respondents were able to explain 'Gambling Disorder' or 'Problem Gambling' accurately. In other words, there is still room for people to increase their awareness and understanding of Gambling Disorder. Hence, it is suggested to strengthen the public education on Gambling Disorder and its related issues so as to reduce the personal and social cost produced by Gambling Disorder." The psyche of a *Problem* gambler is such that "those who frequently lose often insist in believing that they will win in future," chasing all past losses.

While most of the punters in Macau come from Mainland China and Hong Kong, Macau's residents also engage in gambling, although to a significantly lesser degree. Nonetheless, the concern of compulsive and pathological behavior in gambling has led the government, together with other concerned stakeholders, to initiate the "Responsible Gambling Awareness Week," which started in 2009 and was held annually. The Institute for the Study of Commercial Gaming notes that "Responsible Gambling occurs in a properly regulated environment where one's involvement in gambling activities brings no harm to the gamblers, family members, friends, other gamblers, or casino staff; nor would it lead to negative consequences for the local community and residents." (The Institute for the Study of Commercial Gaming 2016).

In other words, the objective of Responsible Gambling is a practice that mitigates gambling-related damages. For example, Manuel's auntie Fanny bets 500 MOP ($62.50) every month as stipulated in her late husband's wish and will that she enjoy some pastime at the *Casino Lisboa* in Macau. Responsible Gambling consists of: (1) understanding the risk of gambling; (2) awareness that there is no way to predict gambling outcomes; (3) knowing the longer one gambles, the more one loses; (4) setting a budget for gambling; (5) setting a time limit for gambling; (6) not gambling when drunk; (7) not borrowing to finance gambling; and (8) seeking help proactively (The Institute for the Study of Commercial Gaming 2016).

At times, Manuel felt guilty when reflecting on the fact that some people like Joe, who were suffering from gambling addiction, were the ones who were contributing to his business profits. He thought to himself: "How could Confucian ideas justify this?"

Manuel recalled that lying at the heart of Confucianism was the practice of ritual (*li*) and began to reflect on how rituals—with their power to shape and determine emotions and behaviors through controlling the social environment—might work to decrease problematic gambling and regulate gambling in ways that would advance the interests of both consumers and companies. Perhaps thinking of gambling as a ritual could draw attention to the specific roles and duties (key aspects of Confucian ethics) attached to both consumers and casinos. From the Confucian, ritual-centered perspective, the gamblers need to respect the rules of the casino and to engage in a leisurely activity and enjoy the experience. On the other hand, one of the roles of the casino is to make sure that individual players do not lose excessively, resulting in a financial disaster. From a Confucian point of view, the Casinos should not think of themselves as aiming solely to maximize profits, but to set policies and act in ways that aim at the good of the players too. In this way, both the casino and the players can be conceived as participating in a ritual practice that results in benefits to both parties. On the one hand, players get to experience the excitement and fun that moderate gambling, as a form of entertainment, can provide. On the other hand, casinos, with their positive mathematical edge, enjoy profits. But, just as every participant in a Confucian ritual must uphold a set of duties generated by the nature of one's role, both casinos and players also must fulfill certain obligations. Reconceiving the relationship between casino and player in this way by appealing to Confucian rituals could reduce the amount of problematic gambling and increase the probability of a more mutually beneficial exchange of goods and services. Casinos, by caring about the good of their customers, could actually benefit financially in the long-run, by promoting gambling as a safe form of entertainment and also by ensuring that gambling does not ultimately result in economic drain for the society.

One concern that troubled Manuel was that by thinking of gambling as a ritual, it might make it a more routine and socially encouraged behavior, leading to even more problematic gambling. But, while rituals are sometimes conceived as unreflective, routinized behavior, the conception of ritual from the Confucian perspective was not that of mindless, repetitive activity, but a social practice carried out with care and attention that advances the common good. Ritual should, on this picture, be understood as a deeply moral activity that cannot be detached from the moral ends it serves.

In fact, Manuel recalled that he had read the Mission statement of SJM Holdings, the owner of the *Casino Lisboa*, stating that "In 1962, Dr. Stanley Ho promised: Our purpose is to bring a new prosperity to Macau and to improve the welfare and living standards of its citizens" (SJM Holdings Limited 2016).

How could the concept of ritual be positively employed to shape the attitudes and behavior of managers and employees in *Ouro* Hotel? Again, Manuel believed that reflecting on rituals could highlight the duties that casinos have towards the gamers. Concretely, this means training *Ouro*'s customer-facing employees to treat guests as friends and remind them with phrases like "Don't gamble away all your money" or "save for next time." Since the power of rituals partly resides in the way that they reinforce certain patterns of thought and action, instituting such phrases in casinos could provide subtle, psychological cues that could nudge gamers away from problematic gambling and excessive loss. Manuel believed that it is important to manage the often conflicting goals of long-term customer relationships with the hotel's Revenue Management (RM)'s short term goal.

Besides addressing the challenges of *Ouro* Hotel, Manuel wanted to serve Macau's stakeholders by being a pioneer in establishing an association that shows how Confucian values, especially ritual practice, could serve to promote Responsible Gambling for Casino operators. He believed that he could lead the effort in providing the specialized training and workshops for employees of Casinos in Macau to interact effectively in preventing punters from becoming *Problem* gamblers. Moreover, the management should set a limit for hosts or promoters to follow in order to prevent gamblers from excessive gambling, which in turn will affect the sustainability of the business as well. Manuel also felt that the exclusion law on gambling about revocation by gamblers should be amended further.

Managers are tested when the going gets tough for those belonging to the same industry subject to the same conditions. Such is the case in Macau, where satisfying the various stakeholders' interests can be a major challenge.

Manuel continued to observe that casinos are a tried-and-tested money-making formula on which thousands of families in Macau depend. Casino workers—especially the local dealers—cannot be retrained for a different job overnight. What are the implications for the casino workers in *Ouro* Hotel, should Manuel decide to end the gaming concession? Should Manuel insist, rather, on "family-friendly" casinos? How could the Confucian values be of help in these decisions? Should Manuel's decision for *Ouro* Hotel be based on long-term considerations, such as the end of the 50-year Special Administrative Region for Macau in China? Exhausted, Manuel decides to go home. Going over the poems of Du Fu, he reflects on *What a Night!*[2] (Young 2008):

> What a night this is—old year out, new one in,—long watch, bright candles—
> none of their light wasted;—here in the local Inn;—what pastimes do we have?
>> we can throw dice to keep ourselves amused
>> one man leans across the table, begging for five to come up,
>> another rolls up his sleeves before he throws and loses,
>> all the politicians roll dice too, and lose
>> but an accidental meeting just might bring good fortune;
>> don't laugh at that! remember that nonentity, Liu Yi,
>> penniless, and willing to risk millions!

Manuel could not avoid the recurring question—"Who were the losers in the game of gambling?" Vexed and confused, Manuel calls Katrina for her sound advice. She simply asked Manuel to remember the wisdom of Pushkin in *The*

Queen of Spades: "Play interests me very much but I am not in the position to sacrifice the necessary in the hope of winning the superfluous" (Seltzer 2004).

After inheriting a profitable hotel business that generates revenue from gambling, Manuel Vong faces a number of moral challenges. One is how Confucian values can be made consistent with his business practice, given that many suffer from gambling addiction that can ruin the lives of individuals and families. Manuel reflects on the possibility of applying the Confucian concept of ritual (*li*) to gambling activity to help mitigate the harmful effects of gambling. By reconceiving gambling as a ritual, the duties and responsibilities of both casinos and players are more clearly outlined. Moreover, since rituals are social practices that aim at the common good, they can help draw attention to the moral elements of gambling (e.g., the dire consequences of problematic gambling), instead of thinking of it as a solely profit-driven activity.

• Confucian ethics stress the cultivation of certain character traits and virtues. In the story of Manuel, there are considerations that relate to respecting the virtue of ritual propriety (*li*). For the government of Macau, it is a role of fostering social cohesion. For the gaming establishments, it is to provide a venue for legitimate exercise of relaxation in the form of responsible gambling. For the individual players, it is the clamor of emotional fulfillment. For everyone, it is a balance of moral virtue, considered governance and overall material welfare for all constituents.

Guide questions

1 What is the relationship between profit and virtue according to the early Confucians? Do you agree with their view? Why or why not?
2 What are positive lessons for business practices that can be drawn by reflecting on the social enterprise, Carpenter Tan?
3 Confucian ethics stresses the cultivation of certain character traits and virtues. Analyze how both Confucian ethics can shape and influence business leaders in Macau, in general, and those in the Gaming Industry, in particular.
4 If you were in Manuel's situation, what decisions would you have made, and why? Provide realistic assumptions and information to support your position.
5 Are there any special challenges that Confucianism—with its emphasis on families, communities, rituals and respect for elderly—will need to face when it comes to business practices? How might Confucians address such difficulties?

Notes

1 All translations of the Mengzi (Mencius) are from Bryan W. Van Norden's Mengzi: With selections from traditional commentaries, (Indianapolis: Hackett), 2008.

2 The poem was written by Du Fu to celebrate New Year's Eve, probably in the year 746 (Young, 2008), capturing the Chinese amusement for gambling with the heightened anticipation of the risk of winning or losing.

References

Angle, S. 2009, *Sagehood: The contemporary significance of neo-confucian philosophy*, New York: Oxford University Press.

Gaming Inspection and Coordination Bureau. 2017, *Monthly gross revenue from games of fortune*. (www.dicj.gov.mo/web/en/information/DadosEstat_mensal/2016/index.html, Accessed September 27, 2017).

Gough, N. 2015, 'Macau gambling industry faces challenges on multiple fronts', *The New York Times*, 26 November.

IAS. 2017, 'Report on 'A study of Macao people's participation in gambling activities 2016'' *Institute of the Study of Commercial Gaming of the University of Macau* (www.ias.gov.mo/wp-content/uploads/2013/10/2016-11-29_174305_65.pdf, Accessed February 17, 2017).

Ivanhoe, P. 2000, *Confucian moral self cultivation*, Indianapolis: Hackett Publishing Company.

Macau Daily Times. 2015, 'Casino revenues fall 32PCT amid ongoing pressure on VIP market' (http://macaudailytimes.com.mo/gamingcasinorevenuefalls32pctamidongoing pressureonvipmarket.html, Accessed February 2, 2017).

Macau Daily Times. 2016, 'Wynn, Melco hold 'Riskiest Slice' of region's gaming business', (http://macaudailytimes.com.mo/wynn-melco-hold-riskiest-slice-regions-gaming-business.html, Accessed September 27, 2017).

MacIntyre, A. 2007 [1981], *After virtue* (3rd ed.), London: Duckworth.

Mengzi. 2008, *Mengzi with selections from traditional commentaries* (Van Norden, B., trans.), Indianapolis, IN: Hackett Publishing.

Seltzer, T. 2004, *The Queen of Spades* by A. S. Pushkin, Best Russian Short Stories, September 11; Produced by D. Starner, K. M. Eckrich, and the Project Gutenberg Online Distributed Proofreaders Team; Compiled and Edited by Thomas Seltzer; EBook #13437; (www.gutenberg.net).

SJM Holdings Limited. 2016, 'ABOUT US' – Our Mission. (www.sjmholdings.com/en/aboutus/our-mission, Accessed June 13, 2017).

Tang, J. 2008, 'From social gambling to pathological gambling', in A. Lai (ed.), *Counsellors' reflections on gambling: Hong Kong's experience*, Hong Kong: Caritas, 2–5.

The Institute for the Study of Commercial Gaming. 2016, 'About responsible gambling', University of Macau (www.umac.mo/iscg/Events/RG_symposium/rg_home.html, Accessed February 17, 2017).

Van Norden, B. 2007, *Virtue ethics and consequentialism in early chinese philosophy*, Cambridge: Cambridge University Press.

Xunzi. 2016, *Xunzi: The complete text* (Hutton, E., trans.), Princeton, NJ: Princeton University Press.

Yearley, L. 1990, *Mencius and aquinas: Theories of virtue and conceptions of courage*, Albany: State University of New York Press.

Young, D. 2008, *Du Fu: A life in poetry*/Poems by Du Fu (Young, D., trans.), New York, NY: Alfred A. Knopf.

Yu, J. 2007, *The ethics of Confucius and Aristotle: Mirrors of virtue*, New York: Routledge.

INDEX

Note: page references with an *f* are figures.

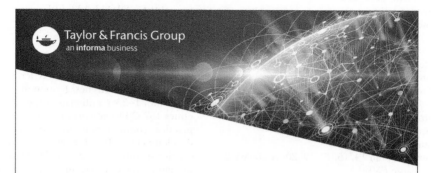